D1582594

CONTEMPORARY
ASPECTS OF PHILOSOPHY

CONTEMPORARY
ASPECTS OF PHILOSOPHY

Edited by

GILBERT RYLE

ORIEL PRESS
STOCKSFIELD
LONDON   HENLEY ON THAMES   BOSTON

Series Editor Dr P W Kent
© 1976 Board of Management of the Foster & Wills Scholarships,
Oxford University, England
First published in 1976
by Oriel Press Ltd (Routledge & Kegan Paul Ltd)
Stocksfield, Northumberland, England NE43 7NA

Set in Baskerville and
Printed in Great Britain by
Willmer Brothers Limited, Birkenhead

ISBN 0 85362 161 6

FOREWORD

ONE OF THE PURPOSES of this series of Symposia is to provide each year a forum where leading scholars in related aspects of a sphere of academic interest can meet for impartial discussions of an inter-disciplinary kind in unhurried circumstances. The Symposia have no dominant themes but rather it is hoped that in them and in the volumes which result, contributors will develop hypotheses which are considered by them to be of importance to contemporary thought.

It is timely and happy that in 1975 philosophy came to be the area for exploration and that so many distinguished philosophers from Europe and America were able to participate. The Symposium was fortunate and honoured to have its deliberations guided from the chair by Gilbert Ryle and further so for his editorship of this book. To him and to all the participants a deep debt of gratitude is owed. From the formative stages of the enterprise, a number of Oxford philosophers generously gave advice and wise counsel about the structure of the Symposium and particular thanks are extended to David Pears, Alan Montefiore, Anthony Kenny and Professor R. M. Hare in this connexion. On the financial side, the most generous financial support, provided by Kulturabteilung of the German Foreign Office, and the Stifterverband für die Deutsche Wissenschaft, is gratefully acknowledged. Particular thanks are due to Herr Risler, Dr M. L. Mruck, Mrs Farenden and to the Steward of Christ Church.

P. W. Kent,
Van Mildert College,
Durham

TABLE OF CONTENTS

Exegeses and Critiques

Meta-Philosophy

PREFACE

THE OXFORD INTERNATIONAL SYMPOSIUM of 29 September–4 October 1975 was held in Christ Church, the college at which the late M. B. Foster had been a tutor in philosophy. The symposium was arranged under the auspices of the Foster-Wills and Theodor Heuss Scholarships. Oxford University, and the Deutscher Akademischer Austauschdienst (DAAD). The organizer of the symposium was Dr Martin L. Mruck, Director of the London Branch of the German Academic Exchange Service, 11–15, Arlington Street, London, SW1A IRD.

This time it was philosophers who were conferring, with their discussion themes hospitably covered by the title "Contemporary Aspects of Philosophy". The number of participants invited was deliberately kept small, partly in order that debates might be of seminar dimensions rather than of public meeting dimensions. The participants came from Finland, the U.K., France, Germany, Norway, Canada, Sweden, Yugoslavia and the United States. Almost all of the participants produced contributions, abstracts of which had been circulated before the conference began. The contributions, which compose this volume, often incorporate additions and alterations made to meet points that had arisen in the public discussions or the personal conversations which were the symposium's actual and intended life. As had been understood from the beginning, English was the language both of the papers delivered and of the discussions.

The members of the symposium were, to their approval, given accommodation and lecture room facilities in Christ Church, but it was the Dining Hall, in which the main meals were served, that received special admiration. It was in this Hall that was held the noble banquet given by the German Academic Exchange Service, on 2 October; this was preceded by an impressive reception at which

His Excellency the German Ambassador and Lord Blake with Frau von Hase and Lady Blake received the symposium members as well as the representatives of the two bodies under the auspices of which this symposium, like the others, had its being. Dr Mruck was of course present, but alas! for the last time in his capacity of Director of the Academic Exchange Service. The Dean of Christ Church and Mrs Chadwick gratified the visitors by their presence; they could be, and were, both welcomed and welcoming.

The papers here assembled have been grouped according to some sometimes rather tenuous affinities of theme. Thus half a dozen predominantly exegetic critical papers are grouped together, despite the dissimilarities between the thoughts of, e.g. Quine, Lukács and Paliard. The sequence of contributions terminates with a couple of "metaphilosophical" articles, but the reader of them will not long suspect collusions between their authors.

Gilbert Ryle,
Plenary Chairman

I

NORMS OF INQUIRY: METHODOLOGIES AS NORMATIVE SYSTEMS

K. E. Tranöy

1. THE IDEA of regarding methodologies as normative systems is not original with me. See Kaufmann (1944), Popper (1945), Merton (1968), and also Tranöy (1953). But I know of no sustained attempt to work out the presuppositions and implications of this idea.

The attempt presupposes an approach to the philosophy of science, in some ways different from that which dominates in Anglo-Saxon philosophy. Thus, I shall take "science" in a wider sense than is now usual in English. It is perhaps not necessary to do so but it is natural to one whose native language is Norwegian where the word for science, *vitenskap*, is a close synonym of the German *Wissenschaft*. It is also natural for another reason. The essential and disputed differences between physical and non-physical sciences, between empirical and non-empirical disciplines, do not seem to lie in the normativity of their methodologies (although they are often thought to be related to differences in *methods*; cf. sect. 2 below).

There is, however, another change of aspect or emphasis which *is* a necessary presupposition of the new approach. It requires that we look at science as an activity. This I take to contrast with the view which focusses on science as a product of such activity; as one or more bodies of knowledge, their internal "logic" and conceptual structure, etc.

If methodological rules are regarded as norms, i.e. as essentially permitting, enjoining or forbidding agents to perform certain actions, then the normative approach invites us to pay attention to the kinds of action involved in the doing of science. Norms are addressed to specific acts and agents. "Find the truth!" is about as helpful a rule as "Do good!"

To avoid misunderstanding, I shall use the general term "systematic cognitive inquiry", or simply "inquiry". There are, of course, many kinds of inquiry, and even of cognitive inquiry, important

1

enough in our lives, but which are not systematic in the way—for instance—science and philosophy are.

"Systematic cognitive inquiry" is still too vague, so let me be more specific. *Inquiry*, in the sense here intended, *is the systematic and organized search for, as well as the acquisition and communication of knowledge and insight.*

Knowledge I take to be a necessary but not sufficient condition of insight. Cf. sect. 4 below.

2. I must now say a little more about the nature and contents of methodological normative systems. By a normative system I mean a finite and ordered set of norms and values. I distinguish between *general* and *specific* methodologies. History differs from physics, and economics from biology, in virtue of what we often call methods. Rules, norms and values tied to such methods are essential in what I call specific methodologies.

Specific methodologies all presuppose largely the same common and shared general methodology. What I mean by a (or the) general methodology will, I hope, appear from the following condensed survey and from subsequent sections.

The general methodology of inquiry must be anchored in the value of accepting true (confirmed) and rejecting false (groundless) propositions, i.e. in the *value* of truth, of knowledge, of insight, or however we phrase it. Methodological rules, norms and ideals in a stricter sense of these terms can then be understood as partly derivable from, and instrumental to the realization of this basic and constitutive value of the methodology. Thus we require our products to meet certain requirements, as for instance : consistency, coherence and system; simplicity, completeness and decidability (intersubjective controllability). In their relations with each other, and with the rest of the world, these norms of inquiry require scientists and scholars to be honest, sincere and openminded in what they make public. Persons professionally engaged in inquiry should be impartial, objective, dispassionate and "sachlich", not given to capricious arbitrariness of judgement. Interpersonal relations are important in this community of knowledge seekers (they are not only scientists) : I trust my friend, the physicist, as a truth-teller, and he appears to reciprocate when he turns to me for information. We take it for granted that a colleague normally has good reasons when he asserts something, reasons which he is able and willing to let others check if they should want to.

And, finally, the products of cognitive inquiry—theories,

hypotheses, findings, data, etc. which are publicly asserted as being true or at least acceptable—must have such properties as relevance and fruitfulness coupled with originality. *Creativity* is one of the star virtues of our tribe.

This is no more than indications, slogan-like and telegraph-style. A detailed and systematic presentation demands more space than I have for this whole paper. (An attempt can be found in Tranöy (1974).)

3. Actions (activities) and norms are linked by the notion of *legitimation* (justification). Tentatively, an action *a* is legitimated (justified) for the agent *x* if there is a norm N which permits or commands *x* to do *a*. "There is" a norm N if N is accepted by *x* and/or those who have legitimate power or authority over *x*. Norms as *guiding* activities can be understood in terms of legitimation. Let *y* have legitimate power or authority over *x* with regard to *a*. Then *y* can be said to guide *x* with regard to *a* if he uses his power or authority to make *x* perform, or abstain from performing, *a*—for instance, by ordering, permitting, or forbidding *x* to do *a*.

There is an element of necessity in the connection betwen actions and legitimation in so far as any action must be capable of legitimation. For any *a*, it must be possible to ask whether or not there is a norm N by reference to which the performance of *a* is permitted.

According to this definition, there will be positive as well as negative legitimation, an awkward linguistic consequence, perhaps. The point is that I need a general term for submitting *a* to moral or other normative or axiological judgement.

It now follows that inquiry must be capable of legitimation. Consequently, there must be a set of norms and values by appeal to which it can be legitimated (approved or condemned) and guided. This set of norms and values I shall call the *ideology of inquiry*; "ideology" being a synonym for normative system; cf. sect. 2. (For a survey of this ideology, see Tranöy (1976).) Haberer (1969) uses the term "the scientific ideology". A methodology is a sub-set of this ideology.

Methodological norms and values do not suffice to legitimate all types of actions and activities involved in inquiry defined as the search for, and the acquisition and communication of knowledge.

Search for knowledge has two aspects : I call them the aspect of *discovery* and the aspect of *verification*. By the latter I mean the systematic and critical examination (testing, criticism, etc.) of propositions considered for acceptance or rejection. "Discovery" is

3

meant to refer neither to the psychology of creativity, nor to the dubious venture of issuing prescriptions for the production of good ideas. What I here mean by discovery is, in part at least, what is also called science and educational policies, and includes such things as research strategies. The direction in which one looks makes a difference to what one sees. It would be odd to exclude from systematic, organized search for knowledge such things as the choice, planning and administration of research and educational projects, or the training of scientists, or the planning, organization, and administration of institutions of research and learning. (Verification and discovery thus represent, broadly, an individualistic and a social aspect of search for knowledge.)

Methodologies clearly have their proper functions in connection with search in the sense of verification. In order to legitimate and guide search in the sense of science and educational policies we need norms and values which relate to human welfare in general. Norms concerning simplicity, completeness, and objectivity (for instance) which have important functions in the context of verification, hardly even make sense—certainly not the *same* sense—when applied to the making and execution of policies, where values of public welfare (economic, social, cultural, etc.) are directly relevant, as such values cannot be when one is engaged in the execution of a chosen research project. (Research strategies may now appear as a borderline area.)

This argument seems to hold no matter what one happens to believe about the right relationship between science and politics in general. It may even be thought to be bordering on the trivial. Did any reasonable person ever think that science and educational policies could and should be *wertfrei* and "value neutral"? Not Max Weber, certainly, who, when he wrote about *Wertfreiheit*, had something else in mind. (Weber (1917), cf. Tranöy (1972a).) Yet I suspect that some of the heat and controversy generated by the contemporary criticism of science is due to a failure to observe the distinction between the two senses of "search for knowledge". Claims that science is value neutral may appear reasonable when science is understood as a body of true knowledge and the activity (the research) directly producing it. The same claims must appear untenable to one who understands science in the broader sense and as including such things as policy making and the application of results. In the former case one must also take it for granted that methodologies are "value free" although from the present point of view they are not. On the contrary, one of their main functions is to legitimate certain aspects of inquiry, but they do so by way

4

of norms and values other than those which have appeared to be so problematic, both for science and for ethics.

To proceed, *acquisition* can be seen as the acts of accepting and rejecting propositions (truth claims)—and doing neither : "suspending judgment", as we often say. Search terminates in acceptance or rejection, as reflected in methodological norms linking the two types of activity. For instance :

"One should not accept p if p has not been tested (or : if the evidence for and against p is unknown)."

The point is not whether this formulation of a generally accepted norm is adequate or not; the point is the methodological flavour of the norm.

Communication as part of cognitive inquiry can be broken down into the acts of publicly asserting and denying propositions (truth claims), in speech or in writing. There are rules which link communication and acquisition. Samples : "One ought not to assert p unless one accepts p." "If one accepts p (which has been properly tested, etc.), then it is permitted to assert p."

Again, the formulations are not important. My point is the necessity of assuming such rules, their functions in legitimating cognitive activity, and their obviously methodological flavour.

Of course, it has happened that a scientist has preferred to accept and assert p as against q because p had been tested, accepted and asserted by one of "his own group", while the protagonist of q belonged to some other and alien group. But consider a rule legitimating this practice, for instance : "It is permitted to accept p as against q if p is tested, accepted, and asserted by non-communist researchers and q, correspondingly, by communist scientists." The norm remains unacceptable no matter what political value we substitute for "communist".

To sum up : a methodology is a sub-set of the ideology of inquiry. It can provide legitimation for some but not for all actions and activities which constitute inquiry. Above all, methodologies legitimate what I shall now call *basic cognitive acts* : (a) the testing and critical examination of truth claims (propositions), and (b) the acceptance and rejection as well as (c) the assertion and denial of propositions so examined. (On the normative aspect of truth claims see Habermas (1973).)

4. Implicit in my argument is the familiar distinction between

5

internal and *external* norms of inquiry. Methodologies are internal. Norms and values required to legitimate science policies are external.

The external norms of inquiry accepted by the scientific community—or, more aptly, by knowledge seekers in the west—have changed considerably in the course of history. Around the year 1600 a fairly undivided faith in inquiry as a means to personal, individual "self-realization"—the tradition of perfectionism, as Rawls (1974, p. 4) says—was supplemented if not replaced by a new faith in public and collective, material and external welfare to be achieved through a science based on technological control of nature. This pattern of legitimation is now under fire. The contemporary criticism of science is directed at the choice of external norms of inquiry, although it is often presented as attacks on objectivity, truth for its own sake, etc., i.e. on internal norms.

Now, internal and external norms of inquiry can hardly be completely disconnected. A point, well taken, in the criticism of science deplores precisely the sharp "ivory tower" separation of the two.

If these two sub-sets of the ideology of inquiry, methodological norms and policy norms, are really completely separate, then a traditional and now so often disputed view of science is not only defensible but incontrovertible. For then the activity of research, for instance, must be guided and legitimated by a set of norms completely dissociated from that which performs corresponding functions for planning and policy making, for the use of the results of research activity. If the two activities are thus normatively distinct, this means that responsibility in science can be divided between two distinct sets of people. The active scientist is and should be guided and legitimated solely by methodological norms. Others will worry about science policy and the application of results. (It is this conception that Chomsky (1968) and others have felt to be a self-imposed schizophrenia.)

This conception of the absolute divisibility of responsibility breaks down if it turns out that methodological norms are essentially incomplete and useless without a working reference to *external* norms of inquiry.

This may appear to be a somewhat strange contention. How could one hope to show such completeness or incompleteness? The sense in which methodological norms may be said to exist is, of course, by no means clear—although we all speak and act as if they do, indeed, exist, notably when we act as critics of each other and as examiners and supervisors of our juniors.

I suggest that the normative system of general methodology exists

6

an unwritten consensus between colleagues, in the scientific community. It exists roughly as anthropologists take cultures and sub-cultures to exist. Professional knowledge seekers are a sub-culture, one of the specialized tribes of the modern world.

This mode of normative existence is unlike that of legal systems, but perhaps not so unlike that of morality. Laws are systematically composed, enacted, and enforced through a complex network of institutions. The idea that one should strive for a similar formalization and institutionalization of methodological norms (or of the norms of morality) feels awkward, on several counts. (To whom, for instance, should we delegate the power to prepare, formulate, and enact the required codex, and who should be in charge of the enforcement?) One important objection is that it is hardly compatible with another element in the ideology of inquiry : the freedom of inquiry, and related ideals of individual and institutional autonomy which are, as a matter of fact, considered an important trait in the institutionalization of inquiry as we now find it in universities, academies, etc.

Nevertheless, it may be theoretically illuminating to attempt to construct, or reconstruct, a system of general methodological norms. I have tried to do so (Tranöy (1974)), on the strength of participant observation, checking my own intuitions and ideas against those of colleagues. There may be something to learn from this.

In practically every single case, one is faced with a variety of different, non-equivalent formulations of the norms one must try to bring to expression in language. Let me illustrate.

Granted that the basic purpose of a methodology is to further the acquisition of knowledge. The more truth and the less falsehood it helps us accept, the better. This fundamental or constitutive value of cognitive activity gives rise to norms relating to the basic cognitive acts (cf. sect. 3). Consider the following five norm-formulations concerning the acceptance and rejection of propositions.

TN1 : "It is not permitted to accept p if p is known to be false."
TN2 : "It is obligatory to reject p if p is known to be false."

Both appear acceptable although they are not equivalent : (1) follows from (2) but not *vice versa*.

TN3 : "It is permitted to accept p if p is known to be true."
TN4 : "It is obligatory to accept p if p is known to be true."
TN5 : "It is permitted to accept p only if p is known to be true."

7

Of these, (3) appears to be trivial (although I am not sure it is, for

TN3' : "It is permitted to accept $-p$ if p is known to be true"

obviously is not acceptable. That is, although (4) implies (3) but not *vice versa*, in practice (3) may be acceptable only where (4) also is). (5) obviously is too restrictive. (4) does seem to be in order, especially if we give it a more felicitous formulation, "One ought to accept p," etc.

There is an ambiguity in "known to be true". If X knows that p is true in the sense that he knows a proof for p, it is odd to say that it is obligatory for X to accept p. It is, rather, in that case impossible for X not to accept p. But if X knows that p is true in the sense that he knows there is a proof for p without knowing the proof, X may be held to be under an obligation to accept p or, at least, not to reject it. Most of the knowledge any of us has is of the second-hand variety. It is reasonable, then that it should be second-hand knowledge which is surrounded by methodological norms. (For instance, there is no obligation and hardly a permission to accept p if it is known simply that p is accepted. It is only if X knows that p is accepted for good reasons or by competent judges and a qualified consensus (Habermas (1973)) that it becomes legitimate for X to accept p.) Note also how the distinction between the two senses of "known to be true" (and, of course, "known to be accepted for good reasons") can clarify the notions of knowledge and insight. It is above all in the case of first-hand knowledge that there is also insight.

Another example. Assume TN1, the weakest of the five norms, and combine it with the law of contradiction. We can then derive a new norm,

CN1 : "It is not permitted to accept or to assert a proposition of the form $(p \& -p)$,"

for one of them must be false, and I would thus violate TN1. (The law of contradiction says something about what is (necessarily) the case with regard to the distribution of truth values over two contradictory propositions, it says nothing about accepting or not accepting them. So, it is not itself a norm.)

When we consider "acceptance values" weaker than "(known to be) true", e.g. "probable" or "confirmed", we seem, most of the time, to obey

CN2 : "It is not permitted to accept or assert p if p is (known to be) less probable than $-p$." Or, further,

CN3 : "It is not permitted to accept or assert p unless one has evidence for p."

CN4 : "It is not permitted to reject (deny) p without evidence for $-p$."

CN5 : "If neither p nor $-p$ can be given a weight, then one ought to suspend judgment regarding both."

The CN-norms are concerned with the distinction between being persuaded and being (rationally) convinced, a basic cognitive concern. And "known to be true" is a species of evidence.

I do not quite know what to make of this kind of result : it seems interesting and I am not sure I see why. Perhaps it constitutes some kind of *reductio ad absurdum* proof for the tribes-eye view of methodologies (and morals) : the appropriateness of the unwritten consensus. If so, it also tells us something about the difference between law and morality. A certain vagueness is not objectionable in moral and methodological matters. "Ought" and "may", "right" and "wrong" are better and more adequate terms in some contexts than the sharper and more precise "permitted", "obligatory", and "forbidden". The former belong to the everyday language of the tribe, a language which is in order as it is.

5. Now let me return to the contention (p. 6) that methodological norms are essentially incomplete without a working reference to external norms of inquiry. Traditionally, it has been thought that there is a close tie between (knowledge of) truth on the one hand, and moral and other values on the other. "The truth shall make ye free" is a Biblical formulation. It is only (?) in our own century that philosophers have argued for some kind of absolute separation between truth and moral values.

It is just not the case that acceptance (or knowledge) of true propositions is *always* a value, let alone an overriding one. Detailed knowledge of my own future is not a value. We disagree about the value and rightness of letting the dying know that they are dying. I have no duty to tell the would-be rapist the whereabouts of my daughter. Three special cases? Enough to prove my point, in any case. And there are other arguments.

There is something awkward about the notion of *counting* truths (even assuming it is possible and meaningful from a logical point of view). To state the basic aim of inquiry as the acceptance of *as*

9

many true and *as few* false propositions as possible does not make good sense. On the contrary, we strive to reduce the number of (logically distinct) truths—we regard it as progress when we can show that p and q are reducible to r. It is the *quality* of truths that counts. The basic aim of inquiry must, then, be something like optimizing the truth-value of inquiry. Pursuit of truth or knowledge strictly for its own sake may have nothing to match it in reality.* This is not to deny that curiosity is a basic human urge; sometimes that *is* what we mean by "pursuit of truth for its own sake".

If we ascribe to knowledge of truth a value in itself, we shall have a problem in justifying the preference of one kind of truth to another. But was it ever seriously thought that *all* truths are of equal value from a moral (or, generally, a practical) point of view? Some truths, some kinds of truth, are better than others, and we have always thought so in our culture, although the kinds of value and, consequently, the kinds of truth given top priority have changed over time. For Plato, truths about the Forms were more important and valuable than other truths, and the values were those of "perfectionism" or self-realization. For Bacon truths about causal connections in nature ranked highest, and the value was collective human welfare. Today, such priority rankings are expressed in our science and educational policies.

In our methodologies the crucial connection between internal and external norms—the tie with *policy*—is established through demands for relevance and fruitfulness. If my point is not clear, try the following thought experiment. Let us now, in a systematic and organized manner, search for, acquire, and communicate the whole truth about umbrellas in Western Norway (where it rains a lot). Let us collect data about the properties of umbrellas and the properties of their users, let us correlate and compute, as creatively as possible, with all the originality at our command. The resulting body of knowledge might have most of the desired properties of worth-while knowledge : system, simplicity, coherence, and so on. If it is all irrelevant, it will be no good, not even to makers and marketers of umbrellas. Methodological perfection is not enough.

---

* It is compatible with this to hold that acceptance of a false proposition is always bad. For the possibility of neither accepting nor rejecting remains open, in theory. The ideal practical version of this would be blissful ignorance, although in real life, e.g. when you want to conceal the truth from a dying patient, the attempt to maintain ignorance may often imply inducing a false belief. So Rawls (1974, p. 3) may still be right when he points out that falsehood is a sufficient ground for rejecting p. Cf. norm TN2, p. 10 above.

6. In conclusion, let me say something in justification of the normative approach adopted in this paper. It will be natural if the defence appeals to criteria of relevance and fruitfulness rather than to formal perfectionism.

(a) Those who are interested in the theory-and-practice problem area may find in this approach something familiar, but with a difference. I have argued that systematic truth-seeking necessarily presupposes the acceptance of certain norms and values—the ideology of inquiry. This ideology is, then, in an obvious sense, part of the foundations of science and of other forms of systematic and organized cognitive inquiry. Such forms of inquiry have often been considered as paradigms of *rational* human activity. Now, on my reasoning, it would be awkward to hold that the acceptance of norms and values is the outcome of arbitrary decisions which are themselves beyond justification. The reflective acceptance of norms and values must, then, be just about as rational and reasonable as the acceptance of propositions deemed to be acceptable on the strength of norms of inquiry. Which is to say that it appears pointless to ask, which comes first, theory or practice. They are both "given" together, in the constitution of rational animals and their worlds.

(b) Norms and values were once held to be utterly "non-cognitive" and non-rational. The corollary that science in part rests on non-rational and non-cognitive foundations was, I believe, accepted by some. (In at least one sense by Popper (1959, pp. 34–38).) In the light of preceding arguments, another alternative—modifying our understanding of human rationality—seems more attractive. This may involve having to make sense of the notion of normative validity, but that should not be an objection any longer. (For a partial attempt, see Tranöy (1972b).)

(c) Dispassionate examination of the ideology of inquiry may throw light on problems in theoretical ethics as well. Some such points have already been made, and I shall mention one more. Recently, a distinction between act- and rule-utilitarianism has attracted the interest of moral philosophers. Material drawn from the ideology of inquiry may provide another illustration. The norms of inquiry are best understood in the spirit of rule-utilitarianism. If for every single and separate act performed in the course of inquiry we demand that it should be judged on the merit of its utility, two undesired consequences seem likely to ensue. The usefulness and value of cognitive inquiry on the whole will diminish. And so will the freedom of inquiry.

(d) I believe, finally, that—dispassionately pursued—the norma-

11

tive approach may contribute to a clearer view of the criticism of science of the last decades, both in terms of the contrast between external and internal norms of inquiry, and above all, perhaps, through a better understanding of the contents and structure of the internal ones, the methodologies. By criticism of science, I am not only thinking of left wing criticism but also of demands and queries from the general public as well as from government institutions.

That particular subset of the norms of inquiry which I have discussed here, general methodological norms, can be described as an ideology (*not* only in the sense of "false ideology") which we "academics" have in common and which makes us identifiable as a group, as a cross-cultural sub-culture. They are deeply internalized norms in most of us; and therefore it is not easy to bring them to the surface. But who is better placed to make the attempt than we ourselves are? To do so may now seem to be useful for several reasons. For one thing it is perhaps a necessary condition of our being *rational* about the acceptance and rejection of particular norms of inquiry. (We do not accept them blindly, do we?) And this, in turn, may be useful for a variety of purposes in the present world, e.g. for being able to offer a good justification, to ourselves, certainly, and perhaps to others as well, for what we are doing. I shall confess, moreover, that for one philosopher at least it is also an interesting inquiry, in itself.

Note. For the term "norms of inquiry" I am indebted to Professor Roderick M. Chisholm.

Professor K. E. Tranöy
University of Bergen, Norway

BIBLIOGRAPHY

Chomsky, Noam (1968) "Philosophers and Public Philosophy" in *Ethics.* 79, 1–23.
Haberer, Joseph (1969) *Politics and the Community of Science.* New York: Van Nostrand Reinhold Co.
Habermas, Jürgen (1973) "Wahrheitstheorien" in *Wirklichkeit und Reflexion.* Festchrift für Walter Schulz, Ed. H. Fahrenbach. Pfullingen: Neske, 211–265.
Kaufmann, Felix (1944) *Methodology of the Social Sciences* London: Oxford University Press
Merton, Robert K (1968) "Science and the Social Order" (1937) and "Science and Democratic Social Structure" (1942), both in *Social Theory and Social Structure* Enlarged ed (New York: The Free Press, 1968), pp 591–615

K. E. TRANÖY

Popper, Karl (1945) *The Open Society and Its Enemies*, esp Vol I, p. 241 and Vol. II, p. 220. London: George Routledge and Sons.
Popper, Karl (1959) *The Logic of Scientific Discovery*. London: Hutchinson and Co.
Rawls, John (1974) *A Theory of Justice*. Cambridge, Mass.: Harvard University Press.
Tranöy, Knut Erik (1953) *On the Logic of Normative Systems*. Part II, "The Normative Aspect of Methodology". Ph.D. dissertation, Cambridge 1953.
Tranöy, Knut Erik (1972a) "The Ideology of Scientific and Scholarly Conduct" in *Contemporary Philosophy in Scandinavia*, 331–349, ed. Olson, R. M. and Paul, A. M. Baltimore and London: The Johns Hopkins Press.
Tranöy, Knut Erik (1972b) " 'Ought' Implies 'Can': A Bridge From Fact to Norm?" in *Ratio*, Vol. XIV, 115–130.
Tranöy, Knut Erik (1974) "Om almenvitenskapelige metodologiske normer og verdier: forsök på en systematisering" ("On general methodological norms and values: an attempted systematization"), 15 pp. Mimeo. Institute of Philosophy, University of Bergen, April 1974.
Weber, Max (1917) "Der Sinn der 'Wertfreiheit' der Sozialwissenschaften" in Weber, *Soziologie, Weltgeschichtliche Analysen, Politik*. Kröners Taschenausgabe, vol. 229. Stuttgart: Albert Kröner, 1956.

13

II

RATIONALITY IN SCIENCE AND SOCIETY: A CONSENSUAL THEORY

K. Lehrer

WHAT IT IS REASONABLE for a person to do in the interests of producing as much good and as little harm as he can depends on his estimate of what is good and what is harmful. Analogously, what it is reasonable for a person to accept in the interests of accepting as much truth and as little error as he can depends on his estimate of what is true and what is erroneous. Both objectives contain internal stress. The production of good is likely to produce some harm and the acceptance of truths is likely to yield some error. There are a variety of decision rules that resolve such conflict in different ways. The application of such rules presupposes, however, an answer to a more fundamental question. How are we to decide whether the estimates themselves are reasonable?

Postulation or Subjectivity. There are two familiar approaches to this question. The first is to postulate *a priori* principles specifying what is intrinsically good or intrinsically evident. It has been urged that such postulation is necessary to escape from skepticism and subjectivism. The other approach is to concede that estimates are subjective and to impose no restraints on such estimates other than coherence and consistency. Those favoring this approach aver that the first alternative is dogmatic and undemocratic. Both approaches have defects. *A priori* postulation, in addition to being dogmatic, neglects the insights of those who demur. The postulated principles are a codification of current opinion and may ignore the reflective judgment of sensitive and informed iconoclasts. Subjectivism, in addition to being excessively latitudinarian, has a corresponding defect. The individual may ignore entirely the judgment of those who are expert. Those who are informed should not be ignored, whether they are an iconoclastic minority or an expert majority. Indeed, no opinion should be ignored. Each should be weighed to

14

elicit from the individual whatever wisdom or information he might have to offer.

Weighted Opinion. The foregoing reflections suggest that we may avoid both *a priori* postulation and unqualified subjectivism. Every opinion about what is good or what is true is a potential source of information that it is reasonable to weigh. But not every opinion should be given the same weight, for some are better informed than others. The subjective estimates of individuals should be restricted by the properly weighted opinions of others. Such a properly weighted opinion is on my analysis a logical construction. The logical construction, though it involves some honest toil, will suffice to replace the theory of *a priori* postulation.

There are two primary problems for the proposed analysis. The first is to propose a method for finding the proper weight to be assigned to each member of the group. The second is to find some reasonable method for using those weights to restrict subjective estimates.

We shall, admitting that this is an idealization, be concerned with those estimates and weights that a person assigns as an impartial and disinterested seeker after what is true and what is good. We discount thereby the biases of prejudice and egotism. We do, in fact, attempt to discount such factors when we weigh the estimates of others. Thus we shall consider the weight that a person gives to the scientific or verific estimates of another, those estimates that another would make as a disinterested and impartial seeker of what is true. Analogously, we shall consider the weight that a person gives to the ethical or bonific estimates of another, those estimates that he would make as a disinterested and impartial seeker of what is good. Moreover, we shall suppose the weights to be assigned impartially and disinterestedly as well.

Ramsey's Method. For our analysis, we require a mathematical representation of estimates. Estimates of what is true are subjective probabilities. Estimates of what is good are subjective utilities. A method for assigning subjective probabilities and utilities was invented by Frank Ramsey.[1] There are two basic elements in Ramsey's method. First, Ramsey assumes that a reasonable person is one who maximizes expected utility. The expected utility of an

[1] See "Truth and Probability," in *The Foundations of Mathematics and Other Logical Essays* (Kegan Paul, London and Harcourt Brace, New York, 1931) by Frank Plumpton Ramsey.

alternative is calculated on the basis of some partition, a partition being a set of possible states of the world that are incompatible in pairs and logically exhaustive. This is a technical way of saying that exactly one of the states must occur.

We calculate expected utility e of an alternative A_i on a partition of states $S_1, S_2, \ldots$ and S_n, letting 0_{ij} be the outcome of choosing A_i when S_j occurs, p be a probability function, and u a utility function by the formula $e(A_i) = p(S_1)u(0_{i1}) + p(S_2)u(0_{i2}) + \ldots + p(S_n)u(0_{in})$. Ramsey provided a method for assigning values to the functions p and u.

The second element in the method is to measure estimates in terms of preferences between gambles. We can determine by behavior or reflection whether we would, if offered the choice, prefer one gamble to another. Any choice between alternatives when the outcomes are uncertain is a gamble. What Ramsey showed is that if we can decide what gamble we prefer in any choice of gambles, then we can measure probabilities and utilities as finely as we desire. The method is extremely simple. If we assume some probabilities, for example those associated with the toss of a fair coin, we can measure utilities. Suppose you consider three outcomes, 0_1, 0_2, and 0_3. You prefer 0_1 to 0_2 and 0_2 to 0_3. Assign $u(0_1) = 1$, and assign $u(0_3) = 0$. These assignments are arbitrary. The problem is to find some nonarbitrary method for assigning $u(0_2)$ The method is this. Ask yourself, to begin with, which of the following you would prefer. First, to have 0_2 for sure or, second, to have 0_1 if the coin falls heads and 0_3 if the coin lands tails. If you are indifferent between the first and the second alternative, then $u(0_2) = .5$. If you prefer the first, $u(0_2)$ is greater than .5; if you prefer the second, then it is less. Suppose you prefer the first. Then you may ask yourself, which of the following you prefer. First, to have 0_2 for sure, or, second, to have 0_1 if the first toss falls heads, and if the first toss falls tails, then to toss the coin again, and if the second toss falls heads then to have 0_1 and if it falls tails to have 0_3. If you are indifferent between these two alternatives, then $u(0_2) = 3/4$. If you prefer the first to the second, $u(0_2)$ is greater than .75, if you prefer the second then it is between .5 and .75. With repeated consideration of gambles you can measure the utility of 0_2 as finely as you desire. The resulting utility function will express the difference in intervals between the outcomes and will be unique up to a positive linear transformation.

To measure utility, we simply assumed that the probability that a fair coin falls heads is .5. Ramsey showed how we may dispense with

16

this assumption, that is, how we may find a proposition to which a person assigns a probability of .5 rather than simply assuming such an assignment. We noted that the person prefers 0_1 to 0_2. We then find a proposition G, say one that describes some repeatable occurrence like a coin falling heads, such that the person is indifferent between the following two gambles. First, to have 0_1 if G, and have 0_2 if not G. Second, to have 0_2 if G and 0_1 if not G. Indifference between these two gambles shows that the person assigns a probability of .5 to G.

The probability of any other statement may then be measured. If you are indifferent between the gamble, first, to have 0_1 if S and 0_2 if not S, and, second, to have 0_1 if G and 0_2 if not G, then, since $p(G) = .5$, $p(S) = .5$. Assuming that G describes some repeatable occurrence like tha flip of a coin coming up heads, you can measure probabilities as finely as you wish. If you prefer the first gamble to the second, then $p(S)$ is greater than $p(G)$, and, therefore, greater than .5. If you want to determine how much greater, ask yourself whether you would prefer, first, to have 0_1 if S and 0_2 if not S or, second, to have 0_1 if the first toss of the coin is heads, and, if the first toss is tails, to have 0_1 if the second toss is heads and 0_2 if the second toss is tails. If you are indifferent between these two gambles, $p(S) = .75$. If you prefer the second gamble, then you have determined that $p(S)$ is less than .75 and greater than .5. With further refinement of gambles, you narrow the interval until you reach indifference enabling you to measure the probability of S.

Probabilities found by this method may fail to satisfy the calculus of probability. However, a genuine truth seeker will revise his subjective probabilities to coincide with the calculus of probability. Subjective probabilities may be interpreted as estimates of relative frequencies, and for such a set of estimates to be correct it must satisfy the calculus. Therefore, a genuine truth seeker will use Ramsey's method to find a coherent set of probabilities, that is, one satisfying the calculus of probability. Once a person has measured his subjective probabilities, he may measure his utilities by the method outlined above.

We may use Ramsey's methods to measure our opinions and preferences concerning what is true and what is good. These opinions and preferences may be biased and egoistic. When we, consider how much weight to give to the opinion of others, however we attempt to discount bias and egoism. We may associate with each person a probability assignment that reflects the probabilities he would assign if he were an impartial and disinterested truth seeker.

That probability assignment is verific in the sense that it represents the best a person can do to provide a guide to truth when he considers all the information available to him. Similarly, we may associate a utility assignment with a person that is bonific in the sense that it represents his preferences concerning what would be good for all concerned. In weighing the opinions and preferences of others in actual situations we attempt to extrapolate to the verific opinions and bonific preferences they would represent if they were to set aside their prejudiced opinions and selfish preferences.

Consensus. We have an account of verific probabilities and bonific utilities. We remain, however, entirely within the domain of individual subjectivity What is probable for one person may be improbable for another, and what has a high utility for one person may have a low utility for any other. No matter how impartially and disinterestedly people pursue what is true and what is good, disagreement may remain. The idea that if we are sufficiently impartial and disinterested, all disagreement will vanish, is a philosophical fiction. This fiction may be supplanted by a logical construction We consider the verific probabilities and bonific utilities of each person as a source of information about what is true and what is good. Not every probability or utility assignment should be given the same weight, for some are more expert and sagacious than others. We require a method for assigning the proper weight to the probability and utility assignments of each person. We use such weights to exploit the information contained in the individual probability and utility assignments. By so doing we shall arrive at intersubjective or consensual probability and utility assignments. Such assignments eliminate the need for *a priori* postulation of objective assignments.

How are we to find the proper weight to be given to the assignments of each individual? To avoid dogmatism, we shall construct the proper weights from the subjective weights that each member gives to other members of the group. People may assign different weights to the probability and utility assignments of the same person. We may judge the same person to be a reliable indicator of what is true but a poor judge of what is best, or *vice versa.* Let us consider a simple situation in which people assign weights to others. Suppose each member of the group is well acquainted with the opinions and preferences of other members of the groups. Moreover, suppose that such a member gives some positive weight to the opinions and preferences of other members.

Weighting Probability. Consider the probability case first. How do I assign weights? I ask myself which member of the group is the most reliable indicator of truth. I then assign to him the value 1. I assign the value 0 to an arbitrary assignment that would be useless as a guide to truth. To the person, b, who is the best indicator of truth I assign the value 1, and to an arbitrary person, z, that is a zero indicator of truth, I assign the value 0. To any other member of the group I assign some number between 0 and 1. To find that number, I use a minor variation of Ramsey's method. I ask myself whether I would prefer, first, to rely the assignment p_b of b if H and assignment p_z if not H, or second, to rely on the probability assignment p_j of the person j in question whether H or not H. If I am indifferent between these two alternatives then I assign $p(H)$ to j, where $p(H)$, is the probability I assign to H. To obtain the normalized weight that I assign to j, I sum the numbers assigned to all members of the group. Let that sum be s. The weight, w_j, I assign to j is $p(H)/s$. The weight, w_b, I assign to b is $1/s$.

In this manner, I assign a set of weights w_1, w_2, and so forth to w_n to the n members of the group including myself. The weights will sum to 1 and all will be positive. Let w_{ij} be the weight that person i assigns to person j in the group by the method prescribed. Each person i then assigns a set of weights w_{i1}, w_{i2}, and so forth to w_{in} to members of the group. We extrapolate the proper weight to assign to each person from the sets of assigned weights. It might appear tempting to take as the proper weight to assign to each person the ratio of the sum of the weights given to that person by everyone over the sum of all weight assigned to all persons. But this simple averaging has a fatal flaw. A person who is given the lowest weight by all other members of the group might give a high weight to someone else. That high weight would have the same effect on the averaging as a high weight given to a person by someone to whom everyone gave a high weight. This should not be. If a very unreliable fellow gives a high weight to me as an indicator of truth, and a very reliable fellow gives a high weight to you as an indictor of truth, the high weight given to you should be counted more heavily than the high weight given to me by a fellow considered to be unreliable. In short, to arrive at a proper weight for a person, we should take into consideration the weight that others give to the weighter giving the weight. There is a mathematical method for obtaining just this result.

Method One. Each person may use the weights he assigns to others to

19

obtain a new set of weights. He may consider the weights that each person gives to some specified person j and arrive at a new weight for j on the basis of these weights by using his own weights to compute a weighted average of the weights initially assigned to j. Let us think of the initial state in which each person assigns weights as state 0 and represent the weight that i gives to j in 0 as w_{ij}^0. Person i may then arrive at a new weight for j in state 1 by the formula: $w_{ij}^1 = w_{i1}^0 w_{1j}^0 + w_{i2}^0 w_{2j}^0 + \ldots + w_{in}^0 w_{nj}^0$. Thus i arrives at the weighted average, using his own weights, of the weights given to j. Suppose that each person uses this method of aggregation to arrive at a new weight for every person in state 1. Then each person might use the new weights that he has arrived at in this way in the same manner. That is, he might find a new weight for each person in state 2 by using the weights he assigns to others in state 1 to find the weighted average of the weights assigned by members of the group in state 1 to person j. He might then repeat this procedure to proceed from state 2 to state 3 and so forth. The general formula by which he proceeds from state m to state m + 1 is as follows: $w_{ij}^{m+1} = w_{i1}^m w_{1j}^m + w_{i2}^0 w_{2j}^0 + \ldots + w_{in}^m w_{nj}^m$. It is a mathematical theorem that as this process continues the weights that each person assigns to a specified person converge toward a common set of weights w_1, w_2, and so forth to w_n that every person assigns to each person in the group.

The situation as we have imaged it yields a regular Markov transition matrix of the following form

$$A = \begin{pmatrix} w_{11} & w_{22} & \cdots & w_{1n} \\ w_{21} & w_{22} & \cdots & w_{2n} \\ \cdots\cdots\cdots\cdots\cdots\cdots\cdots \\ w_{n1} & w_{n2} & \cdots & w_{nn} \end{pmatrix}$$

The method of aggregation from state 0 to state 1 is equivalent to computing A^2, and the use of the general principle to computing A^4, A^8, A^{16}, and so forth. It is a theorem concerning such matrices that as the exponent increases the matrix converges toward one in which every row (but not every column) is the same, hence toward a common row w_1, w_2 and so forth to w_n. By this method, therefore, we obtain a common set of weights by an iterated averaging procedure. The advantage of the method of aggregation employed is that it fully exploits all the information contained in the initial weights. A person to whom everyone assigns a comparatively low weight will have the weight he assigns to others discounted appropriately. In the actual situation, people may be firm in the weights they assign to others and refuse to aggregate in this manner. An impartial and disinterested spectator attempting to use the information imbedded in the weights that one person assigns to another should, however, use exactly this method to find a proper set of weights to assign to each person based on the initial weighting. Other methods would fail to fully exploit all the information summarized in the weights.

Once the proper weights have been found by the prescribed method of aggregation, we still require a method for finding the intersubjective or consensual assignment of probabilities. By using the method in question we arrive at a set of weights W_p for the verific probability assignments of members of the group. Suppose that we have a partition of statements M_1, M_2 and so forth to M_k. Let $p_i(M_j)$ be the probability person i assigns to element j of the partition. Once the set W_p is found, we may use the weights to find the weighted average of the probabilities assigned to an element of the partition by members of the group. Letting p_c be the consensual probability assignment, we may compute it as follows: $p_c(M_j)$ $= w_1 p_1(M_i) = w_2 p_2(M_j) + \ldots + w_n p_n(M_j)$. Calculating the intersubjective or consensual probability of elements of the partition in this manner and of disjunctions of such members by summation, we obtain a coherent probability assignment. The assignment obtained reflects the most complete exploitation of the information contained in the probability assignments of members of the group and the weights they give to each other. The resulting assignment p_c is, with one qualification to be noted, the best guide to truth one can adduce by aggregating the information summarized in the assignment of probabilities and weights.

Method Two. It is interesting to note that the method of aggregation proposed is equivalent to a second method. Consider once again the initial state in which each member i of the group assigns a certain probability p_i^0 to each element of the partition and a weight to each member of the group. Instead of directly aggregating weights to find the proper weight to be assigned to each member of the group, a person might use his initial weighting assignment to arrive at a new probability assignment p_i^1 for an element of the partition by computing a weighted average of the probability assignments of members of the group. He would proceed according to the following formula: $p_i^1(M_j) = w_{i1}^0 p_1^0(M_j) + w_{i2}^0 p_2^0(M_j) + \ldots + w_{in}^0 p_n^0(M_j)$. Once each person finds a new probability assignment at stage 1, he may then use his initial weights to find a stage 2 probability assignment

21

by computing the weighted average of the state 1 probability assignments, and so forth. To move from stage m to $m+1$, he will then be using the following formula: $p_i^{m+1}(M_j) = w_{i1}^0 p_1^m(M_j) + w_{i2}^0 p_2^m(M_j) + \ldots + w_{in}^0 p_n^m(M_j)$. This procedure is equivalent to multiplying matrix A times the following column vector.

$$p^0(M_j) = \begin{pmatrix} p_1^0(M_j) \\ p_2^0(M_j) \\ \ldots \\ p_n^0(M_j) \end{pmatrix}$$

Multiplication yields a new column vector, so at stage 1 we have

$$p^m(M_j) = \begin{pmatrix} p^m(M_j) \\ p^m(M_j) \\ \ldots \\ p_n^m(M_j) \end{pmatrix}$$

It is theorem concerning such multiplication that $p^m(M_j) = A^m p^0(M_j)$, that is, the iterated aggregation procedure amounts to raising the exponent of the matrix by 1 and multiplying by the initial probability vector. This method, method two, yields the same convergence as method one. As the stages increase the probability assignments converge toward a column vector in which each row is the same, that is, toward a single probability assignment for M_j. The probability assignment toward which the process converges is the same as the consensual probability assignment obtained by method one. Method one is a process that converges more rapidly because the next state is reached by multiplying some power of the matrix by itself rather than multiplying some power of the matrix times the original matrix.

Method two is an intuitively plausible procedure. A person starts with a set of weights representing his comparative judgments of how reliable members of the group are as indicators of truth. It is reasonable for him to use those weights to find a new probability assignment, a weighted average of the assignments of members of the group. If, however, such a procedure is reasonable, it is equally reasonable to proceed to the next stage. To refuse to do so is equivalent to assigning a weight of 0 to everyone except oneself, a weight of 1 to oneself, and aggregating. Thus, the refusal to aggregate at any stage is equivalent to adopting the dogmatic position of refusing to give any positive weight to the probability assignments of others at that stage. In some circumstances, for example, ones in which one expects new experimental information shortly, one may reasonably prefer to wait for such information rather than relying on the estimates of others. Nevertheless, an impartial and disinterested inquirer with no guide to truth except the probabilities and weights assigned by members of the group, should, with one qualification to be noted shortly, use precisely this method of aggregation. By so doing he would fully exploit the information to which he has access. Both methods yield the probability assignment that an impartial and disinterested truth seeker would extract from the total information.

Method Three. There is, however, one remaining method that might be appropriate in special cases. Suppose that method one is used to find the set of proper weights, W_p. An impartial observer might note that the probability assignments of members of the group for M_j tend to cluster around two values, many members assigning values around .2, many assigning values around .9. He might conclude that one or the other of these values is the best estimate and that some value intermediate between the two is unlikely to be at all reliable. The analogy here is when two groups of scientists get widely divergent measurements of some quantity. It may seem most reasonable to suppose that one group has made some error and, therefore, unreasonable to take the mean of the two measurements as the best guide to truth. In this special instance, the most reasonable method might be to use converging weights as the basis for a lottery. All the weights in W_p might be reduced to a common denominator D and a lottery of D tickets constructed with a number of tickets for each person equal to the numerator of weight. One might then draw a ticket and select a winning probability assignment. The expectation of finding the truth by this method is the same as by using methods one or two, but method three would not generally lead to the selection of the same probability assignment as the other methods. When there is a polarization of opinion among divergent groups of competent people, method three may be appropriate.

Communication and Total Information. We have so far assumed that members of the group all have positive respect for each other. This is an unrealistic assumption for most groups. More commonly, some members of a group will be totally ignorant of the opinions of others, or, even if they are informed, may not be willing to assign any positive weight to them. Fortunately the assumption of universal positive respect is unnecessary. Some members of the groups may assign a weight of 0 to other members without blocking convergence. All that is required for the matrix A to converge is that the weights be non-negative and such that respect is communicated indirectly from each person to every other person. Let us say that person i directly respects person j if and only if person i assigns a positive weight to person j. Person i indirectly respects j if and only if i does not directly respect j but there is a sequence of members of the group such that every member of the sequence directly respects the next member, the first member is i, and the last member is j. Finally, let us say that i communicates respect to j if and only if either i directly respects j or i indirectly respects j. Notice that it is perfectly possible that i communicates respect to j and j does not communicate respect to i.

To obtain the convergence mentioned in methods one and two, every person must communicate respect to every other person. This may result, however, even though each person assigns positive weight to only one other person. In terms of matrix A, if each person i assigns a positive weight to himself and to the next person in the group, person i + 1, except the last person n, who assigns a positive weight to the first person, person 1, then every person communicates respect to every other person and the matrix converges as the power of the matrix is raised. Assuming that everyone in the group assigns positive weight to himself, communication of respect from each person in the group to every other person is a sufficient condition for the existence of an intersubjective or consensual probability assignment.

When the required communication of respect does not exist the group decomposes into subgroups. Within some of these subgroups the required communication of respect may exist. In that case, we may calculate an intersubjective or consensual probability assignment for the subgroup. An individual who gives 0 respect to all other members of the group and assigns a weight of 1 to himself is an isolated individual, a subgroup of a single member. He may be regarded as intersubjectively unreasonable from the standpoint of the consensual probability of a large group of experts, even though his own probability assignment is perfectly coherent. This does not mean, however, that he is necessarily in error or that his probability assignment is a worse guide to truth than the consensual probability assignment. If he is a brilliant iconoclast, he may hit the mark when the rest fail to discern the target. Yet, at any given stage in human inquiry, the weights and probability assignments people assign in the impartial and disinterested quest for truth summarize

24

the totality of information available to them. It is reasonable to use as much of that information as we can as a guide to truth. By so doing we follow the dictum to use the total information available. The extreme iconoclast, though he may influence us in our initial probability assignments, isolates himself by refusing to assign to others any positive weight at all. He thereby treats others as though they had no relevant information whatever. It is reasonable to follow the consensual probability assignment instead simply because it represents a summary of as much of the total information as we can systematically aggregate.

Utility and Consensus. The same mathematical methods may be used to find a consensual utility assignment. However, the new interpretation raises important issues. First of all, there is the problem of interpreting the weights that yield the matrix A. How do I assign weights to members of the group? I ask myself which member of the group is the most reliable guide to what is good. I assign to him the value 1. I assign the value 0 to an arbitrary person who would be useless as a guide to what is good. To any other member of the group I assign values between 0 and 1 by using a variant of the Ramsey method. The method is exactly analogous to the one used to assign weights in the probability case except that I ask myself whether I would prefer to rely on a utility assignment as a guide to what is good rather than a probability assignment as a guide to what is true. I thus obtain the matrix A for bonific utility assignments of members of the group.

In assigning weights, it is important that these weights represent the weight that I assign to the bonific utility assignment of others rather than to the egoistic utility assignments. The egoistic assignment represents what a person prefers in his own self interest. The bonific or ethical assignment of a person represents his judgments about what would be preferable or best for all concerned. Thus, the weight is an indication of the respect that I have for the opinion of another person concerning what is good rather than a measure of my sympathy or antipathy for his egoistic preferences. There may be someone for whom I have antipathy but whose ethical guidance I highly value. I assign his bonific utility assignment a comparatively high weight in spite of the fact that I abhor many of the things that he likes. An especially salient example would be a person who has excellent moral insight but who is personally cynical in the way in which he conducts his own affairs. On the other hand, there may be someone for whom I have great sympathy but whose judgment I consider almost worthless. An example of such a person would be one who, though thoroughly loving and affectionate, is a very poor judge of needs of others and the manner in which they are most likely to be satisfied. The bonific utility assignment of such a person should be given a low weight corresponding to the comparatively low opinion I have of his judgment.

Having achieved a weighting matrix by using the foregoing strategy, a consensual utility assignment may be obtained by using method one above. Each member finds a new weight for a specified member by taking the weighted average of the weights assigned to that person, each person using as weights the weights he originally assigned. Having obtained a new set of weights, those weights are then used to obtain a new weighted average, and so forth, converging toward a consensual set of weights W_u. To find the consensual utility for an outcome 0_{ij}, the result of adopting policy A_i when state S_j obtains, we again find a weighted average. Where w_k is the consensual weight assigned to k and $u_k(0_{ij})$ is the bonific utility assignment of k to the outcome, we use the following formula to find the consensual utility assignment for the outcome: $u_c(0_{ij}) = w_1 u_1(0_{ij}) + w_2 u_2(0_{ij}) + \ldots + w_n u_n(0_{ij})$. This yields a utility assignment that is consensual and which exploits all the information we can extract from the opinions of members of the group about what is best for all concerned.

There is a strictly technical problem with which we must deal in regard to the consensual utility assignment. I have assumed that utility assignments to outcomes are scaled by the Ramsey method in the interval between 0 and 1. Such methods may mislead us into thinking that there is one standard scale for measuring bonific utilities. Ramsey's method does not yield such a scale. The assignments are only unique up to a positive linear transformation. This means that the utility assignment u_k of person k is equivalent to the transformation of that utility assignment obtained by taking $u_k a + b$ where a is positive and b is any number. Hence, when we use method one we must compensate for linear transformations of utility functions.

Let us refer to utility functions arrived at by the Ramsey method as the r utility function. Thus, r_k is the utility assignment of person k computed by the Ramsey method. For any member i of the group, his r function may be transformed to r* by picking a positive number a_i and any number b_i. $r_i^* = r_i a_i + b_i$. An adjustment in the aggregation procedure is needed to compensate for the different transformations of r functions by different members of the groups.

26

The simplest method is to compute the consensual utility assignment by the following formula: $u_c(0) = (w_1/a_1)r_1^*(0) + (w_2/a_2)r_2^*(0) + \ldots + (w_n/a_n)r_n^*(0) - w_1b_1/a_1 - w_2b_2/a_2 - \ldots - w_nb_n/a_n$. The consensual utility assignment calculated by this formula will yield the same consensual utility assignment as would be obtained by the simpler formula given above for aggregating the Ramsey utility assignments.

The r utility assignment of a person may be obtained as a linear transformation of any other utility assignment u for a person in which the outcome with the highest value has the value t and the lowest has the value b by the following formula: $r(0) = u(0)/(t-b) - b/(t-b)$. By following this procedure we may start from any utility assignment and arrive at the same consensual utility assignment u_c for any positive linear transformation of the original utility assignments.

Conclusion. The formal development of consensual utility is thus completed. We have shown that it is possible to construct a consensual utility assignment by the same method as we constructed a consensual probability assignment. Ethics is not more or less subjective than epistemology. We replace the *a priori* postulation of intrinsic value and intrinsic evidence with mathematical constructions in both domains. The probability or utility assignment of an individual may be unreasonable in the light of the total information available to us as summarized in the consensual probability or utility assignment. Of course, the total information available to us at any time may lead us to the wrong answers. It is a fallible guide to what is true and what is good. The rule to employ the total information available in arriving at conclusions concerning what is true and good is, nevertheless, a fundamental if fallible principle of rationality in science and society.

It is useful, in conclusion, to note some implications of the model. First of all, it indicates the importance of honesty in the communication of information. If individuals are duplicious in their dealings with other men and succeed in deceiving them about their competence and reliability, the assignment of weights will be based on deception. The consensual assignment will be infected with the results thereof. Moreover, those who are less than perfectly honest should be discounted in the weighting and, consequently, the information that they do possess will be lost in the consensual assignment. Secondly, the method shows the importance of increasing respect between members of society. By so doing we may weld together large groups through the communication of respect. The consensual assignment of the larger group will exploit the information of more individuals and thus more nearly approximate the goal of exploiting the total information available to all persons.

Thirdly, it shows how undesirable dogmatism may be when it leads one to totally discount the opinions of those with whom one disagrees. By so doing one decomposes society into subgroups, each having a consensus peculiar to it that fails to encompass the total information available. This fosters irrelevant criticism and misunderstanding. For what is reasonable in terms of the consensus of one group may be unreasonable in terms of the consensus of the other. Rather than the two groups being joined through mutual respect, they remain divided and in a position where each is unreasonable from the point of view of the other. Such segregation, on some few occasions, may have some justification, but by and large a refusal to give others positive respect will create a situation in which there is conflict based on partial information. The argument implicit herein against segregation and elitism in science and society is plain.

Finally, and critically, the method shows how important it is to weigh the reliability of others, not in terms of how closely they agree with oneself, but on their own merits as inquirers after truth and goodness. By so doing, the ultimate consensus will represent the best use of reflective intelligence rather than the willful attempt to dominate others. A consensus based on domination is, of course, useless as a guide in science or society however common the attempt to prevail in this way. For the consensus dominated by an individual or powerful elite represents the information of that small number only. The residual information available is thereby submerged or ignored.

If anyone complains that the consensual theory of probability and utility, of evidence and value, is subject to distortion because of duplicity and dishonesty, I extend my sympathy and my advice to act so as to alter such an unfortunate state of affairs. For to ignore such a consensus is to cast aside the very fruit of human intelligence on which all method and cogency ultimately depend. We should employ the consensual probability and utility assignments to determine what it is maximal to accept as evidence in science and to adopt as policy in society. If those consensual assignments represent an optimal use of information available to us all, we may feel satisfied that we have been reasonable in our quest for what is true and what is good. Some may insist that consensual reasonableness is not enough, that we must have what is necessarily and *a priori* evident and good. They may be left to postulate what satisfies their needs and hopes. The only reason, however, for accepting

28

what they postulate is that it accords with the totality of information we possess. The logical construction I have articulated is a summary of that totality. The rest is epistemic faith and wishful postulating.

Professor Keith Lehrer
University of Arizona

III

HOW A COMPUTER SHOULD THINK*

N. D. Belnap

INTRODUCTION; *the computer.* I propose that a certain four-valued logic should sometimes be used. It is to be understood that I use "logic" in a narrow sense, the old sense: a logic as an *organon*, a tool, a canon of inference. And it is also to be understood that I use "should" in a straightforward normative sense.

My suggestion for the utility of a four-valued logic is a local one. It is not the Big Claim that we all ought always use this logic (this paper does not comment on that claim), but the Small Claim that there are circumstances in which someone—not you—ought to abandon the familiar two-valued logic and use another instead. It will be important to delineate these circumstances with some care.

The situation I have in mind may be described as follows. In the first place, the reasoner who is to use this logic is an artificial information processor; that is, a (programmed) computer. This already has an important consequence. People sometimes give as an argument for staying with classical two-valued logic that it is tried and true, which is to say that it is imbued with the warmth of familiarity. This is a good (though not conclusive) argument for anyone who is interested, as I am, in practicality; it is kin to Quine's principle of "minimal mutilation," though I specifically want the emotional tone surrounding familiarity to be kept firmly in mind. But given that in the situation I envisage the reasoner is a computer, this argument has no application. The notion of "familiarity to the computer" makes no sense, and surely the computer does not care what logic is familiar to *us*. Nor is it any trouble

* This paper and Belnap 1976 are complements. There the introductory paragraphs and Part 1 are heavily abbreviated, while the more technical Parts 2 and 3 are given in full instead of, as here, barely summarized. Thanks are due to the National Science Foundation for partial support through Grant SOC71 03594 A02.

for a programmer to program an unfamiliar logic into the computer. So much for emotional liberation from two-valued logic.

In the second place, the computer is to be some kind of sophisticated question-answering system, where by "sophisticated" I mean that it does not confine itself, in answering questions, to just the data it has explicitly in its memory banks, but can also answer questions on the basis of *deductions* which it makes from its explicit information. Such sophisticated devices barely exist today, but they are in the forefront of everyone's hopes. In any event, the point is clear: unless there is some need for reasoning, there is hardly a need for logic.

Thirdly, the computer is to be envisioned as obtaining the data on which it is to base its inferences from a variety of sources, all of which indeed may be supposed to be on the whole trustworthy, but none of which can be assumed to be that paragon of paragons, a universal truth-teller. There are at least two possible pictures here. One puts the computer in the context of a lot of fallible humans telling it what is so and what is not; or with rough equivalency, a single human feeding it information over a stretch of time. The other picture paints the computer as part of a network of artificial intelligences with whom it exchanges information. In any event, the essential feature is that there is no single, monolithic, infallible source of the computer's data, but that inputs come from several independent sources. In such circumstances *the* crucial feature of the situation emerges: *inconsistency threatens*. Elizabeth tells the computer that the Pirates won the Series in 1971, while Sam tells it otherwise. What is the computer to do? If it is a classical two-valued logician, it must give up altogether talking about anything to anybody or, equivalently, it must say everything to everybody. We all know all about the fecundity of contradictions in two-valued logic: contradictions are never isolated, infecting as they do the whole system. Of course the computer could refuse to entertain inconsistent information. But in the first place that is unfair either to Elizabeth or to Sam, each of whose credentials are, by hypothesis, nearly impeccable. And in the second place, as we know all too well, contradictions may not lie on the surface. There may be in the system an *undetected* contradiction, or what is just as bad, a contradiction which is not detected until long after the input which generated it has been blended in with the general information of the computer and has lost its separate identity. But still we want the computer to use its head to reason to just conclusions yielding sensible answers to our questions.

Of course we want the computer to report any contradictions it finds, and in that sense we by no means want the computer to ignore contradictions. It is just that in these cases in which there is a possibility of inconsistency, we want to set things up so that the computer can continue reasoning in a sensible manner even if there is such an inconsistency, discovered or not. With respect to the latter, even if the computer has discovered and reported an inconsistency in its baseball information such as that the Pirates both won and did not win the Series in 1971, we would not want that to affect how it answered questions about airline schedules; but if the computer is a two-valued logician, the baseball contradiction will lead it to report that there is no way to get from Bloomington to Chicago. And also of course that there are exactly 3,000 flights per day. In an elegant phrase, Shapiro calls this "polluting the data." What I am proposing is to Keep Our Data Clean.

So we have a *practical* motive to deal with situations in which the computer may be told both that a thing is true and that also it is false (at the same time, in the same place, in the same respect, etc., etc., etc.).

There is a fourth aspect of the situation, concerning the significance of which I remain uncertain, but which nevertheless needs mentioning for a just appreciation of developments below: my computer is *not* a complete reasoner, who should be able to do something better in the face of contradiction than just report. The complete reasoner should, presumably, have some strategy for *giving up* part of what it believes when it finds its beliefs inconsistent. Since I have never heard of a practical, reasonable, mechanizable strategy for revision of belief in the presence of contradiction, I can hardly be faulted for not providing my computer with such. In the meantime, while others work on this extremely important problem, my computer can only accept and report contradictions without divesting itself of them.

This aspect is bound up with a fifth: in answering its questions, the computer is to reply strictly in terms of what it has been told, *not* in terms of what it could be programmed to believe. For example, if it has been told that the Pirates won and did not win in 1971, it is to so report, even though we could of course program the computer to recognize the falsity of such a report. The point here is both subtle and obvious: if the computer would not report our contradictions in answer to our questions, we would have no way of knowing that its data-base harbored contradictory information. (We could, if we wished, ask it to give a *supplementary* report, e.g., as follows: "I've been told that the Pirates won and did not win; but of course it ain't so"; but would that be useful?)

Approximation lattices. Always in the background and sometimes in the foreground of what I shall be working out is the notion of an *approximation lattice*, due to Scott (see e.g., Scott 1970, 1971, 1972). Let me say a word about this concept before getting on. You are going to be disappointed at the mathematical definition of an approximation lattice: mathematically it is just a complete lattice. That is, we have a set A on which there is a partial ordering $\sqsubseteq$, and for arbitrary subsets X of A there always exist least upper bounds $\sqcup X \epsilon A$ and greatest lower bounds $\sqcap X \epsilon A$ (two-element ones written $x \sqcup y$ and $x \sqcap y$). But I don't call a complete lattice an approximation lattice unless it satisfies a further, nonmathematical, condition: it is appropriate to read $x \sqsubseteq y$ as "x approximates y." Examples worked out by Scott include the lattice of "approximate and overdetermined real numbers," where we identify an approximate real number with an interval, and where $x \sqsubseteq y$ just in case $y \subseteq x$. The (only) overdetermined real number is the empty set. As a further example Scott offers the lattice of "approximate and overdetermined functions" from A to B, identified as subsets of $A \times B$. Here we want $f \sqsubseteq g$ just in case $f \subseteq g$.

In such lattices the *directed* sets are important: those sets such that every pair of members x and y of the set have an upper bound z also in the set. For such a set can be thought of as approximating by a limiting process to its union $\sqcup X$. That is, if X is directed, it makes sense to think of $\sqcup X$ as the limit of X. (An ascending sequence $x_1 \sqsubseteq \ldots \sqsubseteq x_i \sqsubseteq \ldots$ is a special case of a directed set.) And now when we pass to the family of functions from one approximation lattice into another (or of course the same) approximation lattice, Scott has demonstrated that what are important are the *continuous* functions: those that preserve non-trivial directed unions (i.e., $f(\sqcup X) = \sqcup \{fx: x \epsilon X\}$, for nonempty directed X). These are the only functions which respect the lattices qua *approximation* lattices. This idea is so fundamental to developments below that I choose to catch it in a Thesis to be thought of as analogous to Church's Thesis:

> *Scott's Thesis.* In the presence of complete lattices A and B naturally thought of as approximation lattices, pay attention only to the continuous functions from A into B, resolutely

33

ignoring all other functions as violating the nature of A and B as approximation lattices.

(Though honesty compels me to attribute the Thesis to Scott, the same policy bids me note that the formulation is mine, and that as stated he may not want it, or may think that some other Thesis in the neighborhood is more important; for example, that every approximation lattice (intuitive sense) is a continuous lattice (sense of Scott 1972).)

You will see how I rely on Scott's Thesis in what follows.

Program. The rest of this paper is divided into three parts. Part 1 considers the case in which the computer accepts only *atomic* information. This is a heavy limitation, but provides a relatively simple context in which to develop some of the key ideas. Part 2 allows the computer to accept also information conveyed by *truth-functionally compounded sentences*; and in this context I offer a new kind of meaning for formulas as certain mappings from epistemic states into epistemic states. In Part 3 the computer is allowed also to accept *implications construed as rules* for improving its data base.

Part 1. Atomic inputs
Atomic sentences and the approximation lattice **A4.** Now and throughout this paper you must keep firmly fixed in mind the circumstances in which the computer finds itself, and especially that it must be prepared to receive and reason about inconsistent information. I want to suggest a natural technique for employment in such cases: when an item comes in as asserted, mark it with a "told True" sign, and when an item comes in denied, mark with a "told False" sign. treating these two kinds of tellings as altogether on a par. It is easy to see that this leads to four possibilities. For each item in its basic data file, the computer is going to have it marked in one of the following four ways: (1) just the "told True" sign, indicating that that item has been asserted to the computer without ever having been denied. (2) Just the value "told False", which indicates that the item has been denied but never asserted. (3) No "told" values at all, which means the computer is in ignorance, has been told nothing. (4) The interesting case: the item might be marked with both "told True" and "told False". (Recall that allowing this case is a *practical necessity* because of the fallibility of man.)

These four possibilities are precisely the four values of the many-

34

valued logic I am offering as a practical guide to reasoning by the computer. Let us give them names:

T: just told True
F: just told False
None: told neither True nor False
Both: told both True and False

So these are our four values, and we baptize: **4** = {*T*, *F*, *None*, and *Both*}. Of course four values do not a logic make, but let us nevertheless pause a minute to see what we have so far.

The suggestion requires that a system using this logic code each of the atomic statements representing its data base in some manner indicating which of the four values it has (at the present stage). It follows that the computer cannot represent a class merely by listing certain elements, with the assumption that those not listed are not in the class. For just as there are four values, so there are four possible states of each element: the computer might have been told none, one, or both of "in the class" and "not in the class." Two procedures suggest themselves. The first is to list each item with one of the values *T*, *F*, or *Both*, for these are the elements about which the computer has been told something; and to let an absence of a listing signify *None*, i.e., that here is no information about that element. The second procedure would be to list each element with one *or both* of the "told" values, "told True" and "told False," not listing elements lacking both "told" values. Obviously the procedures are equivalent, and we shall not in our discourse distinguish between them, using one or the other as seems convenient.

The same procedure works for relations, except that it is ordered pairs that get marked. For example, a part of the correct table for Series winners, conceived as a relation between teams and years, might look like this:

⟨Pirates, 1971⟩ *T* or ⟨Pirates, 1971⟩ True
⟨Orioles, 1971⟩ *F*   ⟨Orioles, 1971⟩ False

But if Sam slipped up and gave the wrong information after Elizabeth had previously entered the above, the first entry would become

⟨Pirates, 1971⟩ *Both* or ⟨Pirates, 1971⟩ True, False

To be specific, we envision (in this Part of the paper) the epistemic state of the computer to be maintained in terms of a table giving one of four values to each atomic sentence. We call such a table a *set-up* (following an isomorphic use of Routley and Routley 1972); i.e., a

35

set-up is, mathematically, a mapping from atomic sentences into the set **4** = {**T**, **F**, **None**, **Both**}. When an atomic formula is entered into the computer as either affirmed or denied, the computer modifies its current set-up by adding a "told True" or "told False" according as the formula was affirmed or denied; it does not subtract any information it already has, for that is the whole point of what we are up to. In other words, if p is affirmed, it marks p with **T** if p were previously marked with **None**, with **Both** if p were previously marked with **False**; and of course leaves things alone if p was already marked either **T** or **Both**. So much for p as input.

The computer not only accepts input, but answers questions. We consider only the basic equation as to p; this it answers in one of four ways: Yes, No, Yes and No, or I don't know, depending on the value of p in its current set-up as **T**, **F**, **Both**, or **None**. (It would be wrong to suppose that these four answers are either dictated by the four-valued logic or excluded by the two-valued logic; it is just that they are made more useful in the four-valued context. See Belnap 1963 and Belnap and Steel 1975.)

Warning—or, as N. Bourbaki says, *tournant dangereux* (∩): "told True" is *not* equivalent to **T**. The relationships are rather as follows. In the first place, the computer is told True about some sentence A just in case it has *either* marked A with **T** *or* with **Both**. Secondly, the computer marks A with **T** just in case it has been told True of A *and* has not been told False of A. And similarly for the relation between **F** and "told False." These relationships are certainly obvious, but also in practice confusing. It might help always to read "told True" as "told *at least* True," and **T** as "told *exactly* True."

I now make the observation which constitutes the foundation of what follows: these four values naturally form a lattice under the lattice-ordering "approximates the information in", and indeed an *approximation-lattice* in the sense we described above:

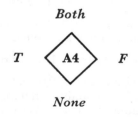

(In this Hasse diagram joins (⊔) and meets (⊓) are least upper bounds and greatest lower bounds respectively, and ⊑ goes uphill. *None* is at the bottom because it gives no information at all; and *Both* is at the top because it gives too much (inconsistent) information, saying as it does that the statement so marked is held both True and False. As we mentioned above, Scott has studied approximation-lattices in detail and in a much richer setting than we have before us; yet still this little four-element lattice is important for much of his work. We remarked above that according to Scott's Thesis the important functions in the neighborhood of an approximation lattice like **A4** are the continuous ones. We do not, fortunately, have to deal with continuity for a while, since in the finite case it turns out that for a function to be continuous is just for it to be *monotonic*, i.e., for it to preserve the lattice ordering: a ⊑ b implies fa ⊑ fb.

For example, suppose a function g on **A4** is such that it takes *T* into *F* and *F* into *T*: $g(T) = F$, $g(\mathbf{F}) = T$. Then given that g is monotonic, since $T \sqsubseteq \textbf{Both}$ we must have $\mathbf{F} \sqsubseteq g(\textbf{Both})$ and similarly $T \sqsubseteq g(\textbf{Both})$. So we must have $g(\textbf{Both}) = \textbf{Both}$. In a similar way, it is easy to calculate that $g(\textbf{None}) = \textbf{None}$—if g is to be monotonic, as all good functions should be.

Compound sentences and the logical lattice **L4**. Now this function, g, is no *mere* example of a monotonic function on the lattice **A4** of approximate and inconsistent truth-values. In fact we are in the very presence of *negation*, which some have called the original sin of logic but which we clearly need in a sufficiently rich language for our computer to use—just to be able to answer simple yes–no questions. To see that g really *is* negation, consider first that the values *T* and *F*, representing as they do the pure case, should act like the ordinary truth values the True and the False, so that obviously we want $\sim T = F$, and $\sim F = T$. And then Scott's Thesis now imposes on us a *unique* solution to the problem of extending negation to the values of our foursome; we *must* have $\sim \textbf{None} = \textbf{None}$ and $\sim \textbf{Both} = \textbf{Both}$ if negation is to be an acceptably monotonic function on the approximation–lattice **A4**.

We can summarize the argument in a small table for negation.

	None	F	T	Both
	m	tt	tt	m
~	None	T	F	Both

Here "tt" in the upper right hand corner means that the value was given by truth table considerations, while "m" indicates that monotonicity was invoked.

Having put negation in our pocket, let's turn to conjunction and disjunction. We start with truth table, considerations for *T–F* portion of the tables, and then invoke monotony (in each argument place) and easy considerations to extend them as indicated.

&	None	F	T	Both
None	None (m)		None (m)	
F		F (tt)	F (tt)	
T	None (m)	F (tt)	T (tt)	Both (m)
Both			Both (m)	Both (m)

V	None	F	T	Both
None	None (m)	None (m)		
F	None (m)	F (tt)	T (tt)	Both (m)
T		T (tt)	T (tt)	
Both		Both (m)		Both (m)

With just ordinary truth tables and monotonicity, it would appear we have to stop with these partial tables; on this basis neither conjunction nor disjunction—unlike negation—are uniquely determined. Of course we might make some guesses on the basis of intuition, but this part of the argument is founded on a desire not to do that; rather, we are trying to see how far we can go on a purely theoretical basis.

It turns out that if we ask only that conjunction and disjunction have some minimal relation to each other, then every other box is uniquely determined. There are several approaches possible here, but perhaps as illuminating as any is to insist that the orderings determined by the two in the standard way be the same; which is to say that the following equivalence holds:

$$a\&b = a \quad \text{iff} \quad a\lor b = b$$
$$a\&b = b \quad \text{iff} \quad a\lor b = a$$

For look at the partial table for conjunction. One can see that T is an identity element: $a\&T = a$, all a. So if conjunction and disjunction fit together as they ought, we must have $a\lor T = T$, all a, which fills in two boxes of the $\lor$-table. And similar arguments fill in all except the corners.

For the corners we must invoke monotony (*after* the above lattice argument). For example, since $F \sqsubseteq \textbf{\textit{Both}}$, by monotony ($F$ & $\textbf{\textit{None}}$) $\sqsubseteq \textbf{\textit{Both}}$ & $\textbf{\textit{None}}$) so $F \sqsubseteq (\textbf{\textit{Both}}$ & $\textbf{\textit{None}})$. Similarly, $\textbf{\textit{None}} \sqsubseteq F$ leads to ($\textbf{\textit{Both}}$ & $\textbf{\textit{None}}$) $\sqsubseteq (\textbf{\textit{Both}}$ & $F)$, i.e. ($\textbf{\textit{Both}}$ & $\textbf{\textit{None}}$) $\sqsubseteq F$. So by antisymmetry in **A4** ($\textbf{\textit{Both}}$ & $\textbf{\textit{None}}$) = **F**. These additional results are brought together in the following tables, where "f" indicates use of the above fit between & and $\lor$, and "m" again indicates monotony.

&	*None*	*F*	*T*	*Both*
None	*None*	f *F*	*None*	f *F*
F	f *F*	*F*	*F*	f *F*
T	*None*	*F*	*T*	*Both*
Both	m *F*	f *F*	*Both*	*Both*

V	None	F	T	Both
None	None	None	T	T
F	None	F	T	Both
T	T	T	T	T
Both	T	Both	T	Both

I don't know if we should be surprised or not, but in fact these tables do constitute a lattice, with conjunction as meet and disjunction as join; a lattice which can be pictured as follows:

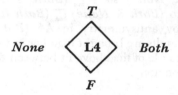

Let us agree to call this the *logical* lattice, **L4**, to distinguish it from the *approximation* lattice, **A4**. The ordering on **L4** we write as a ≤ b; we write meets as a&b, and joins as a∨b. I note that in the logical lattice, both of the values *None* and *Both* are intermediate between **F** and **T**; and this is as it should be, for the worst thing is to be told something is false, simpliciter. You are better off (it is one of your hopes) in either being told nothing about it, or in being told both that it is true and also that it is false; while of course best of all is to be told it is true, with no muddying of the waters. Nevertheless, surely most of you must be puzzled, if you are thinking about it, concerning the rules for computing the conjunction and disjunction of *None* and *Both*: *None* & *Both* = *F*, while *None* ∨ *Both* = *T*. I ask you for now only to observe that we were driven to these equations by only three considerations: ordinary

40

truth tables, monotony, and fit between & and V. But I have shall more to say about this.

We can now use these logical operations on **L4** to induce a semantics for a language involving &, V, and ∼, in just the usual way. Given an arbitrary set-up s—a mapping, you will recall, of atomic formulas into **4**—we can extend s to a mapping of *all* formulas into **4** in the standard inductive way:

$$s(A\&B) = s(A)\&s(B)$$
$$s(A\lor B) = s(A)\lor s(B)$$
$$s(\sim A) = \sim s(A)$$

And this tells us how the computer should answer questions about complex formulas based on a set-up representing its epistemic state (what it has been told): just as for answering questions about atomic formulas, it should answer a question as to A by Yes, No, Yes and No, or I don't know, according as the value of A in s (i.e., s(A)) is **T**, **F**, *Both*, or *None*.

The preceding discussion will have struck you as abstractly theoretical; I should next like to take up negation, conjunction, and disjunction from an altogether different and more intuitive point of view. The question to which we are going to address ourselves is this: given our intuitive understanding of the meaning of the four truth-values as indicating markings of sentences with either or both of the True and the False, what is a plausible way to extend these values to compound sentences when we know the values of the ingredient sentences? Let us take up negation first.

The inevitable thing to say seems to be that ∼A should be marked with the True just in case A is marked with the False, and should be marked with the False just in case A is marked with the True. In other words, ∼A should be marked with at least the True just in case A is marked with at least the False, and marked with at least the False just in case A is marked with at least the True. But then consider the correspondences

None: marked with neither,
  F: marked with just the False,
  T: marked with just the True,
Both: marked with both.

It immediately comes out that we should mark ∼A with *Both* if A is, with *None* if A is, and with *T* or *F* if A is *F* or *T*. For example, if A is marked *None*, i.e., with neither the True nor the False, then

41

$\sim A$ should also be marked with neither. If you know nothing about A, then you know nothing about $\sim A$. And the same reasoning works for **Both**: if you know too much about A, then you also know too much about $\sim A$.

In a similar way, we can give intuitive clauses for evaluation of conjunctions and disjunctions, as follows:

> Mark $(A\&B)$ with at least the True just in case both A and B have been marked with at least the True.
> Mark $(A\&B)$ with at least the False just in case at least one of A and B have been marked with at least the False.

This completely determines how to mark conjunctions.

> Mark $(A\lor B)$ with at least the True just in case at least one of A and B have been marked with at least the True.
> Mark $(A\lor B)$ with at least the False just in case both A and B have been marked with at least the False.

And this similarly uniquely determines disjunction, given our intuitive correspondence between our four values **None, F, T, Both** on the one hand, and markings with neither, one, or both of the True and the False on the other. And furthermore, this intuitive account of the connectives exactly agrees with the theoretically based account deriving from Scott's approximation lattices. For example, consider one of the odd corners, **Both** & **None** = **F**. Well, suppose A has been marked with both the True and the False, and B with neither (corresponding to **Both** and **None**, respectively). Then we must mark $(A\&B)$ with at least the value the False, since one of its components has at least the value the False; and we must *not* mark it with at least the True, since not both of its components are so marked. So we must mark it with exactly the False: So **Both** & **None** = **F**. In other even more informal words, in this circumstance the computer has a reason to suppose $(A\&B)$ told false, but none to suppose it told true. So, although the oddity of **Both** & **None** = **F** doesn't go away, it anyhow gets explained.

Entailment and inference: the four-valued logic. Where are we? Well, we haven't got a logic, i.e., rules for generating and evaluating inferences. (In our case we really want the former; we want some rules for the computer to use in generating what it implicitly knows from what it explicitly knows.) What we do have is four interesting

42

values, with indications as to how these are to be used by friend computer, and three splendid connectives, with complete and well-motivated tables for each. And as we all know, lots of other connectives can be defined in terms of these, so that for our purposes three is enough.

Suppose we have an argument involving these connectives. The question is, when is it a good one? Again I want to give an abstractly theoretical answer, and then an intuitive answer. (And then several more answers, too, were there time enough. For the question is fascinating.)

The abstract answer relies on the *logical* lattice we took so much time to develop. It is: entailment goes up hill. That is, given any sentences A and B (compounded from variables by negation, conjunction, and disjunction), we will say that A *entails* or *implies* B just in case for each assignment of one of the four values to the variables, the value of A does not exceed (is less-than-or-equal-to) the value of B. In symbols: $s(A) \leq s(B)$ for each set-up s. This is a plausible definition of entailment whenever we have a lattice of values which we can think of as somehow being graded from bottom to top; and as I suggested when first presenting you with the logical lattice, we can indeed think of *None* and *Both* as being intermediate between awful F and wonderful T.

Now for an account which is close to the informal considerations underlying our understanding of the four values as keeping track of markings with the True and the False: say that the inference from A to B is valid, or that A entails B, if the inference never leads us from the True to the absence of the True (preserves Truth), *and also* never leads us from the absence of the False to the False (preserves non-Falsity). Given our system of markings, to ask this is hardly to ask too much.

(I note that Dunn 1975 has shown that it suffices to mention truth-presentation, since if some inference form fails to always preserve non-Falsity, then it can be shown by a technical argument that it *also* fails to preserve Truth. Just take the assignment to the propositional variables which *switches* *Both* and *None*, but leaves T and F alone, and show that the value of any compound has the same feature. But I agree with the spirit of a remark of Dunn's, which suggests that the False really is on all fours with the True, so that it is profoundly natural to state our account of "valid" or "acceptable" inference in a way which is neutral with respect to the two.)

Finally we have a logic, that is a canon of inference for our computer to use in making inferences involving conjunction, negation, and disjunction, as well of course as whatever can be defined in terms thereof. I note that this logic has two key features. In the first and most important place, it is rooted in reality. We gave reasons why it would be good for our computer to think in terms of our four values, and why the logic of the four values should be as it is. In the second place, though we have not thrown around many hen-scratches, it is clear that our account of validity is mathematically rigorous. And obviously the computer can decide by running through a truth-tabular computation whether or not a proposed inference is valid. But there is another side to the logician's job, which is codifying inferences in some axiomatic or semi-axiomatic way which is transparent and accordingly usable. If this sounds mysterious, it is not; I just mean that a logician, given a semantics, ordinarily tries to come up with proof-theory for it; a proof-theory which is consistent and complete relative to the semantics.

This job has been done any number of times, though in the beginning the proof-theory came first and the semantics only later. The history of the matter is about as follows. A long time ago Alan Anderson and I in 1962 proposed a group of inferences, which we called *tautological entailments*, as comprising all of the *sane* inferences (involving &, V, ~) which anyone not a psychotic, or not badly trained, would want to make We had various proof-theoretical formalizations for these, and showed that an eight-valued matrix was sufficient to characterize them semantically.

Later T. J. Smiley showed (in a letter to us) that a certain four-valued matrix would do exactly the same work; namely, though with numbers instead of fancy names, precisely the four values I am offering you here. So that's where I learned them. Smiley of course intended his result as merely technical, without logical point, in the sense of "logical" of this paper.

Still later Dunn in 1966 gave a variety of semantics for tautological entailments, some of them highly intuitive, some closely related to the four-valued matrix of Smiley; and to him is due one of the central ideas with which I have been working, namely, the identification of the four values with the four subsets of {the True, the False}. Dunn in 1975 (belatedly) presents much of both the intuitive and the technical significance of this idea. Other semantics for tautological entailments, again with intuitive considerations, are due to van Fraassen 1966b and Routley and Routley 1972. The algebraic structure corresponding to this logic has been investigated in detail by Dunn and others; all this is reported by Dunn in

Chapter III of Anderson and Belnap 1975, wherein also will be found Gentzen calculuses and the like.

My own deeper interest, and the thought that there might be a computer application, came after overlapping with Dana Scott in Oxford in 1970 as guests of Christopher Strachey's—to whom thanks, now tragically posthumous, are due. The four values emerged as an important approximation lattice in Scott's work, and the connection with the Smiley four values was not hard to see. The realization of the importance of the epistemic interpretation is more recent.

Stuart Shapiro has independently argued for the utility of "relevance logics" for question-answering systems, and has suggested implementation in a research proposal; see also Shapiro and Wand 1975.

So much for history. Let me briefly present a group of principles which are semantically valid, and taken together semantically complete. They will also be redundant, but recall that the byword for this exercise is usefulness; I am offering a set of principles for the computer to use in making its inferences.

Let A, B, etc., be formulas in &, $\lor$, and $\sim$. Let $A{\to}B$ signify that the inference from A to B is valid in our four values, i.e., that A entails B. Also let $A{\leftrightarrows}B$ signify that A and B are semantically equivalent, and can be intersubstituted in any context. Then the following have proved to be a useful (complete) set of principles.

$A_1\&\ldots\&A_m{\to}B_1\lor\ldots\lor B_n$
provided some A_i is some B_j (sharing)
$(A\lor B){\to}C$ iff (if and only if) $A{\to}C$ and $B{\to}C$
$A{\to}B\&C$ iff $A{\to}B$ and $A{\to}C$

$A{\to}B$ iff $\sim A{\to}\sim B$
$A\lor B{\leftrightarrows}B\lor A$ $\qquad A\&B{\leftrightarrows}B\&A$
$A\lor(B\lor C){\leftrightarrows}(A\lor B)\lor C$ $(A\&B)\&C{\leftrightarrows}A\&(B\&C)$
$A\&(B\lor C){\leftrightarrows}(A\&B)\lor(A\&C)$ $A\lor(B\&C){\leftrightarrows}(A\lor B)\&(A\lor C)$
$(B\lor C)\&A{\leftrightarrows}(B\&A)\lor(C\&A)$ $(B\&C)\lor A{\leftrightarrows}(B\lor A)\&(C\lor A)$
$\sim\sim A{\leftrightarrows}A$
$\sim(A\&B){\leftrightarrows}\sim A\lor\sim B$ $\sim(A\lor B){\leftrightarrows}\sim A\&\sim B$
if $A{\to}B$ and $B{\to}C$, then $A{\to}C$
if $A{\leftrightarrows}B$ and $B{\leftrightarrows}C$, then $A{\leftrightarrows}C$
$A{\to}B$ if $A{\leftrightarrows}(A\&B)$ iff $(A\lor B){\leftrightarrows}B$

Observations. Some observations now need to be made before pushing further. First, I note that not derivable from these principles, and not semantically valid, are the paradoxes of "implication" $A \& \sim A \to B$ and $A \to B \lor \sim B$. In context, the failure of these principles is evident. The failure of the first simply means that just because we have been told both that A is True, and that A is False, we cannot conclude: everything. Indeed, we may have been told nothing about B, or just that it is False. And the failure of the second is equally evident: from the fact that we have been told that A is True, we cannot conclude that we know something about B. Of course B is *ontologically* either True or False, and such ontological truth-values will receive their due; but for $B \lor \sim B$ to be marked with the True is either for B to be marked with the True or for B to be marked with the False; and it may have neither mark. Or, for a different way of counterexampling $A \to B \lor \sim B$, A may have just the True while $(B \lor \sim B)$ has *both* values because B does.

These inferences are not wanted in a scheme which is designed not to break down in the presence of "contradictions"; and since contradictions really do threaten in the circumstances we describe, their absence is welcome.

I would be less than open, however, if I failed to point out the absence of what at first sight looks like a more harmless principle: $(A \lor B) \& \sim A \to B$. Surely, one would think, our computer should be able to argue that if one of A and B is true, and it's not A, then it must be B. That's true; unless—and of course this is a critical "unless,"—there is an inconsistency around. In fact the inference the canon allows is just exactly

$$(A \lor B) \& \sim A \to (A \& \sim A) \lor B$$

That is, having determined that the antecedent is at least True, we allow the computer to conclude: either B is at least True, or something funny is going on; i.e., it's been told that A is both True and False. And this, you will see, is right on target. If the *reason* that $(A \lor B) \& \sim A$ is getting thought of as a Truth is because A has been labeled as both True and False, then we certainly do *not* want to go around inferring B. The inference is wholly inappropriate in a context where inconsistency is a live possibility.

The second observation is that our four values are proposed only in connection with *inferences*, and are definitely not supposed to be used for determining which formulas in $\&$, $\lor$, and $\sim$ count as so-called logical truths. In fact no formula takes always the value T, so *that* property surely won't do as semantic account of logical truth. There are, on the other hand, formulas which never take the value

46

F, e.g., $A \lor \sim A$; but this set is not even closed under conjunction and does not contain $(A \lor \sim A) \& (B \lor \sim B)$, which can take *F* when *A* takes **None** and *B* takes **Both**. So just don't try to base logical truth on these values.

Thirdly, let us consider ontology vs. epistemology. One of the difficulties which often arises in relating many-valued logics to real concerns is that one tends to vacillate between reading the various values as epistemic on the one hand, or ontological on the other. Does Łukasiewicz' middle value, 1/2, mean "doesn't have a proper truth-value" or does it mean "truth-value unknown"? In informal explanations of what is going on, logicians sometimes move from one of these readings to the other in order to save the interest of the enterprise.

My four values are unabashedly epistemic. According to my instructions, sentences are to be marked with either a *T* or an *F*, a **None** or a **Both**, according as to what the computer has been told; or, with only a slight metaphor, according to what it believes or knows. Does this somehow make the enterprise wrong headed? Or not logic? No. Of course these sentences *have* truth-values independently of what the computer has been told; but who can gainsay that the computer cannot *use* the actual truth-value of the sentences in which it is interested? All it can possibly *use* as a basis for inference is what it knows or believes, i.e., what it has been told.

But we can do better than this. Let us get the ontology into the act by *splitting* our four epistemological values into two, one representing the case in which the sentence is ontologically true, the other the case in which it is false. Obviously we then get eight values instead of four, each of which we may visualize as an ordered pair, the left entry of which is an epistemic value *T*, *F*, **None**, or **Both**, while the right entry is one of Frege's ontological values the True and the False. Giving the usual classical two-valued tables to the connectives, and also and equivalently, interpreting the implicative connective in the usual way, we are led to the following lattice picture (this is *not* an approximation lattice) (See page 48).

The &'s and $\lor$'s can be computed respectively as g.l.b.s and l.u.b.s, while negation-pairs are: two left, two center, two right, and top-bottom (*not* the boolean way). The values of this new many-valued logic have a mixed status: they are in part epistemological and in part ontological. Should we then move to this logic? It is entertaining to observe that there is no need to do so for inferences; for *exactly* the same inferences are valid with this as with our four-valued canon of inference. Nor for two reasons should this be surprising.

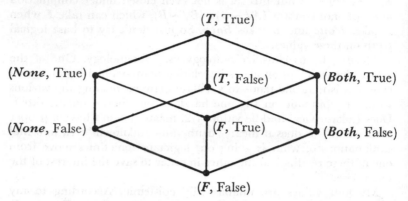

In the first place, as we already observed, the only thing we can actually *use* in inference are the epistemic values *T*, *F*, *None* and *Both*, representing what we know, believe, or in any event have been told by authority we by and large trust. Secondly, and more prosaically, observe that all the inferences sanctioned by the four-valued canon are already approved in two-valued logic; so that adding as a condition that ontological truth is to be preserved is to add a condition that is already satisfied and yields no new constraints. So for practical reasons there is no need to move from four to eight values for judging inferences. In the words of a famous philosopher, "Do not multiply many values beyond necessity."

If, however, for some reason (I do not just now know what) someone wanted an account of logical truth in &, V, and ∼, then one could invoke as a criterion: being always True (by the right entry of the pair) regardless of what you've been told (according to the left entry). Then, not surprisingly, one finds out that the two-valued tautologies are precisely the logical truths on this account. Not surprisingly because we invoke values only ontological, throwing away (in the eight-valued case) all the information of the epistemic values.

Let me say explicitly, if it is not obvious, that I think this codification of truth-functional logical truths not very important to the computer; for what was *wanted* was a way of *reasoning* from and to truth-functional compounds, not a sorting of these compounds.

My fourth "observation" is not so much that as it is an inconclusive discussion of the role of *Both* and *None*. The problem is that one is inclined to the view that they should be identified, that the computer is in the same state having been told that *A* is both

True and False as it is having been told nothing about A. A. Kenny and S. Haack have each, in quite different ways, suggested something like this. If you will be satisfied with a dialectical flourish, I can supply one of the form "Wrong, but understandable." It goes like this. In the first place, it is somehow magnificently obvious that *Both* and *None* should not be identified, as H. S Harris noted in conversation, just because we want the computer to distinguish *for us* when it has been told a contradiction from when it has been told nothing. This is surely essential on anyone's view. In the second, our developments can be taken as explaining the feeling that they should be identified, for just look at the logical lattice **L4**: there *Both* and *None* occupy (distinct but) absolutely symmetrical positions between F and T, and in this sense are "identified." For instance, we allow the inference from neither to F, nor from T to either, and thus treat them alike.

Still, though this response may be helpful, I am not altogether happy with it. And I much prefer to leave the discussion as at this stage incomplete.

My penultimate observation concerns the suggestion that the computer keep more information than I have allowed it to keep. Perhaps it should count the number of times it has been told True or told False, or perhaps it should keep track of its sources by always marking, for example, "told True by Sam at 2200:03 on 4 August 1973." I do not see why these ideas should not be explored, but two comments are in order. The first is that it is by no means self-evident how this extra information is to be utilized in answering questions, in inference, and in the input of complex sentences. That is, do not be misled by the transparency of the idea in the case of atomic sentences. The consequence of this first comment is merely that the exploration lies ahead. The second is the practical remark that there are severe costs in carrying extra information, costs which may or may not be worth incurring. And if there are circumstances in which they are not worth incurring, we are back to the situation I originally described.

Lastly, I want to mention some alternatives without (much) discussing them. A. Gupta has noted that one could define the value of A in s not directly as we have done, but rather by reference to all the consistent sub-set-ups of s. Definitions: s' is a sub-set-up of s if it approximates it: $s' \sqsubseteq s$. s' is consistent if it never awards *Both*. Finally, let s(A) be defined, *a la* Gupta, by s(A) = {s'(A): s' is a consistent sub-set-up of s}, where s'(A) is as already defined. The idea is clearly dual to van Fraassen's definition of true-in-a-valuation by reference to all the complete (i.e., all truth value gaps filled) supervaluations of a given valuation. One notes that if $s(p) = \textbf{Both}$, then the question as to p (on s) will be answered "Yes and No" as before, while the question as to $p\& \sim p$ will be answered just "No," instead of "Yes and No."

This idea could be used, incidentally, to improve on Rescher's suggestion in *Hypothetical reasoning* (North-Holland, 1964). There he suggests reasoning from an inconcsistent set of premisses by looking at all the consistent subsets. The difficulty with that idea, in my judgment, is that it is too sensitive to the way the set of premisses is broken down into separate sentences. Gupta's notion could be used, I think, to present an idea having the initial flavor of Rescher's without its bitter aftertaste.

A related idea is to follow van Fraassen directly by looking at all the complete super-set-ups of a given set-up; this would give always "Yes" to $p\mathsf{V}\sim p$. And carrying this idea to its logical conclusion would combine the two ideas (carefully).

All of these things are possible. One would hope, however, that the discussion of the alternatives would circulate around the question, How in fact do we want the computer to answer our questions? In this way they would not be *mere* possibilities.

Quantifiers. Quantifiers introduce a number of subleties to which I shall merely tip my hat, while recognizing that treating them in detail is quite essential to my enterprise.

There is in the first place the question of whether "the" domain is finite or infinite. Both cases can plausibly arise In the latter case, there is the question of how the computer is to represent infinite information with its finite resources, but one should not infer from the existence of this problem that the computer can't or shouldn't involve itself with quantification over infinite domains. Surely it should be allowed to answer "Is there a number such that . . . ?" queries (if it can).

In the second place, there is the question of whether the computer has a name for everything in "the" domain so that we can employ the substitutional interpretation of the quantifiers, or on the other hand does not have a name for each entity in "the" domain so that the domain-and-values interpretation is forced. Again: both cases can plausibly arise, though attending to standard examples like baseball queries or airline flights might have made one think that in the computer situation everything always has a name. But, for example, in some of Isner's work the computer is told "there is something between a and b" in a context in which it hasn't got a complete list of either the names or the entities against which to interpret this statement. And still it must work out the consequences, and answer the questions it is given. (Of course it is O.K. for the computer to make up its own name for the "something" between a and b; but that is both an important and an entirely different matter.)

In any event, the semantics given for the connectives extend to universal and existential quantifiers in an obvious way, and I suppose the job done. And the various alternatives mentioned above turn out not to make any difference to the *logic* (with the obvious exception of the finite everything-has-a-name case): the valid "first degree entailments" of Anderson and Belnap 1965 do admirably (supplemented, in the finite case, with the principle that a conjunction which runs through the domain implies the appropriate universal statement).

Part 2. Compound truth functional inputs.
My aim in this part and the next is barely to give the flavor of the developments I suggest. They are based much more heavily than are those of Part I on approximation lattices, and in general tend to be more technical. But I think something can be said to give you, as I say, the flavor. Details are to be found in Belnap 1976.

Epistemic states. If we allow the computer to receive as inputs not only atomic formulas but also complexes such as $p \lor q$, a single set-up will no longer suffice to represent its epistemic state. A well-known solution to this kind of problem, going back at least to Carnap 1942, exploited by Hintikka 1962 in epistemic and doxastic logic, and worked out for computers in Isner 1972, 1975, is to employ instead a *collection* of set-ups as the representation of the epistemic state of the computer. Let it be done. Further, it is possible to use approximation ideas to motivate and define how we want the computer to answer our questions about A in each such state; which is to say, where E is such a state, we can compute $E(A)$, the value of A in E, as one of the four values. Let this also be done. (Skippable definition: $E(A) = \sqcap \{s(A) : s \epsilon E\}$.) I note two special epistemic states for use further on: $\text{Tset}(A)$ and $\text{Fset}(A)$ are defined in such a way that they represent what the computer has been told when precisely A has been, respectively, affirmed or denied. (Skippable: $\text{Tset}(A) = \{s : T \sqsubseteq s(A)\}$, and $\text{Fset}(A) = \{s : F \sqsubseteq s(A)\}$.)

More approximation lattices. One of the principal lessons to be drawn

51

c

from Scott's work is that wherever there is one approximation lattice, there are lots of them. In particular, the family of all set-ups forms a natural approximation lattice, **AS**; and then the family of all epistemic states constitutes (or almost constitutes; subtleties omitted) still another approximation lattice **AE**. (Skippable: in **AS**, s ⊏ s' iff s(p) ⊏ s'(p) for all p; in **ES**, E ⊏ E' iff for every s'∊E' there is an s∊E such that s ⊏ s'.)

Formulas as mappings; a new kind of meaning. Now I turn to a question of considerable interest, and a question on which our various approximation lattices can shed considerable light: How is the computer to interpret a truth-functional formula, A, as input? Clearly it is going to use A to modify its present epistemic state; and indeed it is not too much to say that defining how the computer uses the formula A to transform its present epistemic state into a new epistemic state is a way, and a *good* way, of giving A a meaning. Consequently we want to associate with each formula A a transformation, a mapping from epistemic states into new epistemic states. Furthermore, we also want to know what the computer is to do when the formula A is *denied* to the computer; so actually we associate with a formula A *two* functions, one representing the transformation of epistemic state when A is affirmed, the other the transformation when A is denied. Let us call these two functions A^+ and A^-. How to define them?

Recall that A^+ is to map states into states: $A^+(E) = E'$. The key ideas in defining what we want E' to be come from the approximation lattice. First, in our context we are assuming that the computer uses its input always to increase its information, or at least it never uses input to throw information away. (That would just be a different enterprise; it would be nice to know how to handle it in a theory, but I don't.) And we can say this accurately in the language of approximation: E ⊏ A^+(E). Second, A^+(E) should certainly say no less that the affirmation of A: Tset(A) ⊏ A^+(E). Third and lastly, we clearly want A^+(E) to be the *minimum mutilation* of E that renders A at least True. "Minimum mutilation" is Quine's fine phrase, but in the approximation lattice we can give a sense that is *no longer merely metaphorical*: namely, we want the *least* of those epistemic states satisfying our first two conditions. That is, we should define

$$A^+(E) = E \sqcup \text{Tset}(A),$$

for that is precisely the minimum mutilation of E which makes A at least True. (Recall that in any lattice, x ⊔ y is the "least (minimum) upper bound".) Having agreed on this as the definition of A^+, it is easy to see that A^-(E) should be the minimum mutilation of E which makes A at least False:

$$A^-(E) = E \sqcup \text{Fset}(A).$$

The above definitions accurately represent the meaning of A as input, but they do involve a drawback: the Tsets and Fsets may be infinite, or at least large, and so do not represent something the computer can really work with. For this reason, and also for its intrinsic interest, another explication of A^+ and A^- is offered in Belnap 1976, this time inductive, but still very much involving the idea of minimum mutilation. Here we omit it.

Part 3. Implicational inputs and rules
In Part 1 we pretended that all information fed into the computer was atomic, so we could get along with set-ups. In Part 2 we generalized to allow information in the form of more complex truth-functional formulas, a generalization which required moving to epistemic states. Now we must recognize that it is *practically* important that sometimes we give information to the computer in the form of rules which allow it to modify its own representation of its epistemic state in directions we want. In other words, we want to be able to instruct the computer to make inferential moves which are not mere tautological entailments. For example, instead of physically handing the computer the whole list of Series winners and non-winners for 1971, it is obviously cheaper to tell the computer: "the Pirates won; and further, if you've got a winner and a team not identical to it, that team must be a non-winner" (i.e., $(x)\,(y)\,(Wx\ \&\ x \neq y \rightarrow \sim Wy)$. In the presence of an obviously needed table for identity and distinctness, or else in the presence of a convention that different names denote different entities (not a bad convention for *practical* use in many a computer setting), one could then *infer* that "The Orioles won" is to be marked false.

Your first thought might be that you could get the effect of "given A and B, infer C," or "if A and B, then C," by feeding the computer "$\sim A \vee \sim B \vee C$." But that won't work: the latter formula will tend to *split* the set-up you've got into three, in one of which A is marked False, etc.; while what is wanted is (roughly) just to improve the single set-up you've got by adding True to C provided A and B are marked True (and otherwise to leave things alone). It is (roughly) this idea we want to catch.

53

Implicational inputs. Let us introduce "$A{\rightarrow}B$" as representing the implication of A to B; so what we have is notation in search of a meaning. But we have in the previous section found just the right way of giving meaning to an expression construed as an input: the computer is to improve its epistemic state in the minimum possible way so as to make the expression True. So let us look forward to treating $(A{\rightarrow}B)^+$ as signifying some mapping from states into states such that $A{\rightarrow}B$ is true in the resultant state.

Without going into details (to be found in Belnap 1976), the procedure is this. First we atomize the problem by concentrating on a given set-up s. Then we divide the problem by recalling that implication has two parts: B must be at least T if A is, and A must be at least F if B is. So we define two functions, $(A{\rightarrow}_TB)^+$ and $(A{\rightarrow}_FB)^+$, the first *making B* True if A is, the second *making A* True if B is—and in each case by minimum mutilation. Lastly, we put these functions together, in a certain way (omitted here), to come up with $(A{\rightarrow}B)^+$ as a function.

Just a bit more on the part $(A{\rightarrow}B)^+$ which is supposed to minimally mutilate s to make B True if A is. Clearly if A is not True in s, we know what to do: nothing. No mutilation is minimum mutilation. Suppose now that A is True in s: then what is wanted is the minimum mutilation which makes B True—namely, the already defined function, B^+. So putting these clauses together we evidently have a proper definition for $(A{\rightarrow}_TB)^+$ as the minimum mutilation which makes B True if A is.

Rules and information states. This last section of this paper is going to be altogether tentative, and altogether abstract, with just one concrete thought that needs remembering, which I learned from Isner: probably the best way to handle sophisticated information states in a computer is by a judicious *combination* of tables (like our epistemic states) and rules (like our $A{\rightarrow}B$, or a truth-functional formula the computer prefers to remember, or a quantificational formula which it must remember). For this reason, as well as for the quite different reason that some rules, since they may have to be used again (are not permanent, must be remembered), we can no longer be satisfied by representing what the computer knows by means of an epistemic state. Rather, it must be represented by a *pair* consisting of an epistemic state *and* a set of rules:

$$\langle R, E \rangle$$

E is supposed to represent what the computer explicitly knows, and

N. D. BELNAP

is subject to increase by application of the rules in the set R. For many purposes we should suppose that E is finite, but for some not.

Let us dub such a pair an *information state,* just so we don't have to retract our previous definition of "epistemic state." But what is a rule? Of what is R a set? A good thing to mean by *rule,* or *ampliative* rule, in this context might be: *any* continuous and ampliative mapping from epistemic states into epistemic states. As I mentioned above, the set of *all* continuous functions from an approximation lattice into itself has been studied by Scott; it forms itself a natural approximation lattice. It is furthermore easy to see that the ampliative continuous functions form a natural approximation lattice, and one which is an almost complete sublattice of the space of all the continuous functions: all meets and joins agree, except that the join of the empty set is the identity function *I* instead of the totally undefined function. Intuitively: the effect of an empty set of rules is to leave the epistemic state the way it was. The notion of an information state is considered a bit in Belnap 1976, but the explorations there are so tentative that we omit them here.

Closure. Lest it have been lost, let me restate the principal aim of this paper: to propose the *usefulness* of the scheme of tautological entailments as a guide to inference in a certain setting; namely, that of a reasoning, question-answering computer threatened with contradictory information. The reader is not to suppose that Larger Applications have not occurred to me; e.g., of some of the ideas to a logic of imperatives, or to doxastic logic, or even to the development of The One True Logic. But because of my fundamental conviction that logic is (all in all) practical, I did not want these possibilities to loom so large as to shut out the light required for dispassionate consideration of my far more modest proposal.

Professor Nuel D. Belnap, Jr.
University of Pittsburgh

REFERENCES

Anderson, A. R., and Belnap, N. D. Jr. Tautological entailments. *Philosophical studies,* vol. 13 (1962), pp. 9–24: see also Ch. III of Anderson & Belnap, 1975.

Anderson, A. R., and Belnap, N. D. Jr. First degree entailments. *Mathematische annalen,* vol. 149 (1965), pp. 302–319.

Anderson, A. R., and Belnap, N. D. Jr. *Entailment: the logic of relevance and necessity* (vol. I), Princeton University Press, 1975.

COMPUTER-THINKING

Belnap, N. D. Jr. *An analysis of questions: preliminary report*, System Development Corporation, Santa Monica, 1963.

Belnap, N. D. Jr. A useful four-valued logic. *Modern uses of multiple-valued logic*, ed. G. Epstein and J. M. Dunn. Proceedings of the 1975 International Symposium on Multiple-valued Logic. Reidel, forthcoming, 1976.

Belnap, N. D. Jr. and Steel, T. B. Jr. *Erotetic logic: an introduction to the logic of questions and answers*. Yale University Press, forthcoming, 1976.

Carnap, R. *Introduction to semantics*. Cambridge, Mass., 1942.

Dunn, J. M. *The algebra of intensional logics* (dissertation). University of Pittsburgh, 1966.

Dunn, J. M. Intuitive semantics for first degree entailments and "coupled trees". Forthcoming, 1975(?).

Dunn, J. M., and Belnap, N. D. Jr. The substitution interpretation of the quantifiers, *Nous*, vol. 2 (1968), pp. 177–185.

Hintikka, J. *Knowledge and belief*. Cornell Press, 1962.

Isner, D. W. An inferential processor for interacting with biomedical data using restricted natural language. *Proceedings of Spring Joint Computer Conference*, 1972, pp. 1107–24.

Isner, D. W. *Understanding "understanding" through representation and reasoning* (dissertation). University of Pittsburgh, 1975.

Kripke, S. Semantical analysis of modal logic I. *Zeitschrift für Mathematische Logik und Grundlagen der Mathematik*, vol. 9 (1963), pp. 67–96.

Routley, R. and Routley, V. Semantics of first degree entailment. *Nous*, vol. 6 (1972), pp. 335–59.

Scott, D. Outline of a mathematical theory of computation. *Proceedings of the Fourth Annual Princeton Conference on Information Sciences and Systems*, 1970, pp. 169–76.

Scott, D. Continuous lattices: *Toposes, algebraic geometry and logic*. Springer lecture notes in mathematics, vol. 274 (1972), pp. 97–136.

Scott, D. Models for various type-free calculi. *Logic, methodology, and philosophy of science IV*. Proceedings of the Fourth International Congress for Logic, Methodology, and the Philosophy of Science, Bucharest, 1971. Eds. Suppes, Henkin, Juja, Moisil. North-Holland, 1973.

Shapiro, S., and Wand, M. The relevance of relevance. Forthcoming, 1975(?).

van Fraassen, B. Presuppositions, supervaluations, and free logic. *The logical way of doing things*, K. Lambert (ed.), Yale University Press, 1969a.

Van Fraassen, B. Facts and tautological entailments. *The journal of philosophy*, vol. 66 (1969b), pp. 477–87; reprinted in Anderson and Belnap, 1975, $20.3.

IV

POSSIBLE-WORLDS SEMANTICS AS A FRAMEWORK
FOR COMPARATIVE AND CRITICAL PHILOSOPHY

Jaakko Hintikka

IF THERE IS a thematic kinship that unites more twentieth-century philosophy than any other, it is undoubtedly preoccupation with questions of language and meaning. Much of this preoccupation can even be traced back to one and the same precursor, Gottlob Frege. His position in the analytical tradition of contemporary philosophy is generally recognized (Dummett 1973), and his influence on the basic concepts and problems of the founder of the phenomenological tradition, Edmund Husserl, is being spelled out in an impressive way by Dagfinn Føllesdal and his former students. (Føllesdal 1958, 1969, 1972, 1975, Smith and McIntyre 1971, 1975, McIntyre 1975.) Husserl's fundamental concept of *noema* turns out to be both genetically and systematically a direct generalization of Frege's notion of *Sinn*, the second member of Frege's celebrated distinction between reference, *Bedeutung*, and meaning or sense, *Sinn*. (Frege 1892.)

In view of this crucial role of the notions of *Sinn* and noema for the genesis of much of the best recent and contemporary philosophy, it is of interest to find that there is a simple line of thought that takes us from these notions directly to the basic ideas of the so-called possible-worlds semantics. This approach to linguistic meaning and more generally to the philosophy of language came about in the sixties as a generalization of the semantics (model theory) of modal logic developed in the late fifties by several independently working logician-philosophers. (For the early work on the semantics of modal logic along the lines that led to possible-worlds semantics, see Kanger 1957; Hintikka 1957, 1961, 1963; Kripke 1963a, b, 1966. For possible-worlds semantics proper, see Hintikka 1962, 1969, 1975; Lewis 1972.). The generalization was propagated especially energetically by the late Richard Montague; see Thomason (1974).

Frege (1892) characterized his concept of sense (*Sinn*) by saying that it includes more than reference (*Bedeutung*) : it includes also the way in which this reference is given to us. Independently of how Frege himself viewed this characterization, undoubtedly the most natural and the most interesting way of interpreting it is to understand "the way of being given" *functionally*. On this interpretation, the sense of an expression is the function which gives the reference as its value. But what are the *arguments* of this function (meaning function)? What can the reference of an expression in some one world W depend on? The safest but at the same time the most abstract and least informative answer is to say that the reference may depend literally on *everything* in W, that is, is a function of the whole possible world W in which the reference was supposed to be located. (Cf. here Hintikka 1975, chapters 5 and 10.)

But this already is precisely the answer that possible-world semantics gives to the question concerning the logical type of meanings. (Thomason 1974.) Meanings are according to this answer functions from possible worlds to references or extensions of the appropriate sort. In the case of sentences these extensions are truth-values, for singular terms they are individuals, for n-place predicates they are sets of n-tuples of individuals, and so on.

This "transcendental deduction" of possible-worlds semantics shows both how natural it is and how abstract and uninformative it in certain respects remains. These limitations will be commented on later. Meanwhile, in view of the closeness of possible-worlds semantics to the main ideas of Frege and Husserl, it is not surprising that new light can be thrown on Husserl's phenomenology from the vantage point of possible-worlds semantics, even though neither Frege nor Husserl himself came within a mile of taking the admittedly short step which would have assimilated their ideas to those of possible-worlds semantics. On an earlier occasion (Hintikka 1975, chapter 10), I discussed critically another main concept of Husserl's, the concept of intentionality, in the light of possible-worlds semantics. (See Husserl 1950, 1952, 1962, 1966a, b.) Many other Husserlian concepts can be reconstructed and analysed critically from the same perspective. Although such reconstructions and critical analyses would need a much more extended discussion than they can be given here, this subject is too important for the main thrust of my paper to be by-passed completely.

Perhaps the most important single idea of Husserl's which can now be appreciated much better is his notion of constitution with its consequences for his curiously ambiguous position vis-à-vis the traditional idealism—realism contrast (Sokolowski 1970, Kern 1964).

It is clearest in the case of the constitution of individuals. In possible-worlds terms, the fundamental insight here concerns the task of cross-identification, that is, of telling (in principle) of members of different possible worlds whether they are identical or not. Such a task confronts us as soon as we are considering our individuals as members of several possible worlds, and this we are doing as soon as they operate as objects of any intentional attitude or act. The first fundamental insight needed here is the philosophical nontriviality of such cross-identifications. The world lines that connect the embodiments of the same individual in different worlds are as it were "drawn and described" by ourselves. Of course they are not drawn by each of us individually and arbitrarily, but according to certain principles which rely on objective facts like continuity in space and time and which have been built into the presuppositions of the whole language community. The point is, rather, that they could in principle be drawn in different ways.

This yields a much better account of the curious mixture of realism and idealism in constitution than Husserl's own somewhat tortuous explanations. Constitution is like drawing my world lines. It is realistic in the sense that no new "furniture of the world" is created. Each possible world has its individual members, which are neither disembodied nor reified by being compared with the denizens of another world. Ontologically speaking, world lines are thus neither here nor there. They connect worlds, but are not parts of them. In this respect, and in this sense, constitution is on my reconstruction quite as ultra-realistic a process as Husserl sometimes claimed his to be.

At the same time, we do not have objects for any intentional "acts" (in Husserl's sense) until we can in principle cross-identify our individuals, for the common characteristic of the logic of all such acts (propositional attitudes) is that they force us to consider individuals (the objects of these attitudes) as members of several possible worlds. This in turn presupposes cross-identification, i.e., deliberate "drawing of world lines". In this sense, the objects of knowledge, belief, memory, hope, desire, etc. are literally created (better : constituted) by the drawing of world lines, which was seen to be *our* privilege, not Logic's or Nature's. No wonder that Husserl's account of constitution frequently has markedly idealistic overtones.

Many other Husserlian concepts and conceptions can likewise be approached at the same time critically and constructively from the vantage point of possible-world semantics. For instance, the famous transcendence of objects *apud* Husserl becomes from this point of

59

view simply the fact that their known (perhaps especially perceived) properties are always compatible with a broad variety of possibilities ("possible worlds") : we can pin down their attributes only down to this variety, but not all the way down to one world. Instead of transcendence, it would thus be less misleading to speak of inexhaustibility, which anyway is just what Husserl means.

On an earlier occasion (Hintikka 1975, chapter 10), I have criticized Husserl's account of perception, according to which it consists of an act of conceptual thinking, *noesis*, working on certain hyletic data or sense-data. In contrast to this, I have argued that the most spontaneous sense-impressions that can surface in our consciousness are already articulated categorically into individuals, their properties, their relations, etc. I do not think that there is any doubt that Husserl just does not get the phenomenology of perception quite straight. However, possible-worlds semantics offers here a second line of defence to Husserl. For at the very mention of individuals it at once forces us to ask : individuals how cross-identified? Here we come in fact to the one absolutely crucial insight which Husserl missed and which still is not fully appreciated in most contemporary discussions of possible-worlds semantics, although it has been expounded earlier in Hintikka (1969, chapter 8), (1974, chapter 11), and (1975, chapters 3–4). The possibility of drawing world lines differently is not a logician's abstract possibility. We all in our own conceptual practice employ all the time two different overall methods of cross-identification. Sometimes we compare individuals in different possible worlds for their identity by means of their role in the public, objective picture we are trying to form of the world. Such cross-identification is called descriptive, and its success in the case of some particular individual i is testified to by the truth of a statement

I know who (or what) i is.

However, we may forget this overall epistemic *Weltanschauung* of ours and judge the identity of individuals around us instead in terms of their direct cognitive relations to ourselves. Individuals bearing the same relations of this sort to us are as it were declared identical. The clearest cases in point are found in perception, where I can justifiably treat people and physical objects around me as well-rounded individuals (in a logician's sense) even if I do not perceive who or what they are and even though they therefore are not descriptively well-defined individuals. If challenged, I can simply say : But I see (perceive) them ! The successful cross-identification of some particular individual i by this sort of method is thus vouched for by the truth of sentences of the form

I perceive i.

This method of cross-identification may be called perceptual or perhaps rather ostensive. More generally, we may speak of individuation (cross-identification) by acquaintance. My all too brief explanations of the difference have already betrayed the way in which it is expressed in natural language, apart from predictable small fluctuations. The logic of descriptive cross-identification is the logic of subordinate wh-questions with a main verb like "knows", "remembers", "sees", etc., whereas the logic of cross-identification by acquaintance is the logic of the direct-object constructions with these same verbs. The ubiquity of these well entrenched constructions in ordinary discourse ought to be enough to convince philosophers of the reality of the distinction I am making.

From the "idealistic" freedom which we have in drawing the world lines and which I emphasized earlier in connection with constitution it follows that it is nonsense to ask : Which are the *real* individuals, the perceptual (ostensively cross-identified) or the descriptive (descriptively individuated) ones? Whatever differences there may be between the two in theory and in practice, one method of cross-identification does not yield more individual individuals or more real ones than the other, for in both cases we are merely comparing different worlds with each other, not building up any worlds as such.

A failure to make this distinction (or at least a failure to make it clearly and to realize its implications) is one of the most serious flaws in Husserl's philosophy. However, once the distinction is made, it can be put to use to save some of the central ideas of Husserl's theory of perception. For the well-defined individuals which I have argued to be present already in our completely unedited sense-impressions are of course successfully cross-identified perceptually but often not descriptively. No phenomenologically accessible *noesis* is needed to articulate what we see into seeings of people, tables, chairs, books, buildings, bridges, and of other similar medium-sized objects we habitually associate with. However, a *noesis* is definitely needed not only to recognize perceived individuals as definite descriptively cross-identified ones but to constitute the descriptively cross-identified individuals in the first place. The process of their constitution has in fact an interesting resemblance to Husserl's theory of a *noesis*

61

operating on sensory data so as to articulate them into perceptions of well-defined objects. In both cases, a crucial role is played by comparisons between perceptual impressions and other actual or potential sensory data, past, present, and future. This is the partial vindication of Husserl's theory of perception I promised. Only the proper application of the theory is not the articulation of sensory raw-materials into perceptual objects, but to the constitution of descriptive individuals out of perceptually given information. Husserl notwithstanding, this information is not embodied in amorphous hyletic material, but is already articulated into information about perceptual individuals, their properties and relations, and so on.

This possibility of saving a part of Husserl's theory of perception together with the associated necessity of modifying other parts of it is perhaps the most important single example of the consequences for Husserl's philosophy of the duality of individuation (cross-identification) methods which we have uncovered but which Husserl largely overlooked. Perhaps the best evidence of the value of possible-worlds semantics as a framework for comparative philosophy is nevertheless the fact that those aspects of this semantics which one tradition has missed are emphasized and even overemphasized by others. The idea of individuation by acquaintance which Husserl's theory of perception was in effect seen to be lacking was incorporated as its main ingredient in Bertrand Russell's famous theory of knowledge by acquaintance (Russell 1910, 1912). After having discussed this theory in some detail elsewhere (Hintikka 1974, chapter 11) I can perhaps afford to be rather brief. Knowledge by acquaintance is by Russell's virtual admission knowledge of individuals we are cognitively acquainted with or "directly aware of". The primacy of such knowledge is asserted in Russell's thesis of reducibility to acquaintance. Russell's lists of entities of which we can have such knowledge varied somewhat between his different writings, but they all reveal the close connection between Russellian knowledge by acquaintance and what I have called cross-identification by acquaintance. When Russell says that only "logically proper names"—i.e., singular terms picking out the same individual, come what may—are "this", "that", and "I", we are vividly reminded of the role of ostension in perceptual cross-identification. Equally revealing is the role of what Russell, Moore, Broad and others somewhat misleadingly called "sense-data" as the prime examples of objects of acquaintance in Russell. (Moore 1922, 1953; Broad 1923; Marc-Wogau 1945; Hintikka 1969, chapter 8.) These sense-data are ill-named because they are, not *data* at all, but of the logical type of *individuals*. They

62

are *apud* Moore the objects of perception in the sense of being the entities judgements of immediate perception are *about*. As such, they are categorically unlike Husserl's sense-data (hyletic data), which are not objects of sensation or perception at all, but a kind of sensory raw-material which cannot be conceptually separated from the rest of the perceptual situation but which may be thought of as that which can be moulded by the *noesis* into genuine objects of perception. (Thus I could partly reformulate my criticism of Husserl by saying that his sense-data ought to have been in this respect like Moore's.)

Sense-data in Russell's and Moore's sense are indeed especially natural to discuss by reference to possible-worlds semantics. The first approximation is to say that sense-data are simply perceptually cross-identified individuals. The two are in fact cast in precisely the same role. As we saw, for Moore and Russell sense-data are the individuals we judge about in unedited perceptual judgements. Likewise, perceptually cross-identified individuals are individuals considered solely as ingredients of the perceived situation, in abstraction from their identity in terms of the objective (physical or descriptive) state of affairs. Both are literally *what* is perceived, in Moore's and Russell's case by courtesy of their philosophical theory and in my case by courtesy of the connection between perceptual cross-identification and the direct-object construction with "perceives". The role of Russell's sense-data as the prime objects of acquaintance in his theory is only a corollary to this identity of roles.

However, the classical sense-datum theory involves a double mistake. It involves a mistaken reification and at the same time a related mistaken ephemerization. The reification is a typical category mistake. What is involved in cross-identification by acquaintance is that individuals in several possible worlds, typically in those compatible with everything someone (say *a*) perceives or knows, are connected by means of "world lines" which utilize the direct epistemic relations of these individuals to *a*. The objects of acquaintance are individuals thus cross-identified. Classical sense-data come about when these lines of cross-identification, which themselves are literally neither here nor there, are reified into alleged inhabitants of the actual world. In reality, there are not two kinds of entities in the world, descriptive or physical objects and perceptual objects. The contrast between these is merely a distinction between two different ways of comparing several worlds with each other, not a class-distinction among the denizens of any one world. However, traditional sense-datum theories mistakenly turn this interworldly business into an intraworldly one.

Paradoxically this fallacious hypostatization insinuated into the classical sense-datum theory as its consequence an equally fallacious desubstantiation of perceptually cross-identified individuals. When an attempt was made as it were to roll each of the lines of perceptual cross-identification into a ball and put this ball down somewhere in the actual world, it quickly turned out that there was precious little room for such outlandish entities in the world, which was mostly occupied by solid three-dimensional physical objects. The only roles in which they could be thought of as being cast were all more or less precarious and fleeting. Even though attempts were made to identify sense-data with parts of the surfaces of physical objects (Moore 1922, chapters 5 and 7), they mostly remained ephemeral two-dimensional impressions for which *esse* pretty much was *percipi*.

This entailed, and was in turn strongly encouraged by, a very narrow phenomenology of perception according to which the only things directly sensed, for instance seen, were two-dimensional impressions, not (apparent) three-dimensional objects in a genuine visual space.

Because of these fallacies the end product of classical sense-datum theories looks quite unlike my theory of perceptual cross-identification. On my view, it is even slightly misleading to speak of *objects* of perception or *objects* of acquaintance. It would be less misleading to speak of ordinary individuals *considered as* objects of perception, for all that is involved is a special way of comparing individuals in different possible worlds (states of affairs) for their identity. Here my criticism of sense-datum theories converges with my criticism of Husserl. No matter how primitive a layer of sensation we are talking about, as long as it can be consciously beheld, to describe what one perceives is to describe what the objective state of the world would be if one's perceptions were veridical. And this can only be done in the realistic language that speaks of usual commonplace objects, such as persons, physical objects, and their attributes, not of ghostly shadows like the classical sense-data. Hence the dematerialization of sense-data is a mistake logically, ontologically, and phenomenologically.

Realizing the significance of cross-identification by acquaintance opens the door to a further insight which is highly useful for critical and comparative purposes. This insight is difficult to avoid when the subject is reviewed systematically. What I have explained to you so far about perceptual (say, visual) individuation is primarily what it means to cross-identify between the different visual alternatives to the real world, that is, between the different states of affairs compatible with what someone, say a, sees at a certain moment. Very bluntly expressed this compatibility imposes a common geometry on all of them, which enables us to identify the individuals occupying the same slot in a's visual space.

However, this does not tell us yet how to cross-identify between such visual alternatives and the real world. In sufficiently distorted perception, the real world need not have sufficient similarity to trace the world lines back home by means of the same visual geometry as enabled us to cross-identify between the alternatives.

How, then, do we cross-identify in this case? Following Grice (1961) and others I have argued (Hintikka 1975, chapter 4), if the point is not obvious enough, that in this case we go by causal considerations. My "visual individual" i (in the classical terminology, a "sense datum") is identical with an object o in the real world just in case o is in some sense causally responsible for my having i. Even though the precise conditions on this causal link are not easy to write down, the main idea is clear enough. It constitutes a striking "rational reconstruction" of one more philosophical theory within possible-worlds semantics. This theory is the so-called causal theory of perception, which traditionally is often formulated precisely by speaking of sense-data which are caused by external objects. According to this theory, I perceive an object o just when I have a sense-datum S which represents o and is caused by o. According to my version of possible-worlds semantics, it is true to say of one of my perceptual objects, say S, that it is in reality o just when it is caused by o. The match between the two formulations is very good indeed as soon as we can assimilate sense-data to perceptual objects, as I have argued that we can do.

Similar remarks apply to other propositional attitudes. For instance, one of my memory-objects m (individuals that have a niche in my personally remembered past) is in reality o if and only if o caused me to have m.

A realization of the role of causal chains in the semantics of acquaintance has still further repercussions. Rather in the same way as the perfectly valid insight into the role of acquaintance in cross-identification was exaggerated in Russell's theory, equally valid insights into the role of causality in cross-identification have likewise given rise to exaggerations. It is not difficult to grasp what the temptation is. We already saw that for Russell the only really (logically) proper names were "this" and "that" (apart from the questionable "I"). Once the semantical legitimacy of the causal link between the ostension and the ostended object is recognized, this seems to open up the possibility of extending Russell's rather meagre supply of proper names so as to approximate what we actually use. For Russell, ostension could only reach ephemeral entities like sense-data. Causation enables us to reach the real things, not by describing them, but by establishing a causal link with them through ostension or dubbing. Hence causal theories of naming, rigid designators, and suchlike.

This brief sketch of well-known recent developments (Kripke 1971, 1972) does not do full justice to them. It may nevertheless be suggestive enough to indicate the main strengths and weaknesses of theories of this kind. The generalization on Russell is indeed successful. Causal links do enter into the semantical texture of our proper names. The reference r of a proper name n is the individual which causes us to have those beliefs we normally express in terms of n. Our beliefs about Homer may in principle turn out to be as inapplicable to any person as those which for a while were associated with Ossian. This will not spoil the role of the name "Homer" for us as long as there is an appropriate causal link between this ancient character and the information we seem to possess about him, a link of the sort there did not obtain between Ossian and the songs that were for a while attributed to him. To this extent, causal theories of naming are definitely on the right track. As David Kaplan once aptly put the point (if I remember correctly), to use a proper name *is* like pointing to its bearer. Only this pointing-to has the intriguing feature of being independent of the limitations of space and time. It does not require the actual presence of the named object.

However, the exaggerations involved in the currently fashionable theories of naming and necessity are also amply in evidence when they are examined in the possible-worlds framework. The basic fact here is that causal chains can mediate only one very special kind of cross-identification, viz. cross-identification by acquaintance between the actual world and its alternatives. For all the other kinds of cross-world links, other methods have to be used. One of the fallacies involved here is the assumption that once a causal chain has taken us to the real thing in the real world, it can take care of itself as far as individuation is concerned. This fallacy is undoubtedly encouraged by the important role which hard physical realities, such as the continuity of bodies in space and time, in fact play in descriptive cross-identification. (Hintikka 1975, chapters 2 and 6.) However, at bottom the assumption is but an unexamined and invalid dogma. Sufficiently difficult concrete applications ought to make this clear. What, for instance, constitutes personal identity? Bodily continuity or the continuity of memory? Or something altogether different? Although the scientific facts of the case are highly relevant, the answer is not prejudged by them. The last decision is here conceptual, not scientific.

The crucial reason why such questions as the problem of personal identity have a sharp edge here is that they are questions of descriptive individuation. As was already pointed out, causal links of the kind the causal theories of naming utilize have a semantical role only in cross-identification by acquaintance, and only a partial role there, either.

Thus possible-worlds semantics once again enables us to evaluate critically but not unsympathetically an important philosophical development and at the same time enables us to relate it to other interesting philosophical doctrines. I hope that further examples are not needed to convince you of its power to do so. This power has been the main thesis of my paper.

It would be enhanced further if the limitations mentioned in beginning of my paper were removed and the meaning functions that possible-world semantics postulates were somehow concretized. This task has several facets, concerning some of which good progress is already being made. In most cases, the real arguments of meaning functions are not whole big possible worlds, but suitable small parts or aspects of such worlds. This is related to the fact that the meaning functions are not actually dealt with as functions in a mathematician's abstract sense of the term, that is to say, as infinite sets of pairs of associated argument values and function values. They are handled by means of suitable operationalizations which may be compared to algorithms for actually computing a mathematical function or to recipes for finding the function value on the basis of an argument value. It is undoubtedly this importance of the actual recipes for finding the reference of a linguistic expression that in part prevented Frege from adopting that functional interpretation of his concept of sense (*Sinn*) which would have landed him straight in possible-worlds semantics. However, much as I want to emphasize the need of concretizing the present theory of possible-worlds semantics, I nevertheless find Frege's line of thought an illegitimate shortcut. We must find in the end the operationalizations of meaning functions, but not at the expense of overlooking their logical status as functions from possible worlds (or aspects thereof) to extensions. That Frege missed here something worthwhile I hope to have demonstrated in the bulk of this paper.

Jaakko Hintikka
Academy of Finland and Stanford University

67

POSSIBLE-WORLDS SEMANTICS

BIBLIOGRAPHY

Broad, C. D. (1923) *Scientific Thought*, London: Kegan Paul.
Dummett, M. (1973) *Frege: Philosophy of Language*. London: Duckworth.
Føllesdal, D. (1958) *Husserl und Frege. Ein Beitrag zur Beleuchtung der Entstehung der phänomenologischen Philosophie*. Oslo: H. Ashehoug & Co.
Føllesdal, D. (1969) *J. Philos.* 66, 680–687.
Føllesdal, D. (1972) in *Contemporary Philosophy in Scandinavia*, pp. 417–429, ed. Olson, R. E. and Paul, A. M., Baltimore and London: The Johns Hopkins Press.
Føllesdal, D. (1975) in *Handbook of Perception*, Vol. 1, ed. Carterette, E. C. and Friedman, M. P. New York: Academic Press.
Frege, G. (1892) *Zeitschr. Philos. u. philos. Kritik* 100, 25–50.
Grice, H. P. (1961) *Proceedings of the Aristotelian Society*, Supplementary Volume 35, 121–152.
Hintikka, K. J. J. (1957) *Quantifiers in Deontic Logic*, Helsinki: Societas Scientiarum Fennica, Commentationes Humanarum Litterarum, Vol. 23, no. 4.
Hintikka, K. J. J. (1961), *Theoria* 27, 119–128.
Hintikka, K. J. J. (1962) *Knowledge and Belief*, Ithaca, N.Y.: Cornell University Press.
Hintikka, K. J. J. (1963) in *Acta Philosophica Fennica* 16, 65–82.
Hintikka, K. J. J. (1969) *Models for Modalities*, Dordrecht: D. Reidel Publishing Company.
Hintikka, K. J. J. (1974) *Knowledge and the Known*, Dordrecht: D. Reidel Publishing Company.
Hintikka, K. J. J. (1975) *The Intentions of Intentionality*, Dordrecht: D. Reidel Publ. Company.
Husserl, E. (1950) *Cartesianische Meditationen und Pariser Vorträge*, ed. Strasser, S., (*Husserliana I*), The Hague: Martinus Nijhoff.
Husserl, E. (1952) *Ideen zu einer reinen Phänomenologie und phänomenologischen Philosophie. Drittes Buch: Die Phänomenologie und die Fundamente der Wissenschaften*, ed. Biemel, M. (*Husserliana V*), The Hague: Martinus Nijhoff.
Husserl, E. (1962) *Phänomenologische Psychologie, Vorlesungen Sommersemester 1925*, ed. Biemel, W., (*Husserliana IX*), The Hague: Martinus Nijhoff.
Husserl, E. (1966a) *Analysen zur passiven Synthesis. Aus Vorlesungs- und Forschungsmanuschriften, 1918–1926*, ed. Fleischer, M. (*Husserliana XI*), The Hague: Martinus Nijhoff.
Husserl, E. (1966b) *Vorlesungen zur Phänomenologie des inneren Zeitbewusstseins*, ed. Boehm, R. (*Husserliana X*), The Hague: Martinus Nijhoff.
Kanger, S. (1957) *Provability in Logic*, Stockholm: Stockholm Studies in Philosophy, Vol. 1.
Kern, I. (1964) *Husserl und Kant. Eine Untersuchung über Husserls Verhältnis zu Kant und zum. Neukantianismus*, The Hague: Martinus Nijhoff.
Kripke, S. (1963a) in *Acta Philosophica Fennica* 16, 83–94.
Kripke, S. (1963b) *Zeitschr. f. math. Logik u. Grundl. d. Math.* 9, 67–96.
Kripke, S. (1966) in *The Theory of Models*, ed. Addison, J. W., Henkin, L. and Tarski. A., Amsterdam: North-Holland Publishing Company, 206–220.
Kripke, S. (1971) in *Semantics of Natural Language*, ed. Davidson, D. and Harman, G., Dordrecht: D. Reidel Publishing Company, 253–355.
Kripke, S. in *Identity and Individuation*, ed. Munitz, M. K., New York: New York University Press, 135–164.

68

Lewis, D. (1972) in *Semantics of Natural Language*, ed. Davidson, D. and Harman, G., Dordrecht: D. Reidel Publishing Company, 169–218.

Marc-Wogau, K. (1945) *Die Theorie von Sinnesdaten*, Uppsala: Uppsala Universitets Arsskrift.

McIntyre, R. (1975) *Nous* 9 (forthcoming).

Moore, G. E. (1922) *Philosophical Studies*, London: Kegan Paul.

Moore, G. E. (1953) *Some Main Problems of Philosophy*, London: Allen & Unwin Ltd.

Russell, B. (1910) *Proceedings of the Aristotelian Society* 11, 108–28.

Russell, B. (1912) *The Problems of Philosophy*, London: William & Norgate.

Smith, D. W. and McIntyre, R. (1971) *J. Philos.* 68, 541–561.

Smith, D. W. and McIntyre, R. (1975) *Monist* 59 (forthcoming).

Sokolowski, R. (1970) *The Formation of Husserl's Concept of Constitution*, The Hague: Martinus Nijhoff.

Thomason, R. H. (1974), editor, *Formal Philosophy: Selected Papers of Richard Montague*, New Haven and London: Yale University Press.

V

SYMBOLIC ACTS
REMARKS ON THE FOUNDATIONS OF A
PRAGMATIC THEORY OF LANGUAGE

F. Kambartel

PHILOSOPHY of language as well as linguistics, especially formal linguistics, are still widely dominated by a view of language, which we may state as follows : There is a special kind of historically grown or artificially created entities having meaning, i.e. being related by a correspondence to entities in a real or abstract world (for the Tarski-school it should be a world of worlds), such entities e.g. as objects, properties, relations (especially functions). This correspondence enables speakers or writers to make the linguistic entities and their combinations (more precisely their tokens in actual speech performance) represent those other entities and their structural connections. The most developed and formally sophisticated kind of linguistic analysis, which adopts this point of view, is Californian Semantics as worked out by R. Montague, D. K. Lewis, M. Y. Cresswell and others and which has been gaining ground in linguistics during the last years as it seems.

Since Wittgenstein's later philosophy there has been, on the other hand, much emphasis on language being a system of acts. In Wittgenstein's work this insight remained a rather general one without being developed into a systematic theory of the pragmatic constructions constituting those acts, which we are now used to calling "speech acts". Austin and J. Searle then tried to work out some fundamental distinctions, but, alas, they sometimes, Searle more than Austin, depend on traditional grammatical categories developed in logic and linguistics, without previously laying a pragmatic basis for them. Obviously it stands to reason however, that we cannot introduce e.g. acts of referring and predicating by just saying : *predicating* is using a *predicative term* (a *predicator*), *referring* is using a *name term* (a *nominator*). For in a radical pragmatic approach it is forbidden to pursue this explanation by using different semantic correspondences as a basis for understanding the difference between predicators and nominators.

Linguistic pragmatics on the other hand has not yet reached the stage of systematic research, if we leave out modern semantic theory of cotext-dependency, which is but *named* pragmatics without as a rule making the construction of speech acts a subject of inquiry. Thus, in working out methodically the pragmatic view of language, nearly everything concrete still has to be done. (Cf. Schneider 1977.)

In this lecture I am dealing with some distinctions concerning acts, which I propose as fundamental steps towards a pragmatic reconstruction of logical and grammatical categories, a reconstruction, which tries to avoid the difficulties both : of ontological correspondence theories of meaning and of mere surface-grammar (dependent) pragmatics. As in treating *speech* acts we are concerned with *acts*, it is somewhat astonishing that there is still, today, little connection between a general theory of acts and pragmatics in the narrow, language-related, sense of the word. To avoid this defect let us begin by clarifying the concept of act on which our constructions are based.

I hope I need not argue in this circle in favour of a non-scientistic analysis of acts. Therefore I shall simply presume that we have already, with Kant and other intentionalists, agreed upon the existence of *acting subjects*, i.e. that acts are not something just occurring to the agent, but something the occurrence of which is *brought about by the agent*. Citing Kant : We have the "Vermögen, einen Zustand von selbst anzufangen" (*Kritik der reinen Vernunft*, 61, B). I do not think Wittgenstein has in mind anything different, when he says e.g. in *Philosophical Investigations* I, 612 (editors' English translation) : "I should not say of the movement of my arm, for example : it comes when it comes, etc. ... And this is the region in which we say significantly that a thing doesn't simply happen to us, but that we *do* it. 'I don't need to wait for my arm to go up—I can raise it.' " The same view is expressed by von Wright (1974, 51), when he states : "An ability to do things is a 'power to interfere with nature' to make the course of the world (a little bit) different from what it otherwise would be." (Also cf. von Wright 1971.)

Authorities not being a reasonable substitute for methodical reflection, this leaves us with the problem of giving a precise meaning to the term "brought about by an agent". We can do this by realizing that certain acts are not just at our disposal by the favour of nature, but have to be acquired by (sometimes hard) learning.

71

What we acquire then is not the ability to produce one *particular* act, a singular act-*occurrence* or act-*token*, but the capacity, "at will", to initiate or continue occurrences of a certain kind under suitable circumstances.

To act thus is to realize, or, to take a special term, to *"actualize"* an *act scheme,* as W. Kamlah, Lorenzen's co-author, has called it (cf. Kamlah 1972). And to actualize an act scheme means to interfere, in a way disposable at will by a process of learning, with the course of events which otherwise would happen. Using the words of von Wright (1963) you may call act schemes *generic acts,* and their actualizations *individual acts.* Alvin E. Goldman (1970) uses the type-token-terminology instead. Only you have to be careful, not to misunderstand the generic act terms (or those referring to types) in a crude *descriptive* way. For you have to keep in mind that acts in contrast to natural events have an *intentional* character.

What do we or should we mean by ascribing intentions to acts? Conceiving concrete acts as actualizations of act schemes enables us to give a simple answer to this question. Asking for the *intention* of an occurrence, presupposed as an act, means asking for the relevant *act scheme* which is actualized by it. The word "relevant" has to be added, because one act occurrence may be the actualization of several act schemes, i.e. one act-occurrence may have more than one intention. E.g. someone presses the button; by doing this he turns on the light; and by doing this he signals something.

It needs, I presuppose here, no further consideration to see, that intentions are not empirical data observable from outside like the colour of a flower. Ultimately we always have to base an intentional interpretation on interaction, especially dialogues with the agents. Or, if this is not possible, we may reconstruct the cultural background and learning traditions of the groups they belong to.

That acts are governed by intentions is, by the way, an analytical truth. For the very concept of an act implies in our explanation the actualization of an act scheme.

Intentions in the sense just proposed must be distinguished from aims, pursued by acting in a certain way. A person who is running to preserve his health, in this action follows the intention of running, whereas certain conditions of health reached by means of regular running or other activities are then the aim pursued in this person's running.

In my following considerations I shall as a rule use the term "act" in its generic sense, i.e. speaking of the *act* of doing something

72

means then the act *scheme* (as acquired by some agent) of doing this something. And "doing (performing) (the act) *a*" or equivalent expressions are to be understood as "actualizing the act scheme *a*".

Concerning the foundations of language one of the most important relations between acts is, that an act *a* is done by doing one or several other acts $a_1, a_2, \ldots$ of a certain kind. Let us call an act *a mediated* by acts $a_1, a_2, \ldots$ if and only if *a*, by its definition, can be performed by performing one or several of the $a_1, a_2, \ldots$. Then we may speak of a *mediated act a* if and only if *a*, by its definition, can be done only in a mediated way. If an act *a* is mediated by an act *b* I shall call *b primary* relative to *a*.

Simple examples are *complex* acts in the strict (narrow) sense of the word. An act *a*, defined as doing a_1, and then (i.e. thereafter) a_2, is done by doing a_1 and a_2. If we qualify e.g. putting on the light as an act too—I propose to call such acts *causal* acts—then we have another category of mediated acts. Putting on the light can be done only by other acts the effect of which is, under the respective relevant conditions, a state characterized as "light in the room". To put it generally : A (causal) act "bringing about that (the effect) *e*" can be done only by doing acts a_e producing as their effect *e*.

Are there non-mediated acts? I think so. E.g. I do not see how, usually, pressing a button (in turning on the light) can be analysed as mediated. Obviously it is absurd for instance to assume that pressing a button, usually, is learnt as a complex act consisting of the (previously learnt) acts : putting the finger on the button, pressing it just a little bit, pressing it a little bit more etc. On the other hand there is no necessity to believe in the existence of *absolute* basic acts in order to introduce the concept of mediated acts. What is basic in *actual* mediation-structures when learning acts may depend on traditions, knowledge and even individual development.

Let us now analyse the mediation structure of those acts, which form the pragmatic basis of language, as well as of institutional action in general. I propose to call them symbolic acts. Roughly speaking : A *symbolic act s* is constituted by laying down situational conditions or ("vel") pragmatic consequences for the performance of other acts (those other acts becoming by such a convention primary acts in the performance of *s*). Using the new term "symbolic act" avoids connotations which accompany the term "speech act" after the rather vague or theoretically overloaded use it has had during recent years. Furthermore "symbolic act" is the wider concept because it includes e.g. institutionally regulated activities as well as the traditional speech acts.

The definition of symbolic acts still has to be worked out more precisely. First step : Let us say that an act has got a *symbolic use,* if its performance is by tacit or explicit agreement restricted to certain situations or connected with certain pragmatic consequences, i.e. the performance or forbearance of other acts, and thereby is to be understood now just as an actualization of this agreement. (Agreements of such a kind may themselves be valid only relative to certain situations.)

The symbolic use of an act must be distinguished from just *following a rule* in the performance of this act : To prescribe that an act a shall be admitted only in certain situations gives us a rule of acting, $R(a)$. If a person or group is, in performing an act a, (always) obeying $R(a)$, we have the case of a *usage* following $R(a)$. If an act a' is by prescription regulated or regularly performed in just the same way, we are faced with a rule $R(a')$ or the corresponding usage. Obviously $R(a)$ and $R(a')$ as well as the corresponding usages differ from one another.

The symbolic use of an act on the other hand constitutes a *new act*, i.e. a new act scheme. This is done by *abstraction* from the different *concrete* acts $a, a', \ldots$, regulated in the same way by R in the rules $R(a)$, $R(a'), \ldots$: Actualizing the symbolic act scheme corresponding to R, means actualizing *one of the acts* $a, a', \ldots$ regulated by R, without in the end intending to apply $R(a)$ as an a-regulating rule, $R(a')$ as an a'-regulating rule etc. To put it in other words (only in other words) : By actualizing the symbolic act scheme in actualizing a we intend only the underlying agreement, not just a regulated use of a. Let us call a, $a', \ldots$ acts carrying the corresponding symbolic act, which shall be symbolized by expressions like $s_R(a)$, $s_R(a'), \ldots$ or simply $s(a)$, $s(a'), \ldots$, these terms standing of course for *the same* symbolic act. It is now, I hope, obvious, that a symbolic act s is indeed *mediated* by each one of the acts carrying s, these acts thereby becoming primary acts relative to s. Performing a symbolic act s implies performing an act carrying s. Therefore as in the case of other mediated acts we have more than one intention pursued in acting symbolically. We shall call the carrying act scheme a, e.g. a phonetic act, the *direct intention,* and the symbolic act scheme $s(a)$ the *indirect intention,* which is ruling a concrete performance of s as mediated by a, i.e. ruling an a-mediated s-token. (Obviously these distinctions permit the case that a symbolic act s_1 is carried by another symbolic act s_2.)

A symbolically used primary act, in referring to the existence of the conditions, which by agreement allow its performance, has an *informative meaning.* In making operative pragmatic consequences, which by agreement are connected with it, it has a *performative meaning.* We may call *informative* those symbolic *acts*, the performance of which has only or essentially informative meaning. *Performative* symbolic *acts* may be introduced in the same way. Obviously these definitions imply that a symbolic act may have at the same time both informative *and* performative meaning.

Normally in constituting or reconstructing symbolic acts we make use of other symbolic acts already at our disposal. For a methodical understanding of symbolic acts it is, however, necessary to avoid concepts which imply circles or infinite regress. Therefore we have to present "elementary" symbolic acts, which do not presuppose a functioning system of other symbolic acts. I think Wittgenstein already has hinted at a solution of this problem, which only needs some working out. Let us for this purpose recall Wittgenstein's example of the building site :

One of the acts assumed by Wittgenstein as common usage in this situation is the call "slab!" (German : "Platte!"), understood as summoning the addressee to bring things of a certain kind. The sort of symbolic acts exemplified by "slab!" may be introduced in an elementary way not necessarily based upon other symbolic acts. Let us first assume, that the use of "slab!" is by agreement of the users correct only in cases, where there are slabs lying about. Furthermore we take it that calling "slab!" to a participant of the "language game" has normally the pragmatic consequences of a slab being brought by him. By these conventions the phonetic act "slab!" has acquired a symbolic meaning, it has become an act carrying a symbolic act. How can we conceive of this symbolic act as being elementary in the sense already stated? Didn't we use quite a lot of speech to characterize the contents of the conventions defining the symbolic meaning of "slab!"? Indeed we did, but only in order to save unnecessary endeavours, things having been made so pleasant for us in this Christ Church lecture room. Our verbal descriptions of the building site and the conventions, which are valid therein, only serve as a means of making us imagine a situation in which we can do without (other) words and nevertheless learn the symbolic use of "slab!". He who does not believe may leave the lecture rooms and *pragmatically* (as opposed to : only *descriptively*) enter suitable situations.

How then is the elementary learning of the symbolic act "slab!" going on? The answer is simple : just by practising it embedded in acts of handling slabs. No verbal descriptions are necessary to learn in this way "empragmatically" (the term being created by Lorenzen and Schwemmer (1973)), that slabs and not bricks are meant and that in bringing a slab the addressee of "slab!" has acted according to the (indirect) intention of the utterer. As far as elementary symbolic acts imply certain distinctions (e.g. between slabs and bricks), these distinctions can be established pragmatically, without using verbal descriptions.

If we want to reserve the term "distinction" for the symbolic level, we have to state that in pragmatically determining the correct use of an elementary symbolic act *a* we at the same time constitute the distinction, which gives *a* an informative meaning. In German I propose to call such elementary symbolic acts "Weisungen", being derived from "anweisen", "Anweisung" for the more performative ones and "hinweisen", "Hinweis" for the more informative ones among them. It seems difficult to find an appropriate English equivalent. Alas, the term "reference" in its philosophical and logical use often belongs to the semantics of simple or complex nominators (i.e. name or description terms). Neglecting the traditions of English Frege-translations with its terminological consequences as well as the opposition of reference and predication we may for the moment speak of *elementary references*.

It is important to emphasize at this point that elementary references do not imply taking one of the usual logico-grammatical categories as a basis. Wittgenstein e.g. did already see this. In *Philosophical Investigations* I 19 he says (editors' English translation) : "But what about this : is the call 'Slab!' [. . .] a sentence or a word? If a word, surely it has not the same meaning as the likesounding word of our ordinary language, [. . .]. But if a sentence, it is surely not the elliptical sentence : 'Slab!' of our language." Thus elementary references may not be conceived as representing the classical grammatical or logical distinctions. Neither "sentence", nor "word", nor "predicator" ("Peter!" may be an elementary reference as well) will do. Rather, elementary references are to be understood as the fundaments for a radically pragmatic approach to the logico-grammatical form of linguistic expressions. I shall now indicate (suggest) some steps in this direction :

One of the main questions obviously is, how we can get from elementary references to the distinction between, i.e. the different use of, nominators ("this house", "Peter") and predicators ("stone", "red"). The difficulty is that in a radically pragmatic approach nominators or predicators may not simply be imagined as some kind of name-plates being attached to e.g. ontological individuals or semantic functions. Namely such an approach leaves at our method-ical disposal for a starting point only elementary symbolic acts which are by conventions of correctness, empragmatically related to certain ways of *handling,* more generally speaking : of *dealing with,* those things normally distinguished by nominators and predicators (cf. Lorenz 1970). E.g. fetching this cup, pouring water into this cup, touching this cup, pointing at this cup etc. form such a "bundle" of dealing-with-this-cup-acts.

How do we know which acts belong to the bundle? To use the term "this cup" in characterizing the bundle, would be circular. I do not see any other possibility but learning what is dealing with n just *by examples* of acts. On the other hand : to learn what is dealing with n must not be understood as learning an *act* (scheme) : dealing with n. It makes no sense, to require someone just to actualize "dealing with n", without further differentiation.

What then does it mean to exemplify dealing with n by particular ways of dealing with n? What do we learn by these examples if not a general act (scheme) "dealing with n". My argument is that we thus learn the conditions for the correct performance of another act, namely the *symbolic* act consisting in uttering a sound, figure, gesture etc. with a symbolic intention : thus certain well selected acts are, by agreement, distinguished as allowing the thereby defined symbolic intention of uttering e.g. "this cup", "cup". And this agree-ment is settled and communicated by exemplification.

This explanation still makes no distinction between particular n's and general ones. Pragmatically speaking, dealing with *a cup* no matter what particular cup, and handling this *well determined* cup, remain to be distinguished.

Obviously the "general" symbolic act "cup" is related to its individualizations "this cup" etc. in the following way : A correct performance of the individualizations presupposes a situation in which a performance of the corresponding "general" symbolic act is or would be correct. And there are no subdivisions of the individual-izations with this some property. Let us speak of nomination in the "individual" case and of predication in the "general" one. To make nomination cotext—or context—independent we can use *proper names* instead of expressions like "this cup".

Nomination and predication do not attach verbal tickets to indivi-dual objects or abstract entities, not even, as I have already empha-sized, to act schemes, e.g. such act schemes as deal with *a* cup or deal with *this* cup. Rather they constitute *genera* of acts. *Nomina-tion* (namely) enables us to *distinguish* just those acts concerning

77

"a particular object". *Predication* does the same with respect to all objects which can pragmatically be dealt with "in the same way". What is *dealing with (the same) particular object* or *acting in the same way with otherwise different object* cannot be found out by observation of the given, but is constituted by learning symbolic acts of nomination and predication respectively. Nomination- and predication-acts in our construction are *informative* symbolic acts, indeed they are special *elementary references*.

What is the "seat (position) in life" of nomination and predication acts? Are not they just some kind of scholars' fictions? Now, nomination and predication acts do not serve as means of inducing particular acts (as it is the case with Wittgenstein's "Slab!" example), but as means of communicating on *possibilities* of acting. So the predication act "cup" will take us beyond the particular act (e.g. of pointing at a cup) with which it is connected, when being correctly performed. Trusting to the correct performance of this symbolic act just makes us aware that we have the usual cup handling activities at our disposal; e.g. we may then take it for granted that the tea is, at least in part, provided for. Acting according to this expectation then at the same time enables us to control the correctness of the predication act "cup".

Now what about elementary *sentences* of the form $n \varepsilon P$, where uttering n alone under suitable circumstances is a nominative symbolic act and uttering P alone a predicative one? Stating $n \varepsilon P$ may be understood as an informative symbolic act correctly used if all dealing-with-P-acts can be performed as performances of dealing-with-n-acts. To take a higher level example : "Christ Church ε College" means that we are able to perform the usual college activities as Christ Church activities. n being a proper name, elementary statements of the form $n \varepsilon P$, by our analysis, have a meaning apart from the presence of tokens, which can be qualified as dealing with the objects those elementary statements speak about. Using the semantic term we are accustomed to : elementary statements *refer* to our situation *in general*. That raises the question as to how we can *pragmatically control* the correct performance of elementary statements. The answer is : Entering situations with concrete dealings with n, we shall be able to try, if dealing-with-P-acts can be actualized by actualizing schemes of handling n. He who denies that $n \varepsilon P$, may put forward a dealing-with-P-act (scheme), which has no n-operations as its subscheme.

Stating an elementary sentence of the form "$n \varepsilon P$" must not be analysed as performing a *complex* act consisting of performing first a nominative act n, then some kind of connection-act (attached to the ε), finally a predicative act P. Nor are elementary statements at all symbolic acts mediated by the corresponding elementary references. If it were so, these elementary references would be primary acts relative to the respective elementary statement and that means, they would have to be performed in performing this statement. On the other hand elementary references have but an *empragmatic* use, and this use is impossible within elementary statements, because they refer to our situation only in general.

We may call the relation between elementary statements and the corresponding nominative and predicative acts a *pragmatic derivation*. Generally I propose to call an act a *derived from* acts $a_1, \ldots, a_n$ if and only if the *ability* to actualize a presupposes the *abilities* to perform $a_1, \ldots, a_n$. *Derived* acts must not be confounded with *mediated* acts : one need not *perform* an act to make use of the mastery of it in performing another act.

One important remark on elementary statements has to be added : Elementary statements must not be understood as *assertions*, i.e. as provided with *obligations to argue* for them in a well defined manner. The pragmatic cotext they are embedded in is e.g. demanding and giving information, not disputing and defending arguments (not argumentation in the narrow sense of the word). The relation between statements, assertions and propositions gives rise to difficult questions. They form part of the problems linked with the distinction between locutionary and illocutionary acts and similar distinctions. Let me therefore now try to make some clarifying general remarks concerning these distinctions and then examine proposals made by Austin and Searle.

Elementary statements mostly do not occur independently, but as symbolic acts mediating symbolic acts of *higher order*. The elementary *demands* are the best illustration of this. Demands are symbolic acts having a rather simple *performative* meaning. I propose that the pragmatic consequence defining a demand to do something is by agreement the addressee's doing so. I.e. he who demands that something be done or brought about has to expect it to be done; though perhaps the addressee may refuse to act according to the demand. This understanding of demands must not be misinterpreted as being meant imperatively : *D*emands are not *com*mands; commands being formed of demands by performatively embedding them in a context of *sanctions*. For demands, I propose, pragmatic consequences of not fulfilling them shall not be laid down or otherwise established. A person who demands that the salt be given to him, by agreement has to expect *that* the salt is given to him. And this demand has been correctly performed, even if the person asked does not hand over the salt, but is arguing instead that the meal should not be oversalted.

Demands may be learnt in elementary cases as independent symbolic acts, i.e. as symbolic acts which are not mediated by other symbolic acts. We shall here now study the case when a demand is carried by an informative symbolic act s, e.g. an elementary reference or statement. There are two relevant ways in which such an s may mediate a demand. To illustrate the following considerations by an example, you perhaps should keep in mind as an appropriate s the predicative act constituting the *word* "salt". Now, one way of constituting demands as higher order symbolic acts being mediated by s is to establish for s itself an additional symbolic intention s' which is restricted to certain situational cotexts. To actualize s in such situations is then by an additional convention connected with pragmatic consequences. That is done by relating s to certain acts, which by the thus constituted s' one is demanded to perform. In case s is not indicating these acts, one has to learn them by just *exercising s* as carrying the higher order symbolic intention s'.

Especially in cases where it is difficult to separate a demand s' from other actualizations of s, we are accustomed to link a general demand-sign—let us indicate it by "!"—with s. Then a complex act $! \cup s$ takes the place of s in carrying the intention s'. E.g. the "!" may be a phonetic modification of a phonetic act mediating s. This analysis means that demands, which are construed with a special demand sign, must not be understood as being simply an aggregate composed of two independent pragmatic parts, one carrying the so called "propositional content" and the other carrying the demand sense.

For lack of time let me make only very short remarks on the treatment of elementary assertions and questions : An informative symbolic act s is mediating an *assertion s'* if a performance of s by further agreement opens a discourse on the question of this performance being correct. *Questions* of an elementary sort then may be understood as demands to actualize justified assertions out of a range of alternatives indicated by the question considered. This reconstruction of assertions and questions obviously allows us to conceive them as higher order symbolic acts.

The well known considerations of Austin and Searle are not clear enough in their analysis of the mediation structures, which we have just studied. In principle Austin's approach seems nearer to the reconstructions I have proposed to you here. Austin distinguishes, as you know, a *locutionary* act, by which we "say something" from the *illocutionary* acts e.g. of stating, demanding, questioning, which are particular uses of the locutions : "For example, it might be perfectly possible, with regard to an utterance, say 'It is going to charge', to make entirely plain 'what we were saying' in issuing the utterance, in all the senses so far distinguished, and yet not at all to have cleared up whether or not in issuing the utterance I was performing the act of warning or not. It may be perfectly clear what I mean by 'It is going to charge' or 'Shut the door', but not clear whether it is meant as a statement or warning, etc." (Austin 1965, 98).

Austin obviously believes that locutionary and illocutionary acts are not simply put together to form a complex act, in the narrow sense of the word "complex". Rather, we may gather from some of his remarks on this point that he conceives the illocutionary speech acts as *mediated* by the locutionary acts. Pointing in this direction is for example Austin's statement, that "to determine what illocutionary act is [. . .] performed we must determine in what way we are using the locution" (ibid.). Still clearer is Austin's following explanation : "I explained the performance of an act in this new [. . .] sense as the performance of an 'illocutionary' act, i.e. performance of an act *in* saying something as opposed to performance of an act *of* saying something; and I shall refer to the doctrine of the different types of function of language here in question as the doctrine of 'illocutionary forces'." (Austin 1965, 99).

Making use of the distinctions I have explained here Austin's "saying something" is a lower order informative symbolic act s, whereas a corresponding illocutionary act (Austin : "act performed *in* saying something") may be understood as a higher order symbolic act mediated by s. If this interpretation is correct, then Searle's critical work on Austin's intentions rather means a regress.

Searle, like Austin, distinguishes in sentences like "Sam smokes habitually", "Does Sam smoke habitually?", "Sam, smoke habitually!" a "*propositional act*" common to them from the illocutionary acts of stating, questioning, commanding etc. (Searle 1969, 22, 24). And it seems, that like Austin, he understands illocutionary acts as *mediated* acts : "[. . .] in performing an illocutionary act one characteristically performs propositional acts and utterance acts" (ibid. 24). Yet Searle does not sustain his insight into the mediated character of illocutionary acts. One reason is that he seems to analyse the so called propositional acts themselves as mediated by the corresponding illocutionary acts : "The expression of a proposition is a proposi-

81

tional act, not an illocutionary act. And as we saw, propositional acts cannot occur alone. [. . .] When a proposition is expressed it is always expressed in the performance of an illocutionary act." (loc. cit. 29). This leaves us with a pragmatic circle : The propositional acts are to be mediated by the corresponding illocutionary acts, the symbolic constitution of which on the other hand makes use of the respective propositional acts as primary acts. Perhaps Searle wanted to say that propositional acts should not be understood as act schemes at all, i.e. not as learnable apart from their illocutionary use. But then we should not call them *acts*, and it becomes obscure, what is the pragmatic meaning of the letter p in the structural schemes by which Searle characterizes the illocutionary acts as follows :

$\vdash (p)$ for assertions $!(p)$ for requests
$Pr(p)$ for promises $W(p)$ for warnings
$?(p)$ for yes-no questions

Searle's following summary (Searle 1969, 31) then has no pragmatic basis; and that must be contrary to his main intention : "The general form of (very many kinds of) illocutionary acts is $F(p)$, where the variable 'F' takes illocutionary force indicating devices as values and 'p' takes expressions for propositions."

Let us take for example a demand : Either a symbolic act of the form $!(p)$ "contains" a pragmatically independent symbolic part p, which thus may be qualified as an act; or we simply do not know what is the pragmatic sense of stating that the respective p "expresses a proposition", which is the same proposition with all the different symbolic acts having the form $F(p)$. That we have in all these cases a performance of the same phonetic act obviously does not imply *eo ipso* that the phonetic act is carrying an F-invariant symbolic intention.

To sum up : Either Searle's concept of propositional acts leads to a pragmatic circle, or Searle is leaving the pragmatic approach altogether. (Cf. Schneider 1975.)

With the pragmatic reconstructions, which I have proposed for treating illocutionary symbolic acts, this methodical dilemma does not turn up, I hope. The forms $s_1(\vdash \cup s)$, $s_2(! \cup s)$, $s_3(? \cup s)$, ... in our analysis presuppose that the s, being an informative symbolic act, has a separate intention, which is not mediated by the s_1.

In a paper of 1968 Searle has discussed in detail his modifications of Austin's approach. Searle argues that Austin has, in distinguishing illocutionary from locutionary acts, neglected an ambiguity of the word "statement". "Statement" may mean according to Searle either the *"act of stating"* ("statement-act sense") or *"what is stated"* ("statement-object sense"). Searle's examples for the two cases are respectively (Searle 1968, 422) : "1. The statement of our position took all of the morning session. 2. The statement that all men are mortal is true."

In Searle's opinion "statement", used in the act sense, does not refer, as he presumes for Austin, to a locutionary, but to an illocutionary act. Whereas in its object sense the word "statement" stands, Searle thinks, for a proposition. Propositions now have for Searle that illocutionary neutrality which Austin wants, if Searle's arguments are relevant, to ascribe to the locutionary acts of stating : "In the characterization of statement-object we have to add the phrase 'construed as stated' because of course what is stated, the proposition, can also be the content of a question, of a promise, the antecedent of a hypothetical, and so forth. It is neutral as to the illocutionary force which is expressed, but statements are not neutral as to illocutionary force [. . .]." (loc. cit. 431 sq.). In other words of Searle's we are required to distinguish within the entire illocutionary act the *type* of the act from the *content* of the act.

As Austin ranks various kinds of statements (e.g. informations, identifications, descriptions etc.) with the illocutionary acts, he probably understands the locutionary acts as speech acts which mediate the illocutionary acts of asserting, demanding, questioning etc. and which therefore, to avoid a pragmatic circle, must be possible as independent acts. If this interpretation is correct, Searle is still right in stressing the point that locutionary acts in Austin's sense, must not be conceived as acts of assertion. Nevertheless the conclusion he has drawn, namely to introduce an obscure quasi-act "to express a proposition", does not master the dilemma of reconstructing illocutionary acts, which use the utterance of a sentence. A consistently pragmatic approach must first pragmatically reconstruct our speaking of abstract entities like e.g. "propositions" and then make methodical use of it.

It is time to return to the general aspects of a radically pragmatic analysis of language, since otherwise we may be somewhat lost in details. My inquiry had as its subject some mediation (and derivation) relations of rather fundamental speech acts. By means of mediation and derivation, acts (in the sense of act schemes) are intentionally connected. Let me call the working out of these pragmatic connections *intentional constructions*. An intentional construction of an act gives at the same time a possible history of step by step learning (and teaching) this act. If we want to place emphasis on

83

this learning process, we might call an intentional construction of an act a *pragmatic development* of this act.

Intentional constructions need not have only one solution. Namely there may be several ways of mediating an act. Therefore, even if an intentional construction is a *re*construction of well-known act schemes, as is usual in linguistic analysis, it need not necessarily be a copy of the actually established learning processes.

On the other hand intentional reconstructions are not simply a case of free imagination. Indeed they have a double (pragmatic) *fundamentum in re* : Firstly they, by definition, are subject to the pragmatic control that every step must be learnable on the previously laid basis. Secondly reconstructions have to be *pragmatically adequate*, i.e. if we substitute the intention constructed by the reconstruction of an act *a*, which is thus *re*constructed, the relevant *a*-Praxis will be improved, at least not changed for worse.

For symbolic acts this means in both cases that in critically evaluating proposed reconstructions, we have to consider the connections with the performance of other acts. Therefore a pragmatic reconstruction of language in particular raises problems of an interpretation of the action-cotext common to all participants. I.e. a "solution" of pragmatic interpretation problems exists only when some interpretations of some acts are not debated in the community of speakers. If this once were not the case, the participants would not live in the same world. The "natural" world not containing acts, it could obviously not be taken as a basis for judging whether or not we have by means of a reconstruction met the relevant intentions. Furthermore, in that our understanding of nature is itself constituted by action, it would be part of that relativity which has to be overcome to solve the problem.

We are still far from a clear pragmatic development of the symbolic acts embedded in language and other human institutions. And this hermeneutic work will have to be done with the same subtlety hitherto mostly invested in the formalistic analysis of language. If I have at least made a little more precise the kind of task Wittgenstein has left us, I will have realized, not the intention, but the aim of this lecture.

Professor Friedrich Kambartel
Konstanz University
Germany

BIBLIOGRAPHY

Austin, J. L. (1965) *How to do Things with Words*, corrected ed. Oxford: Clarendon Press.
Goldman, A. J. (1970) *A Theory of Human Action*, Englewood Cliffs/New Jersey: Prentice Hall.
Kamlah, W. (1972) *Philosophische Anthropologie*, Mannheim: Bibliographisches Institut.
Lorenz, K. (1970) *Elemente der Sprachkritik*, Frankfurt a.M.: Suhrkamp.
Lorenzen, P., Schwemmer, O. (1973) *Konstruktive Logik, Ethik und Wissenschaftstheorie*, Mannheim: Bibliographisches Institut.
Schneider, H. J. (1975) *Die pragmatische Basis von Semantik und Syntax*, Frankfurt a.M.: Suhrkamp.
Schneider, H. J. (1977) *Ist die Prädikation eine Sprechhandlung?*, in K. Lorenz (Hrsg).: *Konstruktionen versus Positionen*, Frankfurt a.M.: Suhrkamp (forthcoming).
Searle, J. R. (1968) *Austin on locutionary and illocutionary acts*, in Philos. Review 77, 405–424.
Searle, J. R. (1969) *Speech Acts*, Cambridge: University Press.
von Wright, G. H. (1963) *Norm and Action*, London: Routledge & Kegan Paul.
von Wright, G. H. (1971) *Explanation and Understanding*, Ithaca, New York: Cornell University Press.
on Wright, G. H. (1974) *Causality and Determinism*, New York, London: Columbia University Press.

VI

SOME ELEMENTS OF THE FORM OF THEORY PERHAPS USEFUL IN DESCRIBING A LANGUAGE

E. von Savigny

1. A Listener—(or Third Party) Analysis of Linguistic Meaning

WE SHALL FIRST try to explain what it is for a sign to mean something for a certain person and then pass on to what it is for a sign to mean something in a language (i.e. to have conventional meaning).

That a sign x means some certain thing *for a given person* y may be expressed by saying that y understands x in a certain way. E.g., for me an arrow has the meaning of pointing in the direction of its head; I might say instead that I understand an arrow as pointing in the direction of its head. This reformulation is without systematic import; its point is just to permit us to make use of Wittgenstein's and—to a certain extent—Ryle's analysis of what it is to understand something in a certain way.[1] I think I follow these analyses when I assume that the assertion "y understands x in a certain way" attributes to y a dispositional property and that the meaning of this assertion can be rendered by an open list of behavioural regularities, the vast majority of which are true of y if and only if the dispositional assertion is true. How the list looks depends on which sign x is and how y understands it. My example (as all further examples) will be taken from motor-car drivers' non-verbal language in Western Germany—a language of which I am a native speaker. The meaning of the assertion

> y understands the flashing of the headlights of a first driver at a second driver, if the second is waiting to turn left and the first comes from the opposite direction and is slowing down, as an invitation to the second driver to complete his turn

can be given by a list beginning thus :

> (1) If y flashes at a driver in such a situation, he will wait until the latter has completed his turn.

(2) If a driver he has flashed at in such a situation makes no move, he will hesitate before driving on.

(3) If a driver he has flashed at in such a situation makes no move, he will exhibit signs of puzzlement.

(4) If in such a situation the lights are flashed at him and the road has only one lane in the opposite direction, he will complete his turn.

(5) If somebody on the second of two opposite lanes flashes at him while other cars are running on the first lane, he will first turn into the second lane and wait.

(6) If somebody flashes at him in such a situation and does not wait for him to complete his turn, he will get angry.

(7) If the lights are flashed at him in such a situation, he will wave his hand in a gesture of thanks on completing his turn.

(8) If he is waiting behind someone not turning left although the lights are flashed at him in such a situation, he will blow his horn.

(9) If, as a pedestrian, he is about to cross the side road which the waiting driver wants to turn into (in such a situation), he will stop.

And so on. Of course, numerous qualifications have to be added; for somebody to understand the sign in the way indicated, not all behavioural regularities must be true of him nor must they apply to him without exception. But gross changes in the list will attribute to him a different way of understanding the sign. If instead of behaving according to our list the first driver usually turns right himself, looks to see if the second driver follows him, shows signs of puzzlement if he does not, and so on, then this would be good evidence for the hypothesis that he understands the flashing in such a situation as his acceptance of the other driver's request that somebody turn into the sideroad before him. (Driving alone in a road might be taboo for religious reasons; blinking to turn left would then possibly acquire the meaning of such a request.)

What rules are there to govern the step from the dispositional statement to the list of behavioural regularities? Well, no such rules must necessarily be known to anyone. If two persons understand the dispositional statement (attributing to y a certain way of understanding x) in the same way, then they will judge the same behavioural regularities as belonging to the list; if they differ in this respect, then the sentence expressing the dispositional statement is an instance in which their languages differ. Describing y's way of understanding x presupposes a language in which it can be described, and the step from the dispositional statement to one list or another depends upon the language in which the whole procedure is carried on.

That a sign means something in a certain language means that it is correct (in this language) to understand it that way. To introduce correctness is vital because otherwise certain ways of speaking about meaning and understanding cannot be understood. So far, we have been concerned only with expressions like "y understands x in this way, z understands x differently". If x has conventional linguistic meaning, then it makes sense to say things like "y understands x in this way, but that is not correct", or "y understands x correctly, while z doesn't." Now it is quite illuminating that instead of "y understands x correctly" we may equally well say "y understands x", and instead of "y understands x incorrectly" we may equally well say "y doesn't understand x". If it is the arrow's meaning for me to point in the direction of its head, while its meaning for you is that it points in the opposite direction, then you understand it in a different way from me; but if it is the arrow's meaning to point in the direction of its head, then if I understand it this way, my way of understanding it is correct, while if you understand it differently, your way of understanding it is incorrect.

So "x has, in a certain language, a certain meaning" can be rendered as "in that language, that way of understanding x is the correct way". Since a way of understanding a sign is to have a disposition, this means that, for a sign to have a certain meaning in a language, having a certain disposition is correct in that language. Now I hope we may let it pass that if it is correct to have a certain disposition, then it is correct to behave in the ways specified by the list of the disposition's behavioural regularities. E.g., if it is correct to be polite, then it is correct to behave as polite people behave. (I am not sure about the converse, that is, about whether if it is correct to behave as polite people behave, then it is *ipso facto* correct to be polite. But we do not need the converse.) So we arrive at the following hypothetical statement :

If, in the language of Western German drivers, the flashing of the first driver at a second driver, the second waiting to turn left and the first coming from the opposite direction and slowing down, means an invitation to the second driver to complete his

turn, then, in this language, it is correct to behave in the ways
(1) to (9) and so on.

Since Western German drivers' non-verbal language is a natural
language, reference to correctness cannot mean reference to rules
laid down by some authority but only to rules implicitly complied
with by the group of Western German drivers. The most plausible
way of saying what it is for a rule to be implicitly complied with
(that is, regardless of whether anyone can state it or whether it is
laid down or enforced by an authority) seems to me to be Hart's
analysis of the existence of rules. By slightly changing it, we translate
our substitute of "in Western drivers' language, it is correct to behave
in the way (1)", viz.

Among Western German drivers, one complies with the rule to
behave in the way (1)

into the following three conditions :

(a) A first driver who flashes at a second driver, when the second
is waiting to turn left and the first comes from the opposite
direction and is slowing down, generally waits for the second
driver to complete his turn.
(b) If , in such a situation, he does not wait, he is subject to
sanctions on the part of any other drivers (e.g. angry use of the
horn, insulting gestures and so one).
(c) In general, he will accept such sanctions (e.g. by an apologiz-
ing gesture or by admitting his mistake to a passenger).

We shall call this explicit form of stating that (1) is rule-guided
behaviour among Western German drivers. It is an instance of the
following general scheme :

Rule R is complied with in group G

translates into

(a) Members of G seldom openly depart from R;
(b) deviations are subject to sanctions from all other members
of G;
(c) such sanctions are generally accepted.[2]

In our example, R is : "If you flash at a driver, when he is waiting to turn left and you come from the opposite direction and are slowing down, then wait for him to complete his turn."

Hart's conditions for the existence of rules are as follows :[3]

> (0) There must be general conformance to the pattern of behaviour in question;
> (1) deviations incur criticism;
> (2) deviations are accepted as reasons for criticism of the deviations;
> (3) the members of the group must look upon the rule from an "internal point of view".

(0) Corresponds to (a), (1) to (b). (c) is a generalized version of (2). Hart is undoubtedly right that some such condition is necessary; for it helps to distinguish between rules that are deeply entrenched and others that are in dispute. But I fear that this condition either is too narrow—if it is intended to demand that the sanctions and the forms of accepting them be verbal—or its range of application is too narrow if where sanctions are non-verbal it just does not apply. Perhaps (2) and (3) taken together might be construed as equivalent to (c), so that our formulation would not differ in content from Hart's criterion. I must confess that I cannot indeed make anything of the "internal aspect" except that the members of the group treat it as natural and as a matter of no dispute to comply with the rule; and that is surely the case where conditions (b) and (c) are satisfied. Should there really be members of the group not liking the rule but going along with it because of fear of sanctions, then either they are so few that I should have no qualms about ignoring them in the description of the group's rules, or else condition (b) would not be satisfied, since there would be too many members in the group from whom no sanctions would have to be expected. (Somebody may go along with a rule out of prudence in trying to avoid sanctions and in not defending himself against them; but prudence does not demand that he punish others for deviations.)

In explaining the idea of a sign's conventional meaning being the accepted way of understanding it, we have used a Wittgenstein-Rylean concept of dispositional understanding and a Hartian concept of compliance with a rule. We may label it a listener- or third party-analysis, because it attributes the authority for deciding on what has been said neither to the speaker nor to the addressee, but rather to any speaker of the language who might have listened to the utterance (and to speaker and addressee only because they are

E. VON SAVIGNY

such listeners). As a result, we are able to say how a hypothesis stating that an utterance-type in a given language has a certain meaning when uttered in a specific situation must be tested by reference to speech behaviour : A list has to be specified containing behavioural regularities typical of somebody understanding the utterance-type in the appropriate way; for each of these regularities a hypothesis has to be formulated that states in the explicit form that the regularity is rule-guided behaviour among the group supposedly using that language; these hypotheses have to be tested by observing the group's behaviour; and the better a system of hypotheses corresponding to such a list survives the test in comparison with rival systems corresponding to rival meaning hypotheses, the better confirmed is the meaning hypothesis to which that system corresponds.

Such a test procedure seems to provide a means for determining the preciseness of meanings of utterance-types. Perhaps flashing one's headlights (in our situation) means nothing but "Look, here I am".[4] To check this hypothesis, we ought to look whether flashing drivers are held to be committed to things people are not normally committed to just on account of having said "Look, here I am".

Note that the specifications of meanings contain both illocutionary force and rheme (or proposition). So far there is no need to split them up, and the analysis will also apply in cases where no such splitting is possible. So there is no mystery in explaining the conventional meaningfulness of greetings, interjections, and other types of utterances where it is an obvious sort of nonsense to construct propositions in the desperate enterprise of defending the view that saying something meaningful must be commenting on a state of affairs.

2. Constitutive and Regulative Rules of Language

So far we have arrived at two sorts of sentences which are possible candidates for expressing rules of language :

(C) The flashing of one driver at another driver, if the latter comes from the opposite direction and is waiting to turn left and the former is slowing down, means that he invites the second driver to complete his turn.

(R) A driver who slows down and flashes at another driver coming from the opposite direction and waiting to turn left has to wait for this second driver to complete his turn.

I think there is no need to argue that type-(C)-rules express constitutive rules in Searle's sense, while type-(R)-rules quite obviously

91

are regulative rules. Both pass his tests without any difficulty.[5] I hope to show that our analysis will first permit us to describe a quite illuminating ambiguity in the view that languages have rules, and, second, clarify the way in which constitutive rules are connected with regulative rules.

If somebody is asked which of the two rules above may express a rule of Western German drivers' non-verbal language, he will not hesitate to pick out (C); it is just the sort of entry you expect to find in a dictionary. If he is then asked what rule (R) is a rule for and where he expects to find it, he will probably answer that it is a rule for how to be a correct or fair driver and that it might be looked up in the highway code. In short, while (C) looks like what a rule of language should look like, (R) looks like a moral rule.

Now if such descriptions may satisfy a lexicographer, they will surely disappoint a philosopher who thinks, deep in his heart, that language is a social activity and that there is conventional meaning because this social activity is governed by rules. For him, since language is dependent on compliance with such rules, it is they that ought to come out as the rules of language. So our philosopher is apt to make the opposite choice : Language rules are type-(R)-rules— rules compliance with which constitutes a language; and type-(C)-rules have to be explained as something else.

If our analysis is correct, then the difference might be not so great as it appears to be. Let us assume (C) to be correct for a certain group; then (R) expresses a rule that the group complies with. Or to put it another way : If (C) is true (for that group), then it is true that (R) is complied with (by that group). It is quite correct to speak of (C) as true or false; for its content is the empirical proposition that the behavioural regularities (1) to (9) and so on constitute rule-guided behaviour of the group in question. On the other hand, (R) (as distinguished from the assertion that (R) is complied with) cannot be labelled true or false (not empirically true or false, at any rate); assenting to it or denying it is not to assert or to contest an empirical fact. There is indeed an intimate connection between type-(C)-rules and type-(R)-rules; but this connection is neither :

If (C) is true, then (R) is true;

for (R) cannot be true or false; nor is it :

If (C) is valid, then (R) is valid;

for (C) cannot be called valid in the sense of a rule's being valid as (R) can; it is, rather :

If (C) is true, then (R) is complied with,

or simply :

If (C), then (R) is complied with.

Now this means that unless a group complies with some type-(R)-rules there is no type-(C)-rule that comes out true for this group. In other words : If there is no rule-guided behaviour, then any statement to the effect that there is linguistic meaning is false. Type-(R)-rules are rules of language in the sense that unless they are complied with in a group, this group has no language, and that the set of type-(R)-rules complied with determines which language the group has. Type-(C)-rules are rules of language in the sense that they describe, in an indirect way, the rule-guided behaviour on which the existence of the language depends.

To generalize this point, I should like to suggest that the relation between constitutive and regulative rules is in general that between our (C)- and (R)-rules. If there are to be constitutive rules for any sort of activity, then there must be regulative rules which are complied with in that activity; and the constitutive rules are just indirect ways of stating that the regulative rules are complied with, in that they specify open lists of sentences of the form "(R) is complied with". To take an example from soccer, I think the following is a constitutive rule in Searle's sense :

If the ball is not out of play, then its crossing the goal-line of one team counts as a goal for the other team.

(I do not know whether this formulation is quite correct; but I hope it may pass for that.) What does it mean for an event to count as a goal in soccer? Well, of course it means that such an event is called a goal, but that is not the fact we are interested in; it might be called a hoop or a wicket or a point without changing its significance. Somebody who is present at a soccer game for the first time will very soon learn the word by listening to the cheers of one half of the spectators; what else has he to learn in order to know what the significance of the event called by that name is? As far as I know, there are three facts, the first of minor importance, the second and third vital :

(10) After the ball has crossed the goal-line of one team (without being out of play), this team has to kick off unless the playing time is over.

(11) Each player, during the whole game, has to try his best to help get the ball (not out of play) across the other team's goal-line.

(12) Each player, during the whole game, has to try his best to prevent the ball (not out of play) from crossing his own team's goal-line.

The facts our visitor has to learn are that these three rules are complied with by the players in the sense explained above. If he knows that the rules (11) and (12) are complied with, he knows that it is vital, in soccer, to try to win and that for winning or losing it is goals that count. (If the game is played in the course of some competition, there may be more to winning, as for instance by how many goals you win.) In order to check whether the rules are complied with, our visitors must see whether the players generally conform to them, whether deviance is subject to sanctions and whether sanctions are generally accepted. With rule (10), there are no difficulties. If there is a referee, then a goalie who refuses the ball for the kick-off and instead tries to kick from the goal-line after the referee has awarded a goal will be shown the yellow card and will not insist further; if there is no referee, then the reprimands from the players, including his own team, will change his mind. (There is of course the difficulty of deciding whether the ball has crossed the goal-line and whether it was out of play, e.g. offside, or not; whether the rule is complied with can only be checked in cases where the players agree on these points.) Rules (11) and (12) are a little more difficult. A player who quite obviously shows no interest in scoring goals may be punished by the referee for delaying the game; the other players of his own team will reproach him if further goals are still important for them; the opposing team is likely to scorn a team that plays half-heartedly or even break off the match ("You aren't really playing !"). (And likewise for rule 12.) The less plausibly one can say that the rules are complied with in this sense, the less plausible becomes the suggestion that a ball's crossing the goal-line counts as a goal in the sense in which we understand something to count as a goal.[6]

It might be noteworthy, first, that from our regulative rules it follows that you have to try to win, and second, that winning is a thing you must necessarily wish in order to play soccer. Of course, normally you will like to win and you will strive for it. But even if you don't care about it, you have to try anyway.

In this case, it seems rather plausible that the meaning of the constitutive rule is given by the statement that the three corresponding regulative rules are complied with; the list of regulative rules might even be closed, though I am not sure about that. I have, together with colleagues and students, run over many examples taken from everyday social relations and never found a case of an institutional fact (that is, a fact described by invoking a constitutive rule) in which it was not possible to render the meaning of sentences expressing institutional facts ("He is heir to her") or constitutive rules ("He who has been made heir to a person by that person's will is heir to that person") by sentences expressing the compliance with regulative rules in the group for which the constitutive rule is supposed to hold. So I cannot help being rather firmly convinced that institutional facts do not form a second class of facts above, beneath or beside what Searle calls brute facts. For since statements to the effect that a certain regulative rule is complied with in a group surely are statements about brute facts (even if general statements, and even if about dispositions and the like), statements to the effect that a certain constitutive rule holds for a group, as an indirect way of stating compliance with regulative rules, are an indirect way of stating something about brute facts. There are no two kinds of facts; there are two ways of describing facts.

3. Introducing Propositions and Illocutionary Forces for Utterance-types in Specific Situations

Consider the following hypotheses which I am fairly sure are true for Western German drivers :

> (13) The flashing of one driver at another driver, if the second comes from the opposite direction and is waiting to turn left and the first is slowing down, means that the first invites the second to complete his turn.
> (14) The flashing of a first driver at a second driver, if the second is waiting ahead of the former to turn left and the first is forced to wait behind him, means that the first demands of the second that he complete his turn.
> (15) The flashing of a first driver at a second driver, if the second comes from the opposite direction and is starting to turn left and the first is not slowing down, means that the first driver warns the second driver not to complete his turn.

(16) The flashing of a first driver at a second driver, if the first is waiting to turn left and the second comes from the opposite direction and is at a distance such that if he slows down the first will have time to complete his turn, but if he does not the first will not have time to complete his turn, means that the first driver asks the second to permit the first driver to complete his turn.

(17) The flashing of a first driver at a second driver, while the first is completing his turn to the left, this turn being somehow enabled by the second coming from the opposite direction, means that the first thanks the second for permitting him to complete his turn.

These hypotheses, if well confirmed, constitute positive evidence for the more general hypothesis (18) :

(18) The flashing of one driver at another, where one of them is about to turn left, treats of this one's completing his turn.

I am quite sure that (18) is far too general to be true; indeed, I have not bothered about counter-examples since they are too likely to exist. But I have no doubt that there is a correct substitute for (18) (which might even be found), specifying in an economical way situations in which the flashing of one driver at another treats of one of the drivers completing his turn left. (The hypothesis has to specify which one it is.) The substitute might even be more successful in specifying all situations in which the flashing treats of that state of affairs. If we discovered it, we would then know under which conditions the flashing of the headlights treats of that state of affairs.

I have chosen the expression "to treat of" in the hope that it is not very good English or at least sounds a little artificial; for I am not sure that the underlying idea of splitting up meanings of utterances into propositions and illocutionary forces is applicable to all sorts of utterances and, more important, that there is one and the same type of splitting in all cases where it is possible. Becoming upset over a bad English expression could remind one of this suspicion. I have followed the practice of splitting because I know of no better alternative for introducing propositions into the description of a language which can be checked against the language-users' speech behaviour. The remaining illocutionary forces in (13) to (17) are inviting, demanding, warning not to, asking to permit and thanking for permitting.[7]

The hypotheses (14) to (17) are to be tested, in their turn, in the way illustrated for (13). The first step is to specify the open lists of behavioural regularities characteristically exhibited by a person understanding the flashing in the situations in question in the ways indicated; the second step is to formulate the corresponding hypotheses stating in the explicit form that these behavioural regularities are rule-guided behaviour among Western German drivers; the third step is to look whether that is true.

Consider next the following hypotheses which I am again fairly sure are to be true among Western German drivers :

(14) (as above).

(19) The flashing of a first driver at a second driver, if the second is stopped before a traffic light that has already changed to green and the first approaches him from behind, means that the first demands of the second that he accelerate.

(20) The flashing of a first driver at a second driver, if both are driving on the overtaking lane of the motorway and the first is behind the second, means that the first demands of the second that he pull over into the other lane.

(21) The flashing of a first driver at a second driver approaching in the opposite direction in the dark with his bright lights on means that the first demands of the second that he dip them.

(22) The flashing of a first driver at a second driver driving at a speed considerably below the limit, the first driver following him closely with no possibility of overtaking him, means that the first driver demands of the second that he increase his speed.

If hypotheses (14) and (19) to (22) are well confirmed, they in turn constitute positive evidence for the more general hypothesis (23) :

(23) The flashing of a first driver at a second driver, when the second is impeding the first, has the illocutionary force of the first demanding that the second do something.

Though I am a little more confident about the truth of (23) than about that of (18), what counts is only that there are true hypotheses stating in an economical way situations in which flashing has the force of a demand. As with (18), it may be possible to find a complete but economical specification of all situations in which flashing has this force; we would then know under which conditions it has it.

Note that, if "treats of" in (18) is understood in the way indicated above and if "illocutionary force" in (23) is understood in the usual way, then (18) and (23) together entail (14). In general, if there is a hypothesis of the form

> Whenever the situation s has the characteristic C_1, then in s the sign x treats of the state of affairs p_1

and a second hypothesis of the form

> Whenever s has C_2, then in s x has the force f_2,

then together they yield the hypothesis

> Whenever s has C_1 and C_2, then in s x has the meaning f_2-p_1.

The hyphen marks the inverse operation of splitting up the specifications of an utterance's meaning as given in (13) to (17) and (19) to (22) into specifications of force and proposition, and the derivation of (14) from (18) and (23) is nearly as fuzzy as this operation of splitting. But inasmuch as it is unambiguous, the technique provides an economic way of writing down the content of lists of sentences like (13) to (17) and (19) to (22) as soon as there are two or more hypotheses, each linking a certain sign's different propositions to different situations of utterance, and two or more hypotheses, each linking a sign's different forces to different situations. (m hypotheses on propositions and n hypotheses on forces will yield m.n hypotheses on completely specified meanings, m.n being greater than m+n when both m and n are not less than 2 and at least one is greater than 2.)

4. Introducing Propositions and Forces Generally

Let us return to our proposition of a certain driver turning left. Further signs which in some situations treat of this state of affairs are, for instance : waving one's hand in a particular manner, as when you invite somebody to turn left or warn him not to turn left; blowing one's horn, a sign to which much of what has been said about flashing applies; choosing one's lane, as when you announce your intention to turn left by choosing a lane reserved for left-turners; and, of course, blinking to turn left.

Let us assume that for each sign that in any situation treats of a definite driver's turning left we have found a true hypothesis corresponding to a complete version of (18), i.e. an economical and complete specification of all the situations in which the sign treats of a driver's turning left (where the driver must be determined for

98

each situation in the way he is in (18)). Then the task remains of finding an economical way of writing down the content of all of these hypotheses. It will probably be possible to simplify with regard to the situations, since the meaning of drivers' non-verbal utterances heavily depends on the conditions under which the sign is uttered. No substantial simplification will be possible with respect to the signs, since drivers' non-verbal utterances do not exhibit much morphology and syntax. There is some morphology, of course; to express thanks by blowing your horn you have to blow it very short, while to warn somebody you should blow your horn not too short and perhaps with a bit more force. And there are rudiments of syntax; if you want to stop somebody from behind, you have to flash the bright lights several times, with little pauses in between, while following him over a certain distance. This will not yield very much, however, so that economical characterizations of signs will not be possible. Since drivers' non-verbal signs are few, this might not prove damaging.

So let us assume that we have a manageable general hypothesis stating for every sign and every situation that may be relevant to an utterance's treating of that state of affairs under which conditions this state of affairs is treated of. For different propositions, the corresponding hypotheses will be different, while for one and the same proposition all true hypotheses stating for every sign when it is treated of have the same content (relative to the language in which they are formulated, of course). So it is only at this theoretical level of the description of drivers' non-verbal language that an identity criterion for propositions in that language is available.

Illocutionary forces could be introduced in a like way. The illocutionary force of demanding, for instance, ought to be capable of specification by a set of hypotheses like (23).

5. Concluding Remarks

In arriving at identity criteria for propositions, I hope to have shown that there might be a possibility of connecting meanings with speech behaviour in a way that first shows how meaning is tied up with rule-guided behaviour and second how hypotheses about meanings of single utterances or systems of hypotheses describing much more of a language can be tested empirically. Much of current general semantics tells us which form the description of a language should have; but in general, the question of how to decide whether a suggested description of a given language (which is in this form) is correct has remained remarkably untouched.

Propositions and forces are constructed relative to the way of splitting up the lowest-level meaning hypotheses. I do not think that this way can be specified by a relatively precise recipe; inter-subjective agreement about how to split seems to depend heavily on being used to the same or at least to a similar language. If this is true, then the question of which is the proposition an utterance is treating of makes sense only from the point of view of the user of the language used for the investigated language's description. Other observers used to different languages might construct different propositions without there being a sensible question as to what the "real" proposition is.

I have not discussed reference and sense (or predication). This is not meant as a suggestion that a driver cannot refer to another one by using his headlights. If he flashes in the direction of a whole queue of drivers waiting to turn left, he has invited the first one to do so, and nobody else (though the first one in the queue is further off the direction of the flashing than any other driver behind him). In as much as it makes sense to refer to the utterance "The first one may turn left" as a case of reference to the first one, it makes sense to refer to the flashing under the same description. But I am quite sure that if an analysis like the present one is feasible in one form or other, then the construction of something a proposition is about and of something it says about this will be used as an economical way of systematizing the large class of hypotheses stating identity criteria for propositions. Hypotheses stating what is referred to by which sign under which conditions coupled with other hypotheses stating what is predicated by which sign under which conditions should yield hypotheses stating which states of affairs signs treat of under which circumstances. So the reference of an utterance of an investigated language will be relative to the language used for the description; and this relativity is doubled because the way of splitting up the expression of a proposition in the investigator's language into referring and predicating parts is no more determined than the way of splitting up complete specifications of speech acts into forces and propositions. Thus the reference of a concrete utterance might come out differently in two different descriptions of the language that both might be true. That reference is not uniquely determinable does not mean that it is too well hidden, but that it makes no sense to speak of the reference of an utterance without presupposing a certain description of the language the utterance belongs to. Much of the view that, after all, people speak about some definite thing and that it should be possible to find out what this thing is seems to stem from the idea that referring is something people do, something very basic to speaking that ultimately provides the connection between language and the world. But speaking a language isn't like that; it is rule-guided behaviour in connection with easily producible and easily perceptible events of certain kinds. To say that a person refers to something and says something about it is not to give an uncommitted description; it is a way of speaking we can adopt only after deciding on a certain form of describing the speech behaviour of the group he belongs to. It is a way of speaking at a level so far away from speaking about what people actually do that to call such a thing a speech act is far from helpful.[8]

Eike v. Savigny
Universität München
Germany

NOTES

[1] In the *Philosophical Investigations*, understanding in one way or another is well distinguished from understanding in the correct way. (See esp. §§ 151 for the former, 143–145 for the latter.) Since Wittgenstein's analysis of understanding correctly is not very explicit on the point of standards of correctness and of being subject to sanctions for deviations, which is vital to the present analysis, I shall make use only of his dispositional analysis of understanding in one way or another which is part of understanding in the correct way (see esp. §§ 146, 149). The "third party" idea of the present analysis is clearly Wittgenstein's, as I have tried to show in my *Die Philosophie der normalen Sprache*. Frankfurt a. M. (Suhrkamp). rev. ed. 1974, pp. 56–72.

As for Ryle, it is not his concept of understanding actions or motives (*The Concept of Mind*, ch. II(9)) which is relevant here, but his dispositional analysis of knowing how. Knowing how is very close to understanding in the correct way; however, since Ryle's analysis draws heavily on examples where knowing how is to be explained by referring to successful behaviour instead of behaviour conventionally approved of, we shall rely on his analysis only in so far as standards of correctness do not yet come into play.

[2] This explanation covers the cases where the rule demands something. In the cases where it permits something there is a second rule that no one doing the thing permitted be reproached. Our regularities (3), (6), and (8) provide examples.

[3] See *The Concept of Law*, Oxford 1961, pp. 54–56; on the internal aspect, see further pp. 87f, 96, 99–101.

[4] John Searle's example (in discussion).

[5] See *Speech Acts*, 2.5.

[6] Our example is a little tricky because the sentences expressing the three regulative rules still contain the expression "out of play". "The ball is out of play" expresses a statement of institutional fact in Searle's sense; there are constitutive rules that determine under what conditions the ball counts as being out of play;

101

it is or counts as being out of play, for instance, after a foul, or after the ball's leaving the field. To carry our analysis further we should have to show that counting as being out of play is a state of affairs characterised by compliance with regulative rules like "Don't go on playing" or "Do what has to be done according to the rule which in this situation makes the ball out of play" (e.g. corner, kick from the goal-line, throw-in and so on). I do not think that such an analysis would present any grave difficulties.

[7] As we may note incidentally, there are constatives too. If on leaving a tunnel you are flashed at by a driver, he is reminding you of the fact that your lights are still on. (He would not normally be understood as demanding you to switch them off.) If you are flashed at when driving on a main road and there being nothing special about your own car, the flashing driver informs you that there is a radar control not far ahead. (This piece of philosophy might perhaps prove useful for some readers in the future.)

[8] I thank Mr John Guess, M.A., for correcting the English text.

VII

A TERMINOLOGICAL NOTE ABOUT REFERENCE[1]

F. Jacques

TANGENTIAL to mathematical logic, subsists a philosophical logic dealing with fundamental problems such as the relationship between logic and ontology, or logic and epistemology. The most important works from Frege to Quine and other recent contemporaries bear witness to this continuous (up to now at least) association.

In so far as terminology is concerned there is a certain pluralism from one author to another. It is even the case that within individual works a new use is given to traditional notions, perplexing for both historian of logic and philosopher. Within the object language the methods are obvious; in the metalanguage, occasionally used by the philosopher (ordinary language, completed by adequate technical vocabulary) we hesitate on such words as "term", "extension", "denotation", to cite only those most charged with disparate connotations.

Although science of logic is built up above and beyond the work of any particular writer, the semantical strata remain distinct and perceptible. First of all, the traditional vocabulary survives : the couple subject/predicate (P. T. Geach 1962), the opposition between singular and general terms (W. V. O. Quine, 1950). And this even in authors admitting the Fregean heritage, though long after Frege himself has given preference over the first pair to the distinction between function and argument[2] and has shied away from the very notion of term[3].

What is more, most writers seem to be prey to some equivocation. Frege for instance, forcing himself to break with the traditional logic of terms,[4] takes over from Leibniz the word "extension" only to give it the new sense of "range of values". The vocabulary of Boole and Aristotle is used by Frege to introduce a perfectly extensional notion such as the set of truth-cases of a function. "Extension"

103

should no longer be taken as a material collection but in the modern meaning of the domain of definition where the concept takes its arguments. We know that this particular transfer of sense is important, since we are called upon not to mistake the classical relation of the concept to the objects subsumed (that of a common noun to the objects named) for the functional relation which applies the set of individuals distinguished by a conceptual feature to a truth value.[5] Frege decries the false notion of common noun. According to him, any true noun is a proper name, which actually designates an object. A conceptual word which designates no object may not be a name at all. In traditional logic to go back from a concept to its extension amounts to reversing the process of abstracting from the objects of our senses. In so far as Frege relinquishes the epistemological support of abstraction, the fifth law of the *Grundgesetze* remains the only means to determine an extension of concept, by reckoning under which conditions two extensions are identical. The extension of a concept being assimilated by Frege to the range of values of the corresponding function, the range of values of a function is a second-level function such that the value-range $aF(a)$ is identical with the value-range $aG(a)$ if and only if the functions $F(\xi)$ and $G(\xi)$ always have the same value for the same arguments.[6]

Again, notice that Quine deliberately borrows from an apparently scholastic terminology (singular term/general term), from another terminology apparently Fregean (sense/reference) and at the same time from a third terminology properly his own (is true of, open-sentence, and so on).

The difficulty for the historian of logic lies in the fact that this terminology continues to convey peculiar shades of meaning appearing in filigree. The writer may be more or less conscious of this. Such borrowings go from a simple case of *stipulation* (why should the same word "extension" cover both the Aristotelian notion of a collection of material objects falling under a given concept and the Fregean notion of the set of cases in which a function is mapped into a truth-value?) to a case of *overdetermination,* or as far as *utter confusion*. Let us just look at the last two cases.

1°—Quine warns us not to take the word "term" in its medieval sense which he later accounts for.[7] The overdetermination here results from the wish to preserve the continuity of a philosophical heritage. He insists that the distinction between general and singular abstract terms, coming down from medieval logic should be maintained. This is especially true, he thinks, in so far as the distinction can be recovered and reevaluated with respect to quantification theory. Singular terms correspond to the possibility of nominalizing abstracts, which becomes legitimate as soon as abstracts are accessible to positions reserved for quantified variables, in 2nd order quantification theory. On the other hand, part of their rôle is precisely to enable us to postpone recognition of abstract entities as values of our variables. The very move of some logicians (Carnap for instance) who attach so little importance to this transplantation of terminology, has eventually a philosophical motivation.[8]

2°—Now, when Russell uses "denotation" for an equivalent to Frege's *Bedeutung*, his use is somewhat muddled and confusing. His taking a term from Mill's vocabulary to render Frege's original notion is a travesty of the truth. For clearly, whereas for Mill a general term like "white" denotes all white things, for Frege a predicate like ". . . is white" *bedeutet* not white things but the function "x is white". Then, in the Russellian theory of 1903 the phrases "any man" and "some man" which are given as typically denoting phrases[9] are those about which Frege had said it was absurd to wonder what they referred to (*bedeuten*). That is enough to puzzle translators who are bound to make a choice. No wonder they vary in their options. P. Geach and M. Black translate *"Bedeutung"* by the English word "reference", while A. Church prefers the English "denotation", preserved as *"dénotation"*, in the French translation by C. Imbert.[10] The situation becomes even more intricate when Quine takes up again the word to designate the relation of predicates to the objects they are "true of".[11]

The difficulty however should not be exaggerated. The historian may adopt two tactics at once. First, working his way back from the notion to its operative use within one writer's work. Secondly retracing its usage in its stratified historical perspective. No doubt the notions of "term", "extension", "concept", "denotation" are confusing and likely to fade into one another, but equivocation disappears as soon as one takes into account the precise operations, covered and authorized by these notions, the operational methods associated with them. It is then that the elements which had been confused are diffracted and the actual meaning of the term emerges. In this way, Frege and Russell both confuse what is symbolized by a "predicate" with a "conceptual feature" (*Merkmal*), while Quine associates precise operations of substitution with these : one a predic-

105

ate is defined as that which permits certain substitutions, in a formula recognized as valid.[12] Another example : For Quine, the very notion of "extension" corresponds to an interpretation associated with a predicate letter "F". General terms have classes as their so called extensions, and classes recommend themselves as objects for the newly quantified variable "F" to range over. It is the use of "F" in quantified position that changes the status of "F" from schematic letter to variable. This is a long way from Port-Royal indeed, where extension is connected by an absolute link to a corresponding term. Moreover for Quine, a given predicate sends us back to different domains of interpretation or to different sections within one and the same domain. Any ontological link is broken between the term and its extension. I may consider *ad libitum* an interpretation I in a domain D.[13]

The second of the two tactics comes into play with the work of terminological distinction by the historian of logic. By way of illustration, I should like to go back to the origin and clarify the respective implications of three well known dichotomies :

—denotation/connotation, here noted (a)
—extension/comprehension, noted (b)
—sense/reference, noted (c).

The pair (a) is associated with a material sign for the concept, while the pair (b) is associated with the concept itself. The first appears in the *Grammaire générale et raisonnée* of Port-Royal. Here are the texts which are well known to French philosophers at least.[14] Roughly translated it would go like this :

"Adjectives, we read in chapter two, signify things or substances; they have, in addition to that distinct signification, another one, somewhat confused, i.e. the *connotation* of a thing to which the distinct signification is applied. Thus the word "red" has the red as distinct signification (. . .) only in so far as it indicates confusedly the subject of this manner of being, in other words those things susceptible of being red".

106

The pair (b) is introduced by definition in the *Logique* of Port-Royal,[15] which had several reeditions and was to be found in all the English and of course the German libraries as well, from Wolff to Kant to Euler. Here is the text. My translation :

"I call *comprehension* of the idea the attributes it contains in itself and which cannot be taken away without destroying it (...). I call *extension* of the idea the subjects to which that idea applies, also called the *inferiora* of the general term which, with respect to them, is called *superius*".

It is not at all clear whether *inferiora* (the word is used metaphorically) are species or individuals. In their example the writers say "as the general idea of triangle extends to all the various species of triangles." But in the next paragraph, the comment shows that the extension of an idea can be cut down without the idea being destroyed. Which is not true, we all agree, of those species that fall under a *genus*. Anyway they will consider singular propositions as universal propositions, because they alleged that in a singular proposition the idea is taken in all its extension.

On the other hand, with J. S. Mill, it is in his *System of Logic* that we find introduced the pair denotation/connotation. It is no accident since his logic begins with an analysis of *language*. Abstracts such as "white" descriptively designate different things as "being white". It is the "connotative terms" which denote a subject while implying an attribute. In this way "white" is connotative in so far as it denotes the things we call white, while conveying the attribute "whiteness" which these things have in common.[16]

What complicates the problem even more is that a classical use of the pair (a) results from a kind of amalgamation of the Port-Royal doctrine and the interpretation of J. S. Mill. It is commonly said that a *concept* connotes certain features or characteristics and denotes the objects subsumed by the concept. If, however, we pay attention to their historical origin, we are bound to distinguish between the denotation/connotation pair which has to do with the *linguistic* expression of a concept and the extension/comprehension pair which, being a property of it, has to do with the concept itself.

But, put in a Fregean perspective, the pair (b) is inapt for the construction of a truly logical language : bound as it is to a logic of terms, it does not afford us the distinction between concept and object (or between predicative and referential rôles); what is more, it does not allow us to take existence into account. Thus it turns out to be impossible, on these grounds, to form a proposition. It seems we might fare better with the pair (a) dealing with segments of language and no longer with psychological entities such as "idea" (as in *Port-Royal*). Yet in fact it does leave two groups of notions confused, which Frege explicitly tries to distinguish in his ideography.[17] The first group, suggested by "connotation", expresses the depictive power of the concept, contrasting the essential characteristics of the concept to the properties of the objects subsumed. This connexion between properties and characteristics sheds new light on the connexion of comprehension and extension as described by Arnauld and Nicole.

The second group of notions suggested by "denotation" does not belong properly speaking to logic and epistemology but rather to the analysis of language. It scrutinizes the relation between a sign or a group of signs, their sense and finally their reference. The sense is that in virtue of which a sign joins with other signs in forming a higher order semantical unit. Frege, in his account of the composition of senses, has recourse to metaphorical expressions such as "incompleteness", "unsaturation". As for the reference of a sign, it is constituted solely by the object to which it might be coordinated.

For the reader of Frege, the pair (a) is chimerical. The *connotation* of linguistic expression presupposes the *comprehension* of the corresponding concept; it implies that the denoted objects have certain attributes. In virtue of this, it is opposed to *"extension"*. As for the denotation, an indulgent interpretation would have it assimilated to what we call reference, but this would be supposing that a conceptual expression designates or "names" the things falling under it. This, as we saw before, is in contradiction to Frege's interpretation of the *Begriffwort*. The word "denotation" leads us now to a linguistic system and no longer to a psychological one; but then the correlate of "denotation" is no longer "denotation" but sense. If Mill wants to deal with language, without recourse to the psychological notion of idea, his "denotation" must be opposed to "sense".

Actually the author of *The System of Logic* remains a prisoner of a system where it is appropriate to go from the representation to the objects. The pair (c) which aims at analysing the linguistic relationship between signs, their integrating unity in a well-formed expression—and the designated objects—treats of yet another problem. It is no longer a question of going from representation to object but of harmonizing a system of signs independent of any human mind with a system of objects equally independent of any human mind. Signs are to be defined differentially while objects constitute a

108

model. We see here that sense should not be understood as an element of our representation (*Vorstellung*); otherwise we fall back into the very difficulty of representationalism. It must be admitted that sense is the result of the differentiation, within a language, of the signifying material. Accordingly the relevant opposition is with *reference*. That is why the dichotomy (c) is a logico-linguistic one and its analysis must take into account the material of a given language (ordinary language or formula language).

Moreover the main purpose for Frege's making decision (c) is the negative one of setting the notion of sense aside so that the intensional aspects may be kept from obtruding. Thus his whole theory in the *Grundgesetze* might develop at the level of reference and the interpretation of the system might remain wholly extensional.

We can now understand why the translation of "Bedeutung" by "denotation" is confusing. A significant confusion indeed since it conjures away some philosophical distinctions important for both the historian of logic and the philosopher. In the face of this there are two tactics we might consciously adopt. One would be to deliberately take advantage of the amalgamation. This would be to take shelter under two umbrellas. The stakes are high : to restore at whatever price a certain philosophical continuity from Aristotle to Frege and the moderns. This is a loaded option implying a particular way of writing the history of logic.

But one could also take a more drastic stance. We may consider that Russell's usage in 1903 of the word "denote" introduces a deceptive confusion, and that Quine's usage in 1952 of the word "term" introduces a collusion between logical notions belonging to different traditions. A collusion to which we may not want to be a party. It is this last alternative we wish to side with, following on this point Peter Geach, who most aptly said *à propos* of the word "denotation" :

> "High time that so battered and defaced a coin were withdrawn from philosophical currency. I shall avoid it as much as possible."

Francis Jacques
Université de Rennes
France

REFERENCE

NOTES

[1] This text first presented at the Symposium, has been somewhat modified here to include the suggestions made by G. E. M. Anscombe, D. Davidson, H. S. Harris, J. Hintikka, K. Lehrer, A. Kenny and Z. Vendler.

[2] In *Der Gedanke* (1918–1919), Frege withdraws more and more from natural language. He even questions articulating into propositions (cf. *Nachgelassene Schriften*, Hamburg 1969, p. 154) whereas in *Begriff and Objekt* he still takes his "subject" and "predicate" in their linguistic meaning. In his last work, he states that logical books are always cumbered with such considerations as subject and predicate that do not belong properly to logic. Most patently P. Geach himself explains in *Three Philosophers* (G. E. M. Anscombe and P. Geach, Oxford, Blackwell, 1961), how the theory of functions and arguments was first used by Frege to replace the rejected doctrine of subject and predicate. In Frege's system the triad "argument/function/value" is mirrored at levels both of symbol and of what is symbolized. Hence a proposition which contains a name may be regarded as the value of a certain linguistic function for that name as argument. The point is set off with the emphasis it deserved by A. Kenny in his review (cf. *Mind*, vol. LXXIV, no 293, Jan. 1965).

[3] To the point of regretting the wording *"Begriffsschrift"* in an unpublished fragment of July 26, 1919—quoted by van Heijenoort, *From Frege to Gödel*, Harvard 1967, p. 1: "I do not start from concepts in order to build up thoughts or propositions out of them; rather I obtain the components of a thought by decomposition of the thought. In this respect, my *Begriffsschrift* differs from the similar relations of Leibniz and his successors—in spite of its name, which, perhaps, I did not choose very aptly". Recently, P. Geach takes up the same rejection in *Reference and Generality* (Cornell University Press, 1962): "A term as conceived in Aristotelian logic, is supposed capable of being a subject in one proposition and a predicate in another; since only names, not predicables, can be logical subjects, this notion of terms has no application whatsoever".

[4] Cf. his Reply to Schröder, his Introduction to *Grundgesetze*.

[5] The clearest exposition showing that Frege's logic is reorganized on extensional principles are *Grundlagen* § 17, §§ 68–69, *Grundgesetze* I, 3.

[6] *Translations from the Philosophical Writings of Gottlob Frege*, ed. P. Geach and M. Black, Oxford, 1952.

[7] W. V. O. Quine, *Methods of Logic*, chap. XIV, note 1; chap. XVI.

[8] Ibid. chap. XXXIX *in fine*.

[9] Compare B. Russell, *Principles*, § 56, with Frege, *Translations*, pp. 14, 48.

[10] Cf. A. Church, *Introduction to Mathematical Logic*, p. 4; *Ecrits logiques et philosophiques de G. Frege*, trad. fr. par C. Imbert, Paris Seuil 1971.

[11] W. V. O. Quine, *From a Logical Point of View*, Harvard 1953, p. 130.

[12] *Methods of Logic*, § 26.

[13] Ibid., pp. 192, 225.

[14] Arnauld et Lancelot, *Grammaire générale et raisonnée*, Paulet 1969, pp. 25–26, publiée en 1660. English philosophers tend to find their references rather in Mill's *System of Logic*.

[15] Arnauld et Nicole, *La logique ou l'art de penser*, Our quotation is from the critical edition of P. Clair et F. Girbal, P.U.F., 1965, p. 59.

[16] J. S. Mill, *System of Logic*, I, 2, 5.

[17] C. Imbert, op. cit., p. 15.

VIII

A NOTE TO THE PARALOGISMS

Z. Vendler

1. "I COULD have been born in the Middle Ages". Indeed, why not? If I am sufficiently familiar with the period, I can imagine what it would be like to grow up and live in that age. Sigrid Undset and Zoé Oldenbourg must have imagined similar things, otherwise they could not have written their historical novels, whether the story is told in the first person or the third. Not even real historical figures are immune to such intrusions of an alien fancy : think of Robert Graves writing as "I, Claudius".

For that matter, I could have been born in China in this century, too. And I do not mean it in the easy way, to wit, that my parents could have migrated there shortly before my birth. No, I might have had Chinese parents; after all, one in every four persons does. This too is easy to imagine, at least for those who have read Pearl Buck and Lin Yutang. But one does not have to stretch one's imagination as far back as Claudius or as far away as China to appreciate the point : the creation and the understanding of any novel, tale or other fiction, no less than the understanding of a good deal of real history, requires the ability to transcend the limitations of one's actual existence and imagine seeing the world through other eyes. To understand Proust, it is not enough to see him do what he did, with the mind's eye, as it were; one also has to try to see things as he saw them, to feel what he felt, and so on—and one might succeed to some extent. I regard "the transference of this consciousness of mine to other things (die Übertragung dieses meines Bewusstseins auf andere Dinge)" (Kant, *Critique of Pure Reason*, A347) as the manifestation of an absolutely basic, and specifically human ability.

"There but for the grace of God go I" we often say, and we do not merely mean that similar misfortunes could have befallen us in our real lives. Nay, we mean that we could be in those very same

111

dire circumstances ourselves. I was not born blind, retarded or a cripple, yet I might have been; I can imagine what it would be like, and feel sympathy.

J. S. Mill claims that "it is better to be a human being dissatisfied than a pig satisfied; better to be Socrates dissatisfied than a fool satisfied" (*Utilitarianism*, p. 14). And John Rawls asks us to contemplate the kind of society in which we would prefer to live if our individual circumstances were hidden to us by the "veil of ignorance" (Rawls 1971, pp. 136 ff). But if it were inherently impossible for me to be Socrates or a pig, since I am neither, or to be born in a society in which I was not, then I could not prefer one of these things to the other : the impossible cannot be preferred or scorned. As a matter of fact we can make a choice, for we know, in Mill's words, "both sides of the question" (*loc.cit*); we can imagine, to some extent at least, what it would be like to live in a feudal or slaveholding society; what it would be like to be Socrates, a pig, or, with a great deal of effort, perhaps even a bat (see Nagel 1974).

Notice, moreover, that it would not do, in this context, to imagine what it would be like not for me, but for someone in general to be Socrates, a slave or a pig. The question is what I, not some abstraction, would prefer. Thus it is I whom I have to fancy being these things, to be able to respond to Mill's and Rawls's challenge. Later on we will realize, however, that the distinction between imagining myself to be a such and such, and imagining someone in general to be a such and such is an illusive one.

2. My arguments thus far are based on the simple assumption that the impossible cannot be imagined. No one can imagine a square circle, a whole smaller than some of its real parts, the undoing of what has been done, and so forth. Turning to matters of identity, I would not know what to make of a request to imagine the Mississipi to be the Danube, the moon to be the sun, and the like. For the same reason one cannot imagine Robert Graves born as Claudius, or Sigrid Undset living in the Fourteenth Century. Somebody like her (in appearance, talent or character) might indeed have lived in that age, but not Sigrid herself. The Claudius case is even worse. The historical Claudius was not at all like the historical Robert, and even if the mightiest tools of training, scenario and cosmetic surgery had been employed on either end of the relation, the best possible result would be a Claudius similar to Robert, or a Robert very much like Claudius.

Statements of identity, if true, are necessarily true, says Saul

Kripke, and I agree with him (Kripke 1972). And, of course, so are statements of non-identity. Claudius cannot be anybody but Claudius, so he cannot possibly be Robert Graves, nor Robert Graves Claudius.

One has to watch out here though, and not be misled by such locutions as "Claudius, the Fourth Emperor of Rome, might have never become an emperor". This is true, and it follows that Claudius is not necessarily the Fourth Emperor of Rome. In a similar way my mother might not have met my father, so it was possible for my mother not to be my mother. A somewhat extended application of Saul Kripke's notion of a "rigid designator" dissolves this paradox. The phrases "my mother" or "the Fourth Emperor of Rome" may function purely referentially, like a proper name, or may function descriptively. In the former case they denote rigidly, i.e. the reference is kept constant through all counterfactual assumptions, even if these assumptions contradict the "sense" of the phrase, as in "My mother might not have become my mother". Now a statement of identity or non-identity is necessarily true only if it connects two terms that are used as rigid designators; the statements "Cicero is Tully" and "Claudius is not Nero" are necessarily true, but the statement "Claudius is the Fourth Emperor of Rome" need not be : somebody else could have grabbed the Purple in the confusion following Caligula's murder.

Accordingly, Robert Graves could not possibly be Claudius, and indeed one cannot imagine him to be Claudius. Nor could Sigrid Undset have been born in the Middle Ages. The reason for this impossibility is that the counterfactual assumptions one can make with respect to a given individual must stop short of destroying the essence of that individual. Whereas it is possible to say that Sigrid might not have got the Nobel prize, might not have written her novels, or even that she might have died as an infant, it is not possible to assume that she, that very same woman, might have been born even fifty years before she was actually born. In imagining the various possibilities that might have affected the real Sigrid we have to keep the person constant : that infant born to those parents, the result of the fusion of those individual gametes. That origin, that particular "insertion into history" cannot be removed in the imagination without removing the person herself. Once more, then, one can imagine somebody like Sigrid to have been born in the Fourteenth Century, but not Sigrid herself.

Furthermore, since there is nothing special about Zeno Vendler in this respect, it also follows that he could not be another person, could not have been born in another age, or be the offspring of a different set of ancestors.

I have claimed, however, and I still do, that *I* can imagine having been born in another age or to other parents. I also pointed out that other people, like Sigrid Undset and Robert Graves, must have performed similar feats of transference many times in their lives and literary careers. Finally, I argued that since such a transference is imaginable, it must represent a possible state of affairs. But then, we are facing a contradiction. I could be somebody else, but Zeno Vendler could not. Yet I am Zeno Vendler. And although Robert Graves cannot be anybody but Robert Graves, he can imagine himself to be somebody else, which fact shows that it is possible for him to be somebody else, and so forth.

3. "I am Zeno Vendler". This looks like a statement of identity. If so, since it is true, it is necessarily true. In that case, however, I could not imagine myself to be somebody else. Yet I can. Then, perhaps, it is not an identity statement, at least not one of the conventional variety.

Is it, then, something like "Claudius is the Fourth Emperor of Rome"? This, as we remember, can be understood in a contingent way : Claudius might have been overlooked or even killed in the turmoil following Caligula's tragic demise. Understood in this way, the definite noun-phrase "the Fourth Emperor of Rome" is not taken to be a rigid designator, but a mere description, which happens to be true of Claudius. Names, however, are not descriptions, thus such statements as "Claudius is Claudius" or "Cicero is Tully" cannot be read in the contingent sense; they are necessarily true. Unless, of course, one interprets the predicate "is Claudius" or "is Tully" as equivalent to "is called Claudius" or "is called Tully". For in that case there is no necessity : Claudius might have been called Nero. The question then is the following : when I say "I am Zeno Vendler", do I merely tell you my name, or do I identify myself in some stronger sense?

Well, I may be just telling you my name. We meet at a party, are having a conversation, in the course of which I tell you some particulars about me, such as my profession, interests, age, and so forth, and also my name, which, for all I know, may not mean anything to you. On the other hand, I may say the same thing with the intention of telling you who I am. And this is an entirely different enterprise. For, unlike in the previous case, here I presuppose that you already know my name, that is to say, that you already know,

from other sources, who the person is who has that name, and what
I tell you is that I am that person. In this situation the name serves
to identify, to lead your thought to one definite individual with
whom you are already acquainted in one way or another; in other
words, that name *means* something to you.

Ulysses, in telling the suitors his name, did not merely inform
them of a trifling detail about himself; he told them who he was.
For his audience had heard about the wily hero; what they had
not known, and what made them fear and tremble, was that the
shabby individual facing them was that man.

Then it is obvious that in merely being told the speaker's name,
the listener learns a contingent matter : the speaker might have been
named otherwise. In being told who the speaker is, on the other
hand, he learns something which is necessarily so : that beggar facing
them is Ulysses; the two rigid arrows of reference, a name and a
description, hit the same target.

For that matter, Ulysses could have said other things about himself to the same effect; e.g., that he was the husband of Penelope,
the father of Telemachus, the lord of the manor, and so forth. These
too are contingent facts, yet the suitors in learning them would
have been led to the same recognition : that man is Ulysses, the
hero they have good reasons to fear.

Notice, incidentally, that it is not necessary that the name, or the
description, that serves to identify be a real name or a true description. Even if Ulysses and Penelope had never married but lived
in sin, his claim that he was the lady's husband would have produced
the same effect in the suitors' mind, since, being generally *reputed
to be* her husband, he was *known as* her husband.[1] The same about
names. "George Sand is Aurore Dupin" is a true statement of
identity, and as such is necessarily true, even if the lady in question
had been baptized as Yvonne Bertrand, and had taken the place of
the little Dupin girl as a result of an inadvertent switch in the
nursery.

Accordingly, for the purposes of reference and identification, it is
not the link of truth that ties the name or the description to its
designatum, but, as it has been explained in recent literature, a
historical, or circumstantial connection (Kripke 1972, Donnellan
1974). It is sufficient if the person, or thing, is known under that
name or description, or recognizable under that description. Therefore any odd fact, or reputed fact will do, provided it has the
required embedding in history, or the appropriate circumstantial
setting. Then it is not surprising that the contingency of such facts

has nothing to do with the necessity of the corresponding statement of identity : the fact that Alfred Nobel might have failed to invent dynamite does not affect the necessity of the statement that Alfred Nobel is (the same man as) the inventor of dynamite.

It is time to return to our original concern : the statement "I am Zeno Vendler". As I mentioned before, I may say this with a weaker or a stronger intention : merely to tell you my name, or, by doing so, to identify myself to you, i.e. to enable you to locate me in the field of your acquaintances. But whether I intend the first thing or the second, what I say need not be anything more than the statement of my name, thus of a contingent matter. For, obviously, other details about myself may serve the second purpose as well; e.g. "I am the professor who flunked you in Logic at Cornell". Thus there is no reason to think that the statement "I am Zeno Vendler" expresses a necessary truth.

4. At this point, I fear, I might be accused of cheating. At the beginning of this paper I claimed that I could have been born as somebody else, i.e. be somebody other than Zeno Vendler. Yet now I seem to represent my being Zeno Vendler as something equivalent to the trivial fact that I have that name. Now, surely, imagining myself to be somebody else does not merely consist in fancying having another name.

This charge is not quite justified, however. The point of the preceding discussion has been, in fact, to put all the details about me, including my name, on the same level. So in imagining myself living in the Middle Ages, or having been born as Claudius, not only the name goes, but almost everything of the circumstances of my present life. If I were Claudius, I would identify myself by that name, or by some other detail generally known, such as being the nephew of Tiberius, the husband of Messalina (phew!) and so forth. So I would be known as Claudius, as I am now known as Zeno Vendler. And this is all that is necessary to imagine being Claudius rather than some other person. For *I* would remain *I*, of course; that makes the whole exercise possible. Thus whereas the man known as Zeno Vendler cannot be imagined, and cannot be, the man known as Claudius, I, who am known as Zeno Vendler, still can imagine being, and could be, the man known as Claudius.

One might want to object to this conclusion by bringing up the matter of essences. Claudius has an essence, and so do I. He was born in the Imperial Family two thousand years ago, and I was born to my parents in this century. Indeed, even in imagining being

116

Claudius I have to pay respect to his essence. For example, I can imagine being Claudius, yet refusing to marry Messalina, declining the Purple, and so forth. What is impossible is to imagine being that man, Claudius, yet being born, say, to Hannibal. Thus in imagining being Claudius I do not have to take over his life history entire; yet I have to stick to his essence.

But, and this is the crucial question, in indulging in these wild fancies of transference, am I not bound by my own essence, by my own "insertion into history"? How can I, the offspring of my ancestors, take on another essence as it were, albeit in the imagination? How is it possible to leave my essence behind?

The answer is that the "I", the subject of such a transference has no content and no essence; it is a mere frame in which any picture fits; it is the bare form of consciousness. Therefore, although I cannot even attempt to imagine what it would be like to be a rock or a computer, I can try at least to imagine being Claudius, a stone-age man, a bat or a pig. As a matter of fact I happen to be Zeno Vendler, happen to have this essence, but I can imagine being something else, something conscious, that is; thus it is possible for *me* to be somebody or something else, i.e. to have another essence.

If I say "I could have lived another life", what I say is ambiguous. It may simply mean that my actual life might have developed otherwise : I, Zeno Vendler, could have become a watchmaker in Transylvania instead of a philosopher in America. In this case I keep my actual essence intact : that boy, born to those parents. Or it might be understood in the sense of the Kantian transference : I could have been born as Claudius, a slave, or what have you. In this case, of course, the essences too are switched, and only the "I", the "transcendental" I, remains.

5. Descartes reminds us that the statement "I exist" is necessarily true whenever I pronounce it or mentally conceive it. Yet, if my parents had not met, I would not exist; therefore "I exist" is not necessarily true. What I mean in this case is that my "empirical" self, i.e. Zeno Vendler, might not exist. The Cartesian "I", however, is a detached, transcendental "I" : the thinking, conscious thing as such, whatever its individual "mode", incarnation, or, rather "inanimation", may be. And the nonexistence of this is indeed unthinkable, since that very thought, as any thought, implies its existence. I can perfectly well think of myself, i.e. of Zeno Vendler, as not existing now : my father might have died in World War I, or I as an infant. . . . Yet, in another sense, I cannot think of myself as

not existing now, since it is I who must conceive that very thought : the frame "I think . . ." underlies all representations with transcendental necessity. In the first case I think of myself objectively, in the way other people think of me : as a thing among other things located in the texture of the world and history. Thus if history were in some ways otherwise, I, that thing, might not have come into being or might have already deceased. In the second case, however, I think of myself subjectively, as the source of all representations, including all possible alternatives in history. And in this sense my nonexistence is inconceivable. *Cogito ergo sum*; but not *Cogito ergo Vendler est.*

I weigh so many pounds, I am a professor, I live in California . . . All these things could be otherwise without affecting my identity as Zeno Vendler. Data affecting my essence could not. Thus if I had been born in the Middle Ages, or just to other parents, I would not be Zeno Vendler. Yet I can imagine such alternatives. Consequently the "I" underlying these transferences has no essence. The notion of an essence pertains to the objective order : it is the core of an individual (or of a natural kind) that cannot be pared away by the scalpel of counterfactual assumptions while retaining that individual. But, of course, the individual itself can be removed in thought; there are no necessary beings in this world. There is no way, however, of removing the transcendental self, since all possibilities, including the nonexistence of certain individuals, can only be conceived within its all-encompassing frame.

Yet it would be a mistake to conclude that somehow I am two things, a combination of an empirical substance and a transcendental self. The transcendental "I" is not a thing, it does not exist as such : existence, like possibility, is a "category" operating in the field of experience. The transcendental aspect of my being consists in nothing else but in the realization that I, as a subject of experience, am only contingently tied to the senses of this body, that is to say, that the world could be experienced through other eyes, perceived in other perspectives, in one word, it consists in my ability to perform feats of transference.

6. In thinking about other people, and animals to some extent, one can proceed in two ways, which are radically different. And yet, this difference has been largely ignored by most philosophers of the present and the past. Kant, as usual, is the exception, and Thomas Nagel among the contemporaries.

Suppose I am reading about the battle of Cannae. The description is lively, it makes me see the faltering ranks of the Roman legions beset on all sides by African foot and Numidian horse. And there is Hannibal, sitting on a horse, his one eye sweeping the battlefield, the look of triumph on his swarthy face. I can stop, as it were, and contemplate him in detail : see his clothing, weapons, follow his gestures, hear his commands and so forth. I can go even further if I wish : imagine his heart beating fast, his brain working at its peak, and so on.

But then, I can do something else too. I can imagine being Hannibal, surveying the scene with that lone eye, feeling the triumph and the pity mingle in his heart. Thus, for a moment, I am Hannibal himself in the imagination. But I am free to switch again : now I am one of the Romans, sharing his anguish and pain; then a Numidian, sensing every movement of his horse as he presses on towards the enemy. I can do all this, nay, I have to do some of these things, otherwise I would not understand what I am reading. For they are people, not robots, they are subjects too, and not merely objects, of sight and hearing, of feeling, thought, and imagination. And to appreciate this, no representation of their appearance, voice and movement will suffice. It is only through the possibility of transference that movements of bodies are perceived as action and behavior, that some contorted muscles are seen as an angry face, that cold sweat and tears betoken fear and pain. To quote Kant again, more fully this time : "I cannot have any representation whatsoever of a thinking being through any outer experience, but only through self-consciousness. Objects of this kind are, therefore, nothing more than the transference of this consciousness of mine to other things, which in this way alone can be represented as thinking beings" (*Critique of Pure Reason*, A 347).

Think of "torturing" a car and torturing a person or an animal. The first thing may be stupid, but the second is "morally" evil. Why? For the obvious reason : the car does not feel anything, but the person suffers. He, unlike the machine, is a subject of experience. In other words, it is an "I", for that is what it means to be a subject of experience. "But", you say, "it is a different 'I' from yours, so you cannot feel what he feels, can never know what goes on in his mind". You are wrong, I reply, because the "I" itself, i.e. the mere form of consciousness, is "mine" only according to the particular content it has, and since it has that content only contingently, I indeed could be that man, and thus—contrary to Austin's Final Note in "Other Minds" (Austin 1961)—could feel the very same thing he feels. True, I am not on the rack now, and he is; but I can

119

imagine what it would be like being there. My body may be different —stronger, less sensitive. But then, I can imagine being on the rack with more tender limbs. After all, even though I have no sunburn on my back now, I can still imagine what it must feel like being whipped on sunburnt skin. Thus wide range of experience, and the knowledge of physiology and psychology enables one to compensate for the difference found among us in bodily state and personal history. Once the possibility of transference is recognized, the sharing of human experience becomes a manageable task.

7. The nagging worry that still remains is the following : how do I know that there are people, and other conscious beings, in the world besides me to provide the anchors for such a transference. How do I know, in other words, that solipsism is not true?

I give an answer, of the many possible ones, and this consists in a renewed appeal to the fact that there is nothing special about me among the millions of the world's inhabitants. There are other bodies with such constitution and such behavior as to warrant transference. As I said before : I cannot imagine what it would be like to be a rock or a mushroom, but I have no fundamental difficulty in imagining being another member of the human species, and perhaps there is no unsurmountable obstacle even with respect to the higher animals at least. There are dubious cases, of course : embryos, cockroaches, and, maybe, computers of the future. The important point is not where to draw the limit, but rather what to consider in trying to draw one. What is seen is bodily structure and behavior; that is all that can be the object of experience. What is sought for is consciousness, the subject of experience. Given a thing in the field of experience, the question is this : can that thing be a subject, which means, could I imagine myself being that individual? The answer, in some cases, may be hesitant or controversial; in others, however, is as certain as anything can be. If President Ford is not conscious, who is?

"You, and no one else," nags on the devil of solipsism. To quiet him down, I once more evoke the battle of Cannae in my imagination. Since, as the devil tells me, none of the combatants are conscious, I am barred from doing transference. But, surely, I can still view the scene : all those robots fighting on the field. "No," says the demon "how could you? You are not there, for sure, and you cannot be : your very essence prevents you from moving out of your body, and out of your age. Now since you cannot possibly be there, you cannot possibly imagine seeing those things."

And the devil is right, of course : without the possibility of transference I could not imagine something which is not accessible to me in my actual existence. For in imagining, say, the battle of Cannae, I have to imagine being there, and seeing and hearing and feeling things in a body. And that body cannot be this body of mine. The "I" that views that scene cannot be Zeno Vendler, and I cannot imagine him being there. Yet we can imagine scenes of history. Thus transference is possible, thus other minds are possible, and the devil is wrong after all.

Professor Zeno Vendler
University of California, San Diego, U.S.A.

NOTE

[1] Suppose we discover that Shakespeare did not write the plays attributed to him. Then it would be false to say that for centuries he was *known to be* the author of those plays. What would remain true, however, is that for centuries he was *known as* the author of those plays.

BIBLIOGRAPHY

Austin, J. L. (1961) *Philosophical Papers*. Oxford: Clarendon.
Donnellan, K. S. (1974) "Speaking of Nothing," *The Philosophical Review*, LXXXIII, 3–31.
Kant, I. *Critique of Pure Reason*, tr. Kemp Smith N. London: Macmillan, 1953.
Kripke, S. A. (1972) "Naming and Necessity" in *Semantics of Natural Language*, pp. 253–355, eds. Davidson, D. and Harman, G. Dordrecht: Reidel.
Mill, J. S. *Utilitarianism*, ed. Piest, V. Indianapolis: Bobbs–Merrill, 1957.
Nagel, T. (1974) "What Is It Like to Be a Bat", *The Philosophical Review*, LXXXIII, 435–450.
Rawls, J. (1971) *A Theory of Justice*. Cambridge, Mass.: Harvard.

IX

INDIVIDUATION PER SE

R M. Chisholm

1. Introduction

To BE IN a position to individuate, or identify, an individual thing is to know some individuating fact about that thing, something that is true of that thing and of nothing else. We may individuate some things simply by noting certain relations they bear uniquely to still *other* individual things. But if we can individuate anything at all, then there is something that we can individuate without relating it to still other individual things. I will say that, in such a case, we can individuate the thing *per se*. In the present paper, I will consider some of the implications of the fact that we are able to individuate certain things *per se*.

One such implication, I believe, is that each of us knows his own individual essence or haecceity. But it is problematic whether anyone knows the individual essence or haecceity of any individual thing other than himself.

2. Some Definitions

In order to put these points more precisely, it is necessary to set forth certain definitions.

I will first note the sense in which a proposition or a state of affairs may be said to entail certain *properties*. For example, that proposition or state of affairs which is *some dogs being brown* may be said to entail the property of *being brown*, as well as the properties of *being canine* and of *being both canine and brown*. For the state of affairs is necessarily such that, if it obtains, then something has these properties. Let us say, then :

> D1 p entails the property of being F =Df p is necessarily such that (i) if it obtains then something has the property of

being F and (ii) whoever accepts it believes that something is F.

This definition is a schema in which the letter "F" may be replaced by any English predicate expression—e.g., "red" or "such that Socrates is mortal." Thus the proposition that some men are Greeks entails the properties of *being a man* and of *being Greek,* but the proposition that no men are Greeks does not entail either of these properties. (The definition could be taken in such a way that "relation" may replace "property". Then that state of affairs which is Phillip being father of Alexander could be said to entail the relation *being father of;* for the state of affairs is necessarily such that, if it obtains, then something bears the relation *father of* to something, and whoever accepts it believes that something is father of something.)

The point of the second clause in our definiens ("whoever accepts it believes that something is F") is to give us a strong sense of "entail". Without this clause, our definition would require us to say, of any contradictory state of affairs (for example, *there being a square circle*), that that state of affairs entails any property whatever—say, the property of being blue. For *there being a square circle* is necessarily such that either it does not obtain or whoever accepts it believes that something is blue. But given the second clause in our definiens, we avoid this consequence. *There being a square circle* is not necessarily such that whoever accepts it believes that something is blue.

I will use the expression "identifying property" to refer to a property that only one thing can have at a time.

> D2   C is an identifying property $=$Df C is a property such that (i) it is possible that something has C and (ii) it is not possible that more than one thing has C at a time.

Thus the property of being the tallest man is an identifying property; so, too, for the property of being President of the United States; and so, too, I wish to urge, for the property of being identical with me.

The concept of an identifying property should be distinguished from what I will call an "individual essence" or "haecceity". This concept may be defined as follows :

> D3   G is an *individual essence* (or *haecceity*) $=$Df G is neces-

sarily such that, for every x, x has G if and only if x is necessarily such that it has G, and it is not possible that there is a y other than x such that y has G.

Thus the individual essence or haecceity of Socrates, if there is one, has the following characteristics. It is a property which is such that, if anything has it, then that thing has it necessarily; hence Socrates had it necessarily. (But it was not necessary that Socrates have it, for it was not necessary that there be a Socrates.) The individual essence of Socrates is a property which everything other than Socrates necessarily fails to have. And if Socrates had not existed, no other thing could have had his haecceity.

All individual essences or haecceities, then, are identifying properties, but not all identifying properties are individual essences or haecceities. Being the tallest man and being the President of the United States are identifying properties, but not haecceities. I will suggest that being identical with me *is* an individual essence or haecceity. In other words, the English expression "being identical with me", when I use it, has as its intention my haecceity; when another English speaking person uses it, it has as its intention that person's haecceity. There is no contradiction or absurdity in affirming this and also affirming that "being identical with *him*" does not intend anyone's haecceity.

Given the concept of an identifying property, we can say what it is for a proposition or state of affairs to imply, with respect to some particular thing, that that thing has a certain property. This important concept may now be explicated in the following way :

> D4 p implies x to have the property of being F =Df There is a property G such that (i) G is an identifying property, (ii) p entails the conjunction of G and the property of being F, and (iii) x has G.

(The letter "F" in this definition functions as it did in D1; it is schematic and may be replaced by any predicate expression.) An alternative reading of the definiendum would be, "p implies, with respect to x, that it is F." The President of the United States being in Washington may be said to imply, with respect to Mr Ford, that he has the property of being in Washington; and my feeling depressed may be said to imply, with respect to me, that I have the property of feeling depressed.

That proposition or state of affairs which is the President of the

United States being in Washington does not logically imply that proposition or state of affairs which is Mr Ford being in Washington. But that proposition or state of affairs which is the President of the United States being in Washington does imply, with respect to Mr Ford, that *he* is in Washington. For it entails an identifying property, being President of the United States, and the state of affairs is necessarily such that, if it obtains, then whatever has that identifying property is in Washington. My feeling depressed implies the property of being identical with me; and my feeling depressed is necessarily such that, if it obtains, then whatever has that property feels depressed.

Definition D4, then, tells us the sense in which a proposition or state of affairs may be said to *pertain* to a thing. The state of affairs pertains to a thing if it implies the thing to have a certain property. Philosophers have sometimes spoken of "constituents" of propositions and states of affairs. Our definition D4 could be said to define one sense of "constituent": a constituent of a state of affairs is a thing such that the state of affairs implies it to have some property.

We may now say that one has a concept of a thing if one knows a proposition or state of affairs implying that the thing has a certain property uniquely. Thus we may now define a broad sense of the expression "to individuate":

> D5 S individuates x =Df There is a p such that (i) p is known by S and (ii) there is a property p implies x to have.

And so if we individuate a thing, we know a proposition entailing an identifying property of that thing. Our definition of individuation may be somewhat broad, but the above questions turn upon the much more narrow concept of individuation *per se*:

> D6 S individuates x *per se* =Df There is a p such that (i) p is known by S, (ii) there is a property p implies x to have, and (iii) there is no individual thing y such that y is other than x and there is a property p implies y to have.

If I individuate you *per se*, then there is some property which I know you to have uniquely—and the property is not one which consists in your being related uniquely to some other individual thing.

Can I have a concept of myself? This question is often answered in the following way: "You can have a concept of a thing only if you have a way of individuating that thing. And you can individuate a thing only if you know something that is true of that thing and of nothing else. Hence you must be able to pick out the thing from among all other things. But this means that before you can individuate yourself you must be able to locate yourself within a certain class of things; you must pick out the members of that class and be able to specify the various ways in which each of them is uniquely related to you."

But I will argue that, if we can individuate anything, if we can pick out anything, then it is *not* the case that the only way we have of individuating things is by relating them uniquely to still *other* things. And it may well be, in fact, that the only way we have, ultimately, of individuating *anything* is to relate it uniquely to *ourselves.*

3. An Aristotelian Argument

There are some things we can individuate *per se*. This may be shown by a kind of Aristotelian argument.

The first premise of the argument would state that (1) we individuate or pick out certain individual things. Possibly there are sceptics who profess to deny this assumption, but I cannot feel that their position is to be taken seriously. There are many things that I can individuate or pick out. One of them, let us suppose, is you.

One of your identifying properties may be that of being the sole person to the immediate right of Professor Smith; another may be that of being the sole person sitting to the immediate left of Professor Jones. Although each property applies uniquely to you, it does so by implying a certain relation that you bear uniquely to some *other* individual thing. Unless, then, I had an independent way of identifying the other individuals, these identifying properties would not enable me to pick *you* out. I might identify the people sitting next to you by reference to the people sitting next to *them*. And I might then try completing a circle, identifying the last-named individuals as being the sole people, twice removed, from the left and from the right of *you*. Or I could try continuing *ad indefinitum,* pointing beyond at each step to still another as yet to be identifed individual, and letting the whole previous identification process hang upon my subsequent identification of *it*.

And so the second premise of our Aristotelian argument should be this : (2) there are three possibilities with respect to individuating any given thing : (a) we individuate in a circle; (b) we individuate by having individuated an infinite number of things; or (c) we individuate some things without relating them uniquely to still other things and therefore individuate them *per se*.

The third premise is : (3) the first two possibilities considered in the second premise—individuation in a circle and individuation into infinity—are each inconsistent with our first premise, with the fact that we do individuate certain things (with the fact that I have picked you out, for example).

And the conclusion is : (4) we individuate some things without relating them uniquely to other things. There are some things that we identify *per se*.

I have no doubt whatsover about the validity of this argument. The premises are true and the conclusion follows from the premises. We *do* individuate some things without relating them uniquely to other things.

What individual things do we thus identify in this way?

One possibility is that we identify ourselves *per se*. Another is that we identify things other than ourselves *per se*.

4. Individuating Myself Per Se

If I can pick *me* out *per se*, then I do it without identifying myself as standing in some relation to still another individual thing. When I do thus pick me out *per se*, what do I identify myself as being? What is the individuating property that I can attribute to myself?

If I'm now giving a lecture, can I pick me out *per se* as the person who is giving a lecture? No, for I'm not *the* person who is giving a lecture. Or at any rate I cannot *know* that I am. It would seem quite likely that many other people are now giving lectures. Of course, I'm the only person who is giving a lecture in this room, or in this part of this room. But that property—the property of being the only person who is giving a lecture in this room—doesn't individuate me *per se*. It individuates me by reference to the room. If I pick me out that way, I pick me out by reference to the room.

What other individuating property do I know myself to have? That of being the only person having such-and-such a fingerprint pattern? Given the vastness of the physical universe, perhaps I can't be said to *know* that I'm the only one with this fingerprint pattern. At best, I know only that I'm the only inhabitant on the earth that has this pattern, but this is to relate me to the earth. And, in any case, if I identify myself by reference to my fingers, I am identifying myself by reference to individual things other than myself.

So far as I can see, it would seem that, if I identify or individuate myself *per se*, it can only be by reference to the property of *being*

127

me, the property of *being identical with myself*. This is a property that is entailed by ever so many propositions that I know to be true. And it can only be an individual essence or haecceity. It is a property that I cannot fail to have and it is "repugnant to" all other things— "repugnant" in the sense that there couldn't possibly be anything other than I that has it.

To say that I can pick me out as being I, as being the thing that is identical with me, is *not* to say, of course, that I can pick me out as having those unique properties by means of which *others* pick me out. You may pick me out by means of properties that I don't even know I have. And if, as a result of amnesia, I forget the events of my past, I may still know that *I* am now in doubt about my past.

There is a certain obviousness about this answer. If there is *something* that I individuate *per se*, then what better candidate could there be than myself?

What of the doctrine that I cannot really identify myself unless I am in a position to contrast myself with other individual things? We may accept this doctrine if we interpret it in the following way : I haven't identified myself *clearly* until I have contrasted myself with something else. But this point is quite consistent with saying that I individuate myself *per se*. although I may individuate several different things obscurely, I don't individuate any of them clearly until I have contrasted them with each other. That is to say, I may pick out this object obscurely, then pick out that object obscurely, then see that this object is other than that object, and thereby pick out both objects clearly.

5. *Individuating Things Other than Myself Per Se*

Is it possible for me to pick out some *other* individual thing *per se*?

The only other way in which I might pick out an individual thing other than myself *per se* would seem to be something like this : I perceive you and then pick you out as being *that* person. (Of course, I need not pick you out as being a *person*. If I see you approaching from the distance, like Coriscus, I can pick you out as *that thing* that is approaching.) If I try to express the way I pick you out, I will use demonstratives—just as I use the demonstrative "I" to refer to myself. I will say you are "that man" or "that person" or "that thing that is approaching".

It is very tempting to say that, in the type of situation we are considering, I use the demonstrative expression, "that person" and "that thing that is approaching" only to express a certain relation

128

that the thing in question bears uniquely to *me*. "That person", for example, would be "The person that *I* am now perceiving, or pointing at, or thinking about"; and analogously for "that thing that is approaching". The theory of the use of the first-person pronoun which fits most naturally with what has been suggested is this : each person who uses a first-person pronoun uses it in such a way that, in that use, its *Bedeutung* is himself and its *Sinn* is his individual essence. A corollary would be that each person knows directly and immediately certain propositions implying his own individual essence and that no one knows any propositions implying the individual essence of anyone other than himself.[1] But *if* we should decide that, when I individuate something as "that thing", I individuate *per se* some individual thing other than myself, then we would have to take a different view of these demonstrative expressions.

We would have to say that they resemble the word "I" in that they may be used to intend certain individual essences or haecceities. This seems to have been the view of St Thomas and Duns Scotus. According to this way of looking at the matter, if I pick you out as being *that* person or *that* thing, then I pick you out *per se*. For I pick you out as being something that has uniquely a certain property—the property of being that person or that thing. And this property, like the property of being identical with me, will be an individual essence or haecceity. In support of this latter point, one may urge : "If you *are* that thing, then you are *necessarily* that thing. After all, that thing *has* to be that thing and it couldn't be anything *other* than that thing". If we accept this view, we will say that the demonstrative expression "that thing" intends a certain nonrelative property—namely, that of *being that thing*. And this property would be an individual essence or haecceity. Then the sentence "That thing has to be that thing and couldn't be anything else" would tell us, with respect to the thing in question, that being that thing *is* its haecceity.

But "that thing" could also be taken in a relational sense—as relating the thing in question to the person who is using the expression. So interpreted, it could be replaced, as I have suggested, by some such phrase as "The thing I'm now looking at" or "The thing I'm concentrating on". And when it is taken in this way, then, of course, it doesn't intend the individual essence or haecceity of the thing referred to. (In this case, the sentence "The thing I'm now looking at has to be the thing I'm now looking at and couldn't be anything else", might be re-expressed as "There is just one x such that I am now looking at x, x is necessarily identical with x, and

for every y, if y is other than x, then y is necessarily other than x".
But the new sentence should *not* be taken to imply "The thing that
I am now looking at is necessarily such that I am now looking at
it".)

Which interpretation of "that thing" is the correct one, and how
are we to decide? The only way to decide, so far as I can see, is
first to decide whether or not to accept the thesis that I can pick
out *per se* certain entities other than myself. The thesis, then, seems
to remain problematic.

Whether or not we accept the thesis, we should remind ourselves
of one point about the primacy of the self. Usually if I identify *per se*
some individual other than myself (if indeed I ever do this), then
I am also in a position to identify that individual by reference to
some relation that it bears uniquely to me. If I can now pick you out
as being *that person*, then there is some way of perceiving which is
such that I can now pick you out as being the thing I am now
perceiving in that particular way. If I were *not* in a position to
identify you by thus relating you uniquely to me, then I wouldn't
be able to identify you *per se*. (But, one may ask, isn't it also true
that, whenever I can pick you out, *per se,* as being *that person,* then
I can pick *me* out, by reference to you, as being *the one who is
perceiving that person?* No, since for all I know there are other
people who are *also* perceiving you, in which case I cannot pick me
out as *the* person who is perceiving you.)

6. Conclusion

I would conclude, then : (i) I am able to individuate myself *per se*;
(ii) I can do this because I know that I have the property of *being
me*, a property that is my haecceity; (iii) it is problematic whether
any proposition that I can know entails the haecceity of any
individual thing other than myself; and therefore (iv) it is problematic whether there is any individual thing other than myself that
I can identify or individuate *per se*.

I do not know of any plausible alternatives to the first two of these
conclusions. If nevertheless what I have said seems unacceptable to
you, I suggest you try to formulate clearly just what the alternatives
might be.

Professor Roderick M. Chisholm
Brown University

R. M. CHISHOLM

NOTE

I have defended this view in detail in *Person and Object: A Metaphysical Study*, to be published in 1976 by George Allen and Unwin and by the Open Court Publishing Company. Professor Anscombe has recently surveyed possible theories of the use of the first-person pronoun, but she does not consider the theory formulated above. She concludes, negatively, that the first-person pronoun "is neither a name nor another kind of expression whose logical role is to make a reference, *at all*." (But I believe she would recognize the validity of the inference from "I am depressed" and "I am the so-and-so" to "The so-and-so is depressed." The conclusion, surely, does contain a referring expression. It does not seem plausible to suppose, therefore, that the thought expressed by the first premise could be put *without* the use of any referring expression.) What Professor Anscombe says positively is something like this: For every x, the sentences x uses to express x's "I-thoughts" are sentences which, when they can be verified or falsified, are verifiable or falsifiable by reference to the states and activities of x. But if y is a person other than x, then y cannot formulate any of x's "I-thoughts" by using y's own terms for x. It seems to follow, therefore, that, when I say "I am depressed," then either (a) I am not expressing a thought at all, or (b) I am expressing a thought that, strictly speaking, you cannot grasp, or (c) you can understand certain thoughts which you cannot formulate in your language. See G. E. M. Anscombe, "The First Person," in *Mind and Language: Wolfson College Lectures 1974* (Oxford: The Clarendon Press, 1975), pp. 45–65.

X

PROXIMALITY AS A MARK OF THE MENTAL

A. Hannay

1. BOTH the aim and the substance of this paper* strike a rather
reactionary note. In the first place, against the oft-repeated advice
not to look for properties unique and common to a given range of
phenomena, I am proposing, Brentano-like, a criterion of mind, a
sufficient condition of something's being mental. Secondly, my
specific proposal amounts to saying that the mental is what we are
directly conscious of, and that sounds suspiciously like part of the
widely discredited Cartesian package—the notion of mind as a
non-spatial substance transparent to its owner but totally opaque to
anyone else.

On the former point I shall only, first of all, admit that a criterion
of mind doesn't tell you what the mind concretely is, but point out,
secondly, that opinion in contemporary philosophy of mind is
divided not only on how to describe the mental, but also on
whether "mental" characterizes any basic category at all. My
criterion is an attempt to draw a distinction sharp enough to be a
statement to the effect that mind does amount to a basic category.

On the second point I must make it clear that I am assuming
certain now familiar objections to Cartesianism to be decisive. In
particular the following : (1) that Cartesianism precludes the attribution of mental characteristics to matter—in the sense that according
to this view no investigation of material events will turn up mental
properties, or the mind itself; (2) that it precludes mental states from
ever being, even in part, presentations of the material world—in
the sense that, in Ryle's graphic phrase, it interposes a "mental
screen" between the experiencing self and the, on this view, all too
truly outside world; and (3) that it forces us to say that any causal
efficacy we might want to ascribe to persons is imparted *to* and

* I am grateful to Ted Honderich for his helpful response to an earlier draft.

not *by* their physical organisms. These requirements form the core of Cartesian dualism and if that is what one means by Cartesianism, then my own proposal that what is proximal is mental is not Cartesian. In fact what I shall do here is confront my criterion with certain unequivocally anti-Cartesian theses, to see just how far one can accept it without having to return to Descartes. My ulterior aim is to suggest that proximality deserves a more central place in the scheme of things than many modern philosophers are inclined to give it.

2. But why "proximal"? What does this word mean here, and why not pick one of the regulars, like "immediate" or "private", or the newly fashionable "intentional"? Taking the latter point first, the word "proximal" commends itself because the alternatives, including the everyday "mind" itself, are heavily infected with dualist associations from which I would like for the time being to dissociate my criterion. Immediacy and privacy, for example, are often regarded as properties of things which, if they have them, cannot be described as public. I want to allow that the inference here may not be legitimate. In general "proximal" is useful to the extent that it lacks the strongly disjunctive overtones of these two other expressions. As for "intentional", the reader may note certain affinities between current philosophical use of this term and what I mean by "proximal", and in any case I think the respective notions are quite compatible. The advantage "proximal" has for my discussion is that it allows us to concentrate less on mind as thought *about* the world and more on what parts of the world are, or may appropriately be referred to as, mental. In other words the discussion has a bias towards ontology.

To explain what I mean by "proximal" let me begin in the usual way by mentioning pains. Pains, however linked their expressions may be, naturally or logically, to publicly visible and audible behaviour, are not themselves either visible or audible. Usually, however, they are located—at least we locate them—in some part of the body, as in eye-ache. Although the ache is not public, the eye is. Cartesians analyse this by saying that the ache is a state of consciousness while the eye and whatever may be the matter with it "transcend" consciousness. Husserlians prefer to think of what transcends consciousness as functions of meanings, or *noemata*, which they then focus upon exclusively, in the belief that they will find there all that is essential about mind and its relation to matter. I want to turn the conception common to both views on its head and say that aches and pains are non-transcendent physical states which we can call "mental" because they are proximal.

What goes for aches and pains goes equally, and perhaps more convincingly, for depressions and exertions (to pick two central examples). A Romantic prejudice has led us to regard depressions as spiritual states and exertions as bodily ones, but we could only have succumbed to that prejudice because we had already succumbed to another, the dualism which forces us to choose. Left to their own, pains, depressions, and exertions look much of a kind. They are proximal because they are immediate objects, and therefore not public objects, of awareness. They seem to be bodily states none the less.

It should be clear that whatever verb we use to refer to the being aware of proximal states—if we can use that expression—it cannot be a merely intentional one in Anscombe's sense (Anscombe 1968, pp. 171–172). Pains, depressions, and exertions are guaranteed references (I deny that dreamed exertions, e.g. dreamed mountaineering ones, are not exertions; from the proximal point of view and in the short term they can be as good examples of the real thing as any actual mountaineering ones). That might make it look as if I could have put my point by saying that references that are guaranteed are mental, and then gone on to call all and only that which, in a description, is guaranteed a reference "proximal content". But this would prove too restricted a criterion. If someone sees the mountain as a God, I want to say that the corresponding content is proximal precisely because the reference to a divine mountain is not only *not* guaranteed, but that if what here seems to be so were so, we would have to regard the mountain as part of that person's mind.

If it is possible to see things as they are—and surely it is—then in those cases the corresponding contents contain a non-proximal core, which amounts to denying that, e.g., mountains are constructs out of, or entities inferred from proximal data. On the other hand even where a description a perceiver might give of what he sees on the basis of his visual experience contains exclusively non-proximal material, there is I think good reason to assert that the perception has an ineradicably proximal residue. Some would argue that the residue in question is the internal property of being the perception of the person concerned. The "mine-ness" of my experiences, it is sometimes claimed, is a quality with which I am immediately acquainted. I see nothing against postulating this proximal quality if only something more can be said about it. But even if one denies its existence, a case for the inescapable proximality of all experiences can still be made out. The fact that my experiences have to be publicized if they are to be known to others, that they are located at my person but not witnessably so, implies that in a sense in which public events can be publicly "known", experiences cannot. That two people gazing at the same public event give identical descriptions of it strongly confirms that they are having identical visual experiences, but this latter state of affairs is not on a par with the public event. The event of two people having the same experience can only occur, it cannot also be seen to occur. And, unless I am mistaken, the fact that the contents of two statements individually verifiable in experience cannot form a truth-functional compound which is itself verifiable in experience, implies that the content of at least one of them is proximal. If so, we may conclude, as we would like to, that experiences are mental. I shall tentatively call them proximal events.

3. Armed with at least the rudiments of a theory of proximality, let us now confront this notion with three theses which take care of the unattractive Cartesianisms mentioned earlier.

First, then, regarding the radical elusiveness of the Cartesian mind from the point of view of the observer of material events. Here what we need is a liberalization of "mind" sufficient for it to extend to the material topics of human science. Until persuaded to the contrary, I believe we should also *exclude* its application to anything not spatially continuous with the material world. Otherwise we will be faced with an intra-mental dualism which looks every bit as unattractive as its Cartesian cousin. The question now is, under what non-Cartesian conditions can we allow what Descartes denied, namely that matter may be mental? Note that the point is not to try to do without the mind. That would be a more drastic measure to be resorted to only when conceptually more conservative ones fail.

Let us formulate a thesis which covers our requirements. For simplicity I confine it to one, central kind of mental sample, namely the unimpeded exercise of a typical human competence, e.g. taking the front-door key out of one's pocket, unlocking the door, and letting oneself in. The thesis is (1) that in such a case the mental domain, whatever its constitution, is contained within the volume occupied by the human organism during the period through which the action lasts. I appreciate that there are certain difficulties with cutting biographical continua into segments, but I assume they

135

can be safely ignored here. The problem is to specify the conditions under which what happens within the segment can be called mental. My proposal is that in this case it is because the bodily movements are under proximal control and themselves either are or can become proximal content that a certain spatio-temporally locatable biographical segment can properly be described as mental. The following comments must be considered as no more than a sketch of an argument in support of this claim.

Whatever "proximal control" may amount to, the idea of control itself in this context is not hard to pin down. It is simply the idea of doing something physically which one wants or means to do—doing it *as* one wants or means to do it. And an intuitively acceptable description of the above piece of biography can be given by saying that what happens there is that the person in question—in the appropriate sense—did or was doing those things : that is, he took out the key, unlocked the door, and let himself in. Of course, in order to know everything, or even something about every kind of thing that happens in the segment, one would need to know very much more than how to employ (in this case) English. But if all we want to do is to identify, on the one hand, the kind of happening and, on the other, the particular specimen of that kind, it will be enough to understand the behavioural descriptions and the appropriate sense of "did". The latter is not too hard to specify. For instance, it is obvious that the person in question would not be doing the things in the appropriate sense if he was not aware of doing so, or meaning to be doing so, or if at each stage of the action he was not both aware of (though not necessarily focussing his attention upon) and meaning to (though not necessarily planning how to) do what was necessary to bring about its next stage.

First, can these factors be accounted for without reference to proximality?

Here my argument takes what may seem a lamentable short-cut. I am excluding the possibility that a description of whatever proximal content there is will be a description of an act, event, or episode, or of a series of such acts, events, or episodes, which—as a dualist conception would have it—runs parallel with the observable movements and is combined with the latter to produce a kind of joint performance (cf. Ryle 1949, pp. 143 and 161). In this dualist sense the phenomenological evidence at least is that there are no joint performances. I accept the evidence here not because I believe phenomenological appearances disclose substantial truth, but rather because I know of no compelling reason to refrain from the initially plausible attribution of a genuinely basic status to some bodily actions, namely those sometimes *called* "basic", e.g. raising my eyebrows, arm, or voice, where attracting the chairman's attention by these means is not basic. That is, I see no justification for, indeed possibility of, introducing mind-body dualism into an analysis of such actions. It would be quite implausible to say, for instance, that in order to raise my eyebrows I must first *do* something mental which is then the really basic action. One doesn't "do" anything mental in order to raise one's eyebrows when one raises one's eyebrows to attract the chairman's attention. It might be argued that something undeniably mental has to come before, i.e. causally precede, the raising, namely the idea of doing that or of attracting the chairman's attention in that way, or of getting a word in edgeways by doing the second by doing the first. But then the precedence here, if it isn't "actional", doesn't seem to be causal either—at least in any Humean sense. The only alternative seems to be to accept that, except where one is simply toying with the idea, or waiting either for the chairman to wake up or one's inhibitions to vanish—in which case perhaps we should say that what we have is not a mental event preceding the bodily one but simply a bodily inaction—the occurrence of the idea already constitutes the initiation of the bodily action.

Those who accept the genuine basicness but not the proximality of bodily actions have suggested that the alleged "mental" aspect is best represented in language by adverbial forms (cf. Ryle, p. 111). This gets rid of the linguistic appearance of double reference, and with it the myth that (in Rylean terms) unwitnessable events are always attendant upon the witnessable ones. As a defender of genuine basicness I would also like to avoid the appearance of double reference. The question is then whether the action is to be construed as witnessable or as unwitnessable.

Certainly for "frame of mind" adverbs like "consciously", "attentively", "strenuously" etc. and their opposites, there are specific behavioural configurations which, when noted by those familiar with the relevant parts of the mental vocabulary, provide criteria for the proper use of these descriptive terms. Think, for example, of the witnessable changes that occur in the course of a 100-metre event at an athletics meeting, from the initial propulsive exertion to the sustained rhythmic motion of the limbs and then finally the wild flinging and flapping of arms and legs once inertia takes over from effort. But even in this example, which seems to favour a maximally

137

behavioural analysis, it would be absurd to construe the exertion, the sustaining, and the relaxing of effort as exclusively witnessable events, as if they lacked *any* proximal aspects. The exertions, as I argued earlier, are undeniably proximal, and there are other proximal events, for instance the sprinter's hearing the starter's gun and identifying the appropriate finishing line, which are essential to the behavioural sequence occurring as it does. This consideration leads me to propose that, in general, in any case of unimpeded, i.e. unobstructed and unclumsy, action the series of proximal events determines the spatio-temporal path taken by the acting physical organism. Loose stones and cramp may intervene and, *via* the proximal series, activate new sequences (e.g. getting out of the way of one's competitors, trying to avoid being hurt in falling). But once a sequence has been activated and the action proceeds unimpeded, the current proximal series controls (in some sense) the current mental domain. Which is not, however, to say that the limits of that domain are the effects of proximal causes. That would be to assume once again that the bodily exercise of human competence involves two causally distinct levels or stages.

But then the alternative to a behavioural account of an exercise that is genuinely basic in this sense will be one which identifies the exercise as a whole with the controlling proximal series. With a qualification to be added shortly, this seems to me substantially correct. Of course, in allowing that the action as a whole is proximal, we would not mean to imply absurdly that it lacks a public aspect. We would simply be denying that the public aspect is related causally to the proximal series, denying in fact that they form two distinguishable terms. One could perhaps talk of mind-limb identity. Be that as it may, the proximal series is in no way related to the bodily exercise as, in Descartes's nautical simile, the pilot is related to the movements of the ship in his charge. Mind and body are, as Descartes himself recognized—though he could not have approved of the metaphor—much more hand in glove than that.

But then what *about* gloves? If the spatio-temporal path described by our acting human organism is mental, should the mental area not also include those man-made outer layers which perform such minimal extensions of its bodily movements? And not just clothes. What about the key in the door, the door itself, and so on? There is, I think, a good case to be made for describing these things as "mental" in some derivative sense, in so far as it is their function to be various kinds of adjunct to unimpeded human performance. But it is a more basic sense of the word that is employed in our Thesis 1.

138

A sense which excludes all extra-epidermal hard- and soft-ware, as well as some corporeal items such as hard skin, finger nails, paralysed limbs, and hair, but nevertheless includes some elements not listable among the proximal contents of the current proximal series. These elements are the innumerable motor and other skills exercised in at least all overt and perhaps also in some covert human performances. They are not part of the series simply because their activation and exercise are automatic. But they are under the dispositional control of the proximal series, and hence within its range. And necessarily so. For when something goes wrong, e.g. the key won't turn in the lock, it is only if the unanticipated pressure on the hand—a pressure which halts this particular sub-routine and brings it within proximal range—becomes the occasion for a new exercise under proximal control, that the action as a whole (opening the door, or letting oneself in) can continue. Of course the key, too, comes to the door-opener's attention, but it remains outside proximal range. It is the pressure on the hand, not on the key, that is mental. As far as bodily movements are concerned, the mental extends only to the area occupied by neurally alive human organs and limbs. My point then is to suggest that one way of upholding our first anti-Cartesian thesis that mind can be an attribute of matter is to admit as mental any matter which can reasonably be claimed to be, or to be dispositionally capable of being, proximal content. Under certain very usual conditions bodily movements seem to me to satisfy that condition.

4. An evaluation of our second thesis leads us to conclude that much else satisfies our condition. As before, we oppose our unwanted Cartesianism by stating its contradictory : in this case the realist thesis (2) that the contents of visual reports include true descriptions of the physical world, a point we have already touched on in connection with mountains. But why so tentative? Why not say "comprise" instead of just "include"? Well, there lies the rub. Not all visual reports, even when they accurately describe the visual scene as it appears to the subject, are veridical, as the examples of optical illusion and mental imagery testify. Perhaps we shall have to grant then, that the mental screen cannot be withdrawn completely. Maybe that wouldn't matter. Maybe realism will be satisfied just as long as we can pull the screen aside at least enough to let some visual reports be true descriptions of common objects of perception.

Few philosophers have in fact been content to accept only partial

139

removal of the mental screen. Either because they believe that even screen-vestiges require mental location, and once the special mental space is conceded that itself seems screen enough to put realism in doubt. Or, more penetratingly, because they take this whole way of talking to reflect a fundamental error in traditional thinking about mind, namely the unwarranted transference to the mental of a way of talking acquired from our acquaintance with public things and events—e.g. talk of seeing mental images, having thoughts, exercising will, and so on. Screen-removers of this latter kind may have one of two quite different positive proposals in mind. One is that it should be granted (as I believe, does Wittgenstein [1967]) that the mind may be *sui generis*, and hence always radically misdescribed by physical analogies. The other is that the conception of mind as an irreducibly special set of operations, material or immaterial, is in any case wrong, a view elaborately argued by Dennett (1969).

I shall consider this latter position only, since it presents the most radical alternative to the view I am sketching, denying as it does the existence of the traditionally assumed references of a proximal analysis of mind—images, thoughts, beliefs, feelings, wants. It doesn't deny that there are proper uses of the ordinary sentences incorporating the corresponding nouns. But it urges us to consider these sentences as ways of describing complete performances or responses such as saying what one thinks, or sees, or thinks one sees, or wants to do. According to the view, the "what" in each case must not be taken to refer to a reportable inner event or thing, of which the report is a description. Thus when I report, for example, an hallucination, or any other imaging event, I am not referring to or describing an inner picture. Reporting an hallucination is essentially the same kind of performance as having it, which means that really there is no "having" and no "it". That is, to hallucinate is not to have a mental picture in the mind, but is itself a kind of response, a pre-verbal response, to certain inaccurate information fed (to use the terminology) to the input part of the speech centre. The claim is that no part of this response involves an episode in which an inner object with its own characteristics and qualities is noted and described, as one might note and describe the characteristics and qualities of a portrait (cf. Dennett, pp. 111–113). The only "inner" things and events involved are not mental in a Cartesian sense, or proximal in our sense. They are neural events literally inside the brain ("freak" or "abnormal neuronal discharges", pp. 137–138).

Now suppose this were true. I believe that conscientious attention

140

to perceptual—and I mean *perceptual*—experience reveals that the "input states" fed to the speech centre are extensively and ineradicably contaminated with false information. I have attempted elsewhere to distinguish some main kinds of case (Hannay 1971): here it will be enough to mention those where perceptual content is supplemented by elements not traceable to seen features of the public environment. For example, the image supplements which our expectations bring to the over-all perceptual experience—qualities of the kind that can be seen in the environment, and if our expectations are correct, would be seen there, but are not genuinely seen since they lie beyond the presently available vista. But there are also qualities which things in the environment are seen as having, but which they cannot seriously be thought to possess as public perceptual property—e.g., the familiarity that belongs to certain persons, objects, and places and not to others, the divinity of mountains, or the hostility that can attach to an environment, like the Examination Schools, long after the circumstances generating it have vanished. These properties clearly belong in the proximal series, since they don't pick out publicly identifiable characteristics. I think one can extend the list to include characteristics belonging, one might say, to the pervasive manner or feel of one's moral or aesthetic experience of the world (cf. the "aesthetic" works of Kierkegaard). But we don't have to go that far to recognize that human perception incorporates proximal elements which make it depart widely and perhaps radically from the manner in which a "perceiving machine" (cf. Dennett) scans and records the public property of the outside world.

What, then, can be the force of ascribing such proximal content to the feeding of inaccurate information to the speech centre? Is this to say that perception discloses reality only to the extent that its content is not proximal? The trouble with that idea is that if due note is given to the phenomenological evidence we are forced to reintroduce something very like the mental screen. The proximal "injection" (to talk in a grossly simplistic manner) is too pervasive and integral to be regarded as a mere supplement to accurate vision. It has, indeed, a consistency and regularity that suggests it is in some respects the perceptual analogue of the unconscious skills activated in action, and is, like them, essential to the operation as such. Without the activation of more or less enduring dispositions to see, or more generally to experience, the environment in this way or that, perception as we know it would be impossible. Secondly, phenomenologically and perhaps more cogently, the perceptual field is homogeneous in that it presents no division between environmental

141

core and non-environmental supplement. That is one reason why it is not only simplistic but also misleading to talk of "supplements" and "injections". Our environments as we experience them are *essentially* "proximalized"; thus what we often so glibly refer to as *the* environment, as though it were a piece of exclusively public property, is not the environment we individually experience. We should, I insist, resist any temptation to place the public environment *behind* the proximalized one, i.e., construe the notion of a public environment as the real world behind the "mental" one we experience. It is because "mental screen" talk involves succumbing to the temptation that we should reject it under whatever philosophical patronage it is introduced. But the denial of the screen still poses a problem for the realist. He has to account for the fact, for instance, that *my* real world is not entirely public, that some of the properties I would attribute to inanimate as well as animate public objects are proximal and therefore mental.

5. Our third anti-Cartesian thesis proposes uncompromisingly that actions are genuine initiatives—in the libertarian not the character-building sense. Cartesianism of course accepts the thesis as it stands, but locates initiative outside the space bounded by the epidermis. We are trying to accommodate all that matters within that space, so the logical step here would be to include there the capacity to initiate change in the physical universe. Let us therefore formulate our third thesis as follows : (3) the physical human organism is capable of genuine initiatives.

Libertarians will consider this thesis the crux of my case for proximality as a criterion of mind. If they think Thesis 3 cannot be upheld they will opt for a freedom-saving Cartesian alternative : a theory to the effect that libertarian freedom is introduced into the human organism by something other than it. But in fact I am not primarily concerned with finding room for libertarianism. It is reasonable to suppose, of course, that if genuine initiatives occur, they are introduced at the proximal level—as the content of choosings, decidings, deliberate doings, etc. But for present purposes I am content to argue for a slightly less ambitious thesis (a weaker form of [3]) that proximal events and contents (in more usual terms, mental acts and states of consciousness) are efficacious; that is that they play *some* causal role, even if only as a link in a chain. That conclusion would in itself, I think, provide a certain amount of significance for proximal events and contents. But I also suspect that consideration of what these events and contents are leads one more quickly than might be supposed to the conclusion that libertarian freedom exists. This latter contention must remain unsupported here. I shall argue only for mental efficacy, and do that by suggesting— perhaps a little paradoxically—that my monistic account of the relation of physical states to states of consciousness offers better support for advocates of the efficacy of "mental states" than does a dualist one. To expedite matters I hitch my (all too brief) comments to a recent argument by Honderich for a deterministic view of human behaviour (Honderich 1973). Honderich's argument is instructive precisely because in addition to the three premisses which he argues for explicitly and in detail, his case for the determinist conclusion hinges very obviously on an unargued dualist premiss to the effect that any physical state can in principle be completely described "without recourse to descriptions of consciousness" (p. 195). Honderich's three explicit premisses are : (1) "there exists, for each discriminable conscious state, a theoretically discribable physical correlate" (p. 189); (2) "brain states [a species of physical state in the above sense] are effects of sufficient physical conditions" (p. 197); and (3) "actions, which are certain movements, are caused by brain states" (p. 201).

The first premiss (the "Correlation Thesis") poses no problems— even if we accept a refinement crucial to Honderich's claim that states of consciousness are causally idle, namely that the correlation between descriptions of consciousness and brain states is not many-one (p. 191). I see no pressing reason to deny what Honderich regards as a well-confirmed hypothesis, namely that each proximal state has a public (though not necessarily easily accessible) correlate. Nor, in principle, do I see any need to object to the claim that states of consciousness are not to be found among the causal antecedents of brain states, and which is a corollary to the second premiss. Though my justification for this claim would not be Honderich's. He claims that states of consciousness are causally "idle" in respect of brain states. But here I would advocate an extension of the principle applied earlier to the case of bodily movements, which we described as bodily complements of proximal states. There it was suggested that the control exercised on the actual course of an unimpeded action was not causal. Why not say, then, that if, as the Correlation Thesis claims, the brain is a functional part of action, its states must be *neurophysiological* complements of proximal states? In that case proximal states would no more stand in a causal

143

relation to the states of the brain than they do, on this hypothesis, to actual bodily movements—this incidentally being our reason for rejecting Honderich's third premiss, that the bodily movements which constitute actions are *caused* by brain states. The price of the assumption is to add neural conditions to those we have already exempted from the dualist principle that physical states be completely describable without recourse to descriptions of consciousness.

The core of the determinist thesis is in the claims that actions are caused by brain states (the second part of premiss 3) and that brain states are effects of sufficient Honderichian physical conditions. Everyone, including Honderich, must admit that both claims are strongly counterintuitive. Our intuitions tell us that if our actions are determined by anything at all, whether strictly or otherwise, it is by things like wants and beliefs, not by states of the brain. And on dualist premisses it is certainly very difficult to believe that states of consciousness (proximal states) are not among the causal antecedents of particular brain states. Of course if our intuitions were correct on the first point, then Honderich's thesis that states of the brain have exclusively physical antecedents would be worse than counterintuitive; it would have the scientifically unacceptable consequence that brain functions are not necessary for action.

Honderich admits that his second premiss runs counter to our inclination to assign efficacy of some kind to mental states and events (p. 196), and that the case for premiss 2 would be considerably weakened if its proponents could offer no explanation of this apparent efficacy. But because explanations are available (pp. 196–197), resistance to premiss 2 is "ill-formed" (p. 196). It is ill-formed because the intelligibility of the confirmed instances of premiss 2—which give us all the efficacy we need (p. 196)—contrasts overwhelmingly with the "mystery" attached to the view that a particular brain state can have a sufficient genesis in consciousness (p. 197).

Now the idea of a state of consciousness activating a brain state without the brain's assistance is indeed mysterious. In fact I believe we cannot form an adequate concept of such an operation, and that in itself seems good reason for adopting an alternative hypothesis to the effect that the operation does not exist. There are, of course, also theoretical difficulties with the idea. Why should consciousness need the brain's support in some cases and not in others? Why bring in the brain at all? The alleged operation threatens to undermine the whole scientifically confirmed principle of the brain's functional role in human activity. The question is whether to opt for a form of alternative hypothesis that requires us to say that

consciousness simply mirrors physical efficacy or one that allows
states of consciousness to be efficacious themselves (though in the
case of the bodily aspect of basic actions, not causally). The latter
alternative commends itself not merely because it saves our intuitions
here, but also because it has the advantage of permitting the question
of whether, and in what sense, to attribute efficacy to states of
consciousness to be posed in a form which admits the possibility that
among the alleged causal antecedents of states of consciousness
themselves one may find not only purely physical conditions, such as
alcohol-content and hormone balance, but also things like wants,
aims, purposes, beliefs, theories, contents, agreements, and principles.

But, as we have already said, to be able to conclude that states
of consciousness are efficacious would not suffice for acceptance of
our third anti-Cartesian thesis : that the physical human organism
is capable of genuine initiatives. States of consciousness may after
all contribute only to monitor and control actions that are still
effects of sufficient causal antecedents, antecedents which include
those very monitoring and controlling operations—as perhaps in the
example of the highly trained and programmed sprinter. Whether
genuine initiative occurs depends on whether actions can lack
sufficient causal antecedents.

Since we accept that any hypothesized incursions into the causal
sequence could hardly come from outside the proximal domain, a
positive answer to this question would provide the best case for the
claim made at the beginning that proximality does not play such a
subordinate role after all in the scheme of things, provided human
happenings have some significant place in the scheme. So let me
propose that an argument that ordinary human actions are themselves initiatives—in the libertarian sense—would be provided if it
were possible to show that in the proximal series no one stage can
strictly determine the next. In support of this one might point to
the evident difficulty of dividing the series up into stages at all, or
even therefore of regarding it as a "series" in any literal sense
(*vide* the possibility mentioned earlier of the mind being *sui generis*).
Another, more common argument would be that even in the case of
basic proximal contents like wantings and believings, the agent under
their control has a dispositional capacity to alter his wants and beliefs
in response to criticism (cf. Popper 1972, and Koertge 1975), a
response which is then considered not to have sufficient causal antecedents. A supporter of human initiative in this minimal, non-
character-builder's sense might then argue that one place where such
an initiative is required is in actually changing one's wants and

145

beliefs in accordance with the (proximal) realization that to do so is rational. In fact in a potentially character-building context. If this could be upheld, then proximal events would have been found a significant role in one humanly very important kind of event : a person's actual modification of his desires in the direction of the adoption of courses of action that afford longer-term or more widely distributed benefits. But even if, say because the strong version of Thesis 3 turns out to be false, such changes must occur without initiative, the conclusion that people must come to realize the rightness of these changes before they are made would in itself give point to adding to our list of proximal events the realizing of such a thing.

6. Someone perceives, reflects, realizes, and then takes steps. That might be a simple story or a complicated one. But in either event it is surely a narrative of this kind if any that we should call "a description of the mental". Philosophers have offered different analyses of the mentality of such a sequence—different ontologies of mind. Cartesians see it as a series of non-mental effects of mental causes, but their proposal is difficult and implausible, and an alternative is needed. One such is to look upon the human perform-ance from the outside, notice its rationality, its rule-governed nature, etc. and to conceive mentality as the organism's acquired capacity to respond in appropriate ways to its environment. I have suggested another which seems to me to have the crucial advantage of not being blind to phenomenological evidence. It says that seeing and responding are the bodily engagement of proximal states in the public affairs of the world.

Professor Alastair Hannay
University of Trondheim
Norway

BIBLIOGRAPHY

Anscombe, G. E. M. (1968) "The Intentionality of Sensation: A Grammatical Feature", in *Analytical Philosophy*, 2nd Ser. ed. Butler, R. J. Oxford: Blackwell.
Dennett, D. C. (1969) *Content and Consciousness. An Analysis*, London: Routledge & Kegan Paul.
Hannay, A. (1971) *Mental Images—A Defence*, London: Allen & Unwin.
Honderich, T. (1973) "One Determinism" in *Essays on Freedom of Action*, pp. 187–215, ed. Honderich, T. London: Routledge & Kegan Paul.

Koertge, N. (1975) "Popper's Metaphysical Research Program for the Human Sciences", *Inquiry*, 18, pp. 437–462.

Popper, K. R. (1972) *Objective Knowledge. An Evolutionary Approach*, Oxford: Oxford University Press.

Ryle, G. (1949) *The Concept of Mind*, London: Hutchinson's University Library.

Wittgenstein, L. (1967) *Zettel*, ed. G. E. M. Anscombe and G. H. von Wright, trans. G. E. M. Anscombe, Oxford: Basil Blackwell.

F

XI

SOFT DETERMINISM

G. E. M. Anscombe

KEITH LEHRER[1] has the following argument. Consider the three propositions :

A 1 If causal condition C obtains, A will ϕ
2 Unless causal condition C obtains, A can't ϕ
3 C does not obtain.

These three are consistent. But from 2 and 3 there follows "A can't ϕ". 1 therefore cannot be the analysis of "A can ϕ" – no matter what condition "C" is a dummy for. Therefore in particular "A can—i.e. is free to—ϕ" cannot be explained as "If A chooses to ϕ, A will ϕ", where choice is understood as a causal condition. (This is the standard development of the analysis of freedom of will proposed by Moore.)

Lehrer's argument has been criticized by Alvin Goldman[2] on the grounds that it could be used equally well to fault the analysis of "X is soluble in water" as "X will be dissolve if it is immersed in water". "Let X be a piece of sugar, and imagine a magician such that if X is not immersed in water he changes its molecular structure so as to make it non-soluble, whereas if X is immersed in water it dissolves." On this supposition it would seem that three consistent propositions parallel to the A-triad could be framed, and Lehrer's argument used to fault the conditional analysis of "X is water-soluble". But the conditional analysis is certainly right, so Lehrer's argument must be wrong !

Donald Davidson also says : If Lehrer's "reasoning is sound, it shows that no attribution of a power or disposition is ever equivalent to a conditional (whether the conditional is construed as causal law or subjunctive). Thus on Lehrer's argument to say something is water-soluble can't mean it dissolves if placed in water, since it may now

148

be soluble and yet placing it in water might make it insoluble. There are various ways one may try to cope with this point. But for my purposes it will be enough to remark that even if Lehrer's argument showed that no disposition or power is correctly analysed by a sub-junctive conditional, the claim that being able to do something is to have a causal power would not be undermined."³ Davidson be-lieves that freedom to act is a "causal power". A causal power is "a property of an object such that a change of a certain sort in the object causes an event of another sort".

Clearly Lehrer's argument disturbs. Let us examine Goldman's application of it to water-solubility. The three propositions

> B 1 If C obtains, A will dissolve
> 2 Unless C obtains, A is insoluble
> 3 C doesn't obtain

are consistent only if "A is insoluble" is given a sense other than that of the contradictory of 1. Goldman implicitly does this, and Davidson's remarks too imply that it can be done. If we say that, e.g., A's having a certain molecular structure is sufficient for A's insolubility, even though 1 is true, then that is already to abandon 1 as the analysis of "A is soluble".

Someone who held by the hypothetical analysis *should* say that the B-triad is inconsistent. We should then have two opposing argu-ments, one running "The B-triad is obviously consistent, therefore the hypothetical analysis is wrong" and the other : "The analysis is obviously right, therefore the B-triad is inconsistent".

There is, I think, no indication in Lehrer's article that he would want to apply his argument so as to fault the hypothetical analysis of solubility and similar properties. Nor is this to incur Schopen-hauer's stricture on philosophers who treat an argument like a cab—take it as far as you want to go, and then pay it off. It is not so clear as Goldman and Davidson think, that if Lehrer's argument is valid it applies to the analysis of dispositional properties. For there is a quite different application of it to the case of water-solubility, which is the real parallel, and is in various other ways more relevant to the original argument. Consider :

> C 1 If C obtains, A will dissolve (in water).
> 2 Unless C obtains, A can't dissolve (in water).
> 3 C doesn't obtain.

When we put Lehrer's original argument side by side with this one, it hits us on the nose that what he has to defend himself against is the charge of a fallacy of ambiguity. We have, we will suppose:

A 1 If C obtains, A will ϕ.
   2 Unless C obtains, A can't ϕ.
   3 C does not obtain.

All right, A can't ϕ, but how do we know whether *this* is—or entails—the negation of the "A can ϕ" which expresses A's freedom of will? By stipulation?—Lehrer knows that all soft determinists hold that in one sense (the free-will sense) one can act otherwise than one does, while in another sense (deterministic causal necessity) one can't. In the case of the dissolving of A, we see quite clearly that the "possibility" expressed by "solubility" is not what is in question in C2 : "Unless C obtains, A can't dissolve".

"If A is immersed in water it will dissolve" cannot really be adequate to the intentions of those who offer it as an analysis of "A is water soluble". They certainly mean it will dissolve in the water it is immersed in. Hence we have to quantify. I will take : "x is W" to mean "x is ordinary water under ordinary conditions", and I will take "immersion" to cover, say, being soused, being sprinkled, etc. Then, instead of "If A is immersed, it will dissolve", we put :

D 1. For all x, for all t, if x is W then if A is immersed in x at t and left in x, A will start dissolving in x within $t+i$,

where i is some small time interval. And instead of "Unless C obtains, A can't dissolve in water" we put :

D 2. For all t, *if* there isn't an x which is W at t and in which A is immersed and left at t, *then* for all x which is W at t it is not possible that A starts to dissolve in x within $t+i$,

and instead of "C does not obtain" we put :

D 3. There isn't an x such that x is W and A is being immersed in x just now.

From all of which we may infer :

150

It is not possible that A starts to dissolve in water now or dissolves in water within now +i.

We may call this impossibility the lack of a possibility for A, and hence, if we like, the lack of a power, or a sort of impotence, on A's part. But it is not the lack of disposition, a general power or capacity.

There is nothing objectionable about the D-triad or the propositions of our C-triad, explicated in some fashion; certainly they are not incompatible. And there is nothing to object to about the conclusion.

Note that in the C-triad we have an example illustrative of the plausibility of the general principle, that a causal condition of something may be a necessary causal condition of its possibility. Indeed, in our example it is not just a bare possibility that the condition mentioned should be a necessary condition of the possibility of the result. It is *necessarily* the case that it *is* such a necessary condition, because of what dissolving is. We could however construct cases where this was not so. E.g. we could suppose, if we wanted to, that someone would die if he took prussic acid, and that that was the only way he could die. Then, given that there was no prussic acid around for the time being, then just for the time being he couldn't die.

Note also that, once we have granted the consistency of the C-triad, we cannot offer C 1 as an analysis of the "A can dissolve" whose contradictory is the consequent of C 2.

Back now to the original argument. When "A can φ" expresses A's freedom, which is it analogous to, "A is soluble" or "A can dissolve"? Evidently to the latter, in the following way : "A is soluble" may still be true where there is obviously no possibility for A of actually dissolving. But "A can walk" (where this expresses A's freedom in respect of walking) is certainly not true where there is obviously no possibility of walking for A because, e.g., he is tied up.

It might be thought that "A has free will" is analogous to "A is soluble". But this cannot be right. "A is soluble" has a certain relationship to "A (here and now) can get dissolved". What stands in the same relationship to "A (here and now) can φ" would be a proposition like, say "A has a general capacity to φ". E.g. let "φ"="walk". Then "A can walk" may express A's competence to walk; he knows how, he is not a cripple, he has not a broken leg. Freedom of will, or even freedom of will in respect of walking, is thus not the analogue of water solubility. The analogue to that for

151

walking is rather a general capacity for which we haven't got a single term in English; but let us coin one and call it "ambulability". There is no such thing as a general capacity, which we would describe as "freedom of will in respect of walking" which like "ambulability" may be still attributable to someone who can't walk because he is tied up. If he is tied up, he has no "freedom of will" to walk.

We are now in a better position to assess the argument. The suggestion being considered is that choosing is a "causal condition" of any action that is called free. "He can, he is free to, act so—I mean, in the sense of doing it if he chooses" one might say, and this has been taken as an analysis as a conditional, and the analysis interpreted by Lehrer and many others as a statement of a *causal* condition. We now consider the three propositions which, according to Lehrer, must be compatible if C is such a condition :

> E 1 If C obtains (i.e. if A chooses to walk now) A will walk now.
> 2 Unless C obtains, A cannot walk now.
> 3 C does not obtain.

Here it is clear that the "A cannot walk" of E 2 does not refer to A's lacking the general capacity to walk. What E 2 says A can't do, unless C obtains, is *walk now* : the proposition is not to the effect that unless C obtains, A now lacks the general capacity.

The interpretation of Moore considered by Lehrer amounts to this (in the particular case). A can walk : this is supposed to express his freedom of will in respect of walking. Then A has, not only a capacity of walking, but a present possibility of walking; he is is not tied up, for example. Now there is of course a further set of causal conditions, which includes various things going on in his muscles and nerve fibres, such that *if* they are all actualized, A will walk. Among these is supposed to be included a choice on A's part, a choice to walk.

Lehrer's argument is that, for any such condition, it is logically possible that (like not being tied up) it is a necessary causal condition of A's here-and-now ability to walk. The statement that it *is* such a necessary condition of possibility is perfectly compatible with the statement that it is not actualized, and together these would imply that it is not possible for A to walk, that A (here and now) cannot walk.

And now the question is whether this "cannot" contradicts the "can" in the "A can walk" that expresses A's freedom of will in respect of walking. Lehrer's opinion is apparently that it does. That is, that the absence of *any* necessary condition of the possibility of exercising a capacity of walking (say) is sufficient to prove that one is not free to walk. Just as not being tightly chained up is a necessary condition of the possibility of exercising one's capacity to walk, and so in the absence of that condition—i.e. given that one is tightly chained—one does not possess freedom of will, to walk.

The picture of choice as a causal condition of doing something—a causal condition, given which one will do it—is a picture of it as like the last added weight which will start moving the weight on the other side of a pulley. We must emphasize that Lehrer is not arguing that choice *will* then be a necessary causal condition of the event or of its possibility, any more than the addition of this weight a necessary condition of the motion of that one. He is arguing merely that its being a causal condition at all is logically compatible with its being a *necessary* causal condition of the *possibility* of the event. And that, since that is so, its being a causal condition at all is compatible with propositions whose truth would entail a statement of impossibility which is incompatible with the possibility expressed by "A is free to ϕ".

Everyone will allow that "A can walk, i.e. has freedom of the will in respect of walking" would be gainsaid by A's being chained up. If choice is a causal condition *it is then logically possible that the absence of this condition should be just as destructive of freedom to walk as being chained up is.* Assume this logical possibility to be actual, and assume that A does not choose to walk. It will follow that he is no more free to walk than if he were tied up. Therefore—so Lehrer's argument goes—"If he chooses, he will walk", which may be true compatibly with those assumptions, cannot be the right analysis of "He is free to walk".

Now can we say : with these considerations, the charge of a fallacy of ambiguity is rebutted? If being chained up is incompatible with freedom of the will (in respect of walking), then on the assumption that choice is a causal condition, so equally *may* absence of choosing be.

May it? *Why* is being chained up incompatible with freedom of the will in respect of walking—that is, with freedom to walk? Is it because absence of chains is a causally necessary condition of its being possible (here and now) to walk?—If so, won't the absence of *any* causally necessary condition of the possibility of an action be incompatible with freedom to act?

Ah, but that is just what the soft determinist denies. Of course he denies it ! There are many causally necessary conditions of the possibility of walking, and in the absence of any of these, he grants, one cannot walk. Some of them are external, and in the absence of these, he says, one not merely cannot walk, but this "cannot" contradicts freedom. This holds of some internal conditions too; one must not be paralysed, for example. But it does not hold of all internal conditions. There are some in the absence of which—of course—one cannot, but still in the *freedom* sense of "can", one *can*. Lehrer has merely pointed out abstractly the possibility that choice should be, not merely a condition of a man's ϕ-ing, in that sometimes if a man chooses to ϕ, he will ϕ, but also a necessary condition of his ϕ-ing's being possible. If the conditions are causal and if this abstract possibility is actualized, then, for a man who does not choose to ϕ, ϕ-ing *is* causally impossible. "He cannot ϕ" will be true for as long as he does not choose to ϕ. But this, the causal-deterministic sense of "cannot", is *not*, so the soft determinist says, the negation of the free will sense of "can".

And what *is* that sense of "can"? Well, Moore told us, and Lehrer's attack on the neo-Mooran definition and the compatibility of determinism and free will has no more force than use of the C-triad to refute the hypothetical analysis of solubility. He said the A-triad was consistent, and inferred that analysis was wrong. But that assumes that the "cannot" of the A-triad negates the "can" that the neo-Mooran was analysing.

Lehrer's opponent, then, says, or ought to say, that the "cannot" that he was analysing will not fit into such a triad of possible and mutually consistent propositions. Plug his analysis of "A can ϕ" (in the free will sense) into A 2.[4] You get an inconsistent triad:

F   1   If A chooses to ϕ, A will ϕ
      2   If A doesn't choose to ϕ, then not :
        (If A chooses to ϕ A will ϕ)
      3   A does not choose to ϕ.

Now if this is so, we can derive the contradictory of any one of the triad from the other two.[5] And *this* carries the argument a stage further. For if Moore's analysis is correct, we have the right to read "If A chooses to ϕ, A will ϕ", either just as it stands, or replacing it by "A is free to ϕ". And this gives some curious results, of which I will give three. (a) From "If A chooses to ϕ, he will ϕ; and if A doesn't choose, he is not free to ϕ" we can infer that A does choose to ϕ. Now might not a person's choice to do something be a causal condition of his freedom to do it in the following way : if he does

154

not actually choose to do it, there will be external obstacles in his way, which make it impossible for him to do it? It is agreed on all sides that physical constraint and exterior obstacles impair freedom— that if, for example, you physically can't commit suttee because "they won't let you", you aren't free to do it. Suppose, then, that they will let you be burnt on your husband's funeral pyre, but only if you choose. Your choice then becomes a causally necessary condition of the lack of external constraint. Why not then also of your freedom? (b) In the same circumstances, if we know that A does not choose to be burnt, we are apparently able to infer that it is not true that if she chooses to be burnt, she will be burnt. Or again, (c) if we know that if she chooses she will, but that she does not choose, we can infer that no such bizarre circumstances hold. Now all of these inferences are absurd. Therefore

> G 1 If A chooses to ϕ, he will ϕ
> 2 If A doesn't choose to ϕ, A is not free to ϕ
> 3 At T, A does not choose to ϕ

are compatible. But the G-triad is the same as the F-triad, except that F(2) has been replaced by G(2); and these are equivalent, on the neo-Mooran analysis. If, then, the F-triad is inconsistent and the G-triad is consistent, that analysis cannot be right.

It is easy to construct other examples on the same lines. E.g. You are free to go over the cliff edge but don't choose to. Does it follow that there isn't anyone or anything that prevents you from doing it unless you choose to?

Again: A will marry B (will go through a marriage ceremony with B) if he chooses. But if he doesn't choose, the ceremony won't be allowed. There are people who can tell whether he is acting voluntarily or not, and if not they will stop it. So if he doesn't choose, external constraints will render the proceeding impossible. Could one infer from this that A chooses to marry B?

These arguments have a certain oddity about them—to which I will return—and also might seem sophistical in the following way: Consider the first two propositions of the G-triad:

> 1 If A chooses to ϕ, A will ϕ.
> 2 If A doesn't choose to ϕ, A is not free to ϕ.

They have got to be tied to a particular time. There is no question of our constructing analogues of the propositions of the D-triad, where we generalized over all times. What then are to say? Can we put

(1)a If A at T chooses to ϕ, A will ϕ by the time T+i
(2)a If A doesn't at T choose to ϕ, A is not free to ϕ between T and T+i.

?—This perhaps seems unreasonable because if we make the interval long enough to include all the time within which A's choice at T may be implemented, it will often be unlikely that a choice a little later than T could not be implemented within T+i.

However, this is after all irrelevant. For the argument turns, not on the *truth* of any three propositions which would be instances of the G-triad, but on the possibility of there being such propositions. So the objection would stand only if there could never be true instances of (1)a and (2)a. But that can't be claimed. So the argument does not contain a concealed sophistry which will be resolved when we consider time references.

Now for the oddity of the arguments. There seems to be something very queer about G(2) in conjunction with G(1), and it remains queer when we supply examples. It is strange to think of freedom as impaired or destroyed by such physical constraints as those. We picture obstacles to freedom as obstacles that resist efforts to surmount them or ones that it is not the slightest use trying to surmount —but *those* obstacles were none so long as A *chose* to do what they otherwise prevented.

We made out cases in which choice was a causally necessary condition of the possibility of an event (the burning of the widow, the occurrence of the marriage ceremony, the falling over the cliff). But doesn't it turn out that a causally necessary condition of the absence of external constraint is here *not* the same thing as a causally necessary condition of freedom to do the thing? And yet, as we have observed, external constraint is generally agreed to be incompatible with freedom. How can it be, then, that a causally necessary condition of the absence of constraint is ever *not* a causally necessary condition of freedom?

Our answer to the charge of sophistry removes our difficulty, however. When we speak in a loose and popular way of a man's being free to do something, we probably have examples in mind where, as we might say, he's free for quite a little time ahead. If A doesn't choose to ϕ at a given moment, it will then be silly to deny his "freedom to ϕ"—because, after all, he may choose to do

156

it and do it at any time within some indeterminate span we vaguely have in mind, and that's what we meant in thinking of his freedom. But if the Moorean analysis (as usually interpreted) is the right account, we have got to be a bit more exact in our thinking.

Instead of the F-triad we must put :

H 1 If at T A chooses to ϕ, A will ϕ by the time T+i
   2 If at T A does not choose to ϕ, then not (1)
   3 At T, A does not choose to ϕ.

which is plainly inconsistent; and instead of the G-triad :

I 1 If at T A chooses to ϕ, A will ϕ by the time T+i
   2 If at T A does not choose to ϕ, A is not free to ϕ between T and T+i
   3 At T, A does not choose to ϕ

and then our argument can proceed as before. If the I-triad is inconsistent, it appears that in a particular case we could make deductions as to matters of fact from any pair of the triad, which we plainly should have no right to make. Therefore the I-triad is not inconsistent. Therefore I(2) is not equivalent to H(2). Therefore the Moorean analysis is wrong.

This argument could be resisted if it could be argued that propositions (1) and (2) of the relevant triads were already inconsistent with one another. The conjunction of them is certainly rather difficult to understand in the F and H triads, when the antecedent is taken as stating a causal condition, though I don't know how they could be shewn to be inconsistent. A sworn addict of the Moorean analysis might say that the difficulty of understanding the conjunctions shews there is an inconsistency, and then say that this must be transferred to the corresponding conjunctions from the G and I triads. But we have actually shewn and explained how those conjunction might be true, on the assumption that choice is a causal condition. The negation of freedom is guaranteed by *certain* constraints (this is agreed by everyone), and choice could obviously be a causal condition of such constraints.

Let us now take a real case of a condition of voluntary movement. Certain patterns of brain activity are found to occur very shortly before the initiation of a movement in response to an order to perform it (at once). When the performance is "self-paced"—i.e., the subject chooses when to make the movement—there is also such a pattern; I

157

understand that it is more diffuse and there is some small difference of time interval from what you get in the other case.

Taking these facts, it may be reasonable to suppose (a) that unless there is such a pattern of activity in someone's brain there will be no initiation of movement on his part, and (b) that normally (i.e. if it is not prevented) when there is such activity, there will be initiation of movement. If (a) were very solidly confirmed, we'd say that without this activity the subject cannot make the movement. In short we shall have a good example for Lehrer's pattern of argument. We shall have as a consistent triad :

(1) If there is a Z-type pattern of activity in A's brain, there will be initiation of movement on A's part.
(2) Unless there is a Z-type pattern of activity in A's brain, there can't be initiation of movement on A's part.
(3) There is no Z-type pattern of activity in A's brain.

The first two propositions, we may say, are probably true, and presumably the third one is often true. Now won't it be true to say that when all this holds, A can't move? And if that is true, doesn't it follow that A is not free to move?

To answer these questions we have to introduce time references, and here we can quantify universally over times. For the sake of the argument, let us assume a constant interval between the onset of the brain activity and the initiation of movement, and let us call this interval i. Then, taking C as the presence of the relevant brain activity.

For all t, if C does not obtain, beginning at t, no initiation of movement on A's part is possible before $t+i$.

Now let us assume that precisely *now* C is not beginning to obtain. (Perhaps I fire a shot or read a clock to fix the time here meant by "now".)

It follows that no initiation of movement on A's part between that *now* and that *now*+i was possible.

And it also follows that A wasn't able to start to make a movement between that *now* and that *now*+*i*—for this is merely a rephrasing of the preceding proposition.

That being so, how can anyone say that in similar circumstances A is *free* to start making a movement between a *now* and the same *now*+i? Obviously one cannot.

But when we say that A is now free to move, of course we are not thinking in terms of such tiny intervals. The conditions we have laid down do not preclude A's beginning to make a movement as soon as you like after now+i; i is very small, and if A can make a movement after now+i+ $\frac{i}{100}$, that would be good enough. Our assumed facts tell us that if A *does* make a movement then, C will have begun to obtain at now+ $\frac{i}{100}$.

To sum up : as soon as we get quite clear about internal conditions, without which a movement on A's part is impossible, the contrast between internal conditions that make an action impossible, and external ones, like being tied up, proves to be illusory. It trades vagueness and ignorance.

People are divided into two opposing camps, for one of which it seems quite obvious that a physical impossibility of walking (say) contradicts freedom to walk, and that it makes no difference whether the physical impossibility arises from an internal or an external state. For the other, it seems equally obvious that when the internal state is connected with choice, that makes all the difference. A choice is here thought of as an event : it causes (no doubt among other things) another event which is called a "free action". It is possible that, in the absence of the event that would have been a choice had it occurred, one's internal mechanism is such as to render impossible that event which would have been called a free action if caused by a choice. Then the choice was a necessary condition of the possibility of the action, and it was physically impossible that one should (say) walk. But just because it is *choice* that is such a necessary condition, the soft determinist says that this is the sort of impossibility that does not contradict freedom.

But what then is the explanation of "freedom" as it is here spoken of? There is none offered except *via* the Moorean definition. And that we have exploded.

I personally found Lehrer's argument convincing against any hypothetical analysis of freedom. But then I have never thought that freedom was compatible with physical impossibility. I realized that the soft determinist would be untouched by the argument because, of course, he does think freedom compatible with physical impossibility. Naturally, since, being a determinist, he thinks that everything except what actually happened was always impossible. Lehrer's "cannot" is therefore compatible with *this* " 'can' of freedom". Now, having disposed of the supposed explanation of this "can", I am at liberty to say that I believe a " 'can' of freedom" which holds in face of physical impossibility is pure nonsense.

Professor G. E. M. Anscombe
Cambridge University

NOTES

[1] *Freedom and Determinism*, Ed. Lehrer, Random House, p. 196.

[2] *A Theory of Action*, Prentice Hall, p. 199n.

[3] Donald Davidson, "Freedom to Act" in *Essays on Freedom of Action*, Ed. Ted Honderich, Routledge and Kegan Paul. Davidson disclaims dependence on the hypothetical analysis of freedom.

[4] I owe this useful suggestion to my student David Waterman, who used it to confute Lehrer.

[5] But note that if we interpret our conditionals truth–functionally, (2) by itself is inconsistent with (3). This would generally be regarded as a red herring, as these conditionals are thought to be future indicative analogues of subjunctive conditionals and the received opinion is that the "if, then" of subjunctive conditionals cannot be truth-functional. But I do not think that that has really been shewn: see my "Subjunctive Conditionals" forthcoming in *Ruch Filozoficzny*. Briefly, I there argue that what the connectives in subjunctive conditionals connect are not propositions with truth values, but subjunctive clauses which have none; the question whether the connectives are the truth functional ones can therefore only be determined by considering whether the usual equivalences hold, and in fact they do hold.

XII

CAUSAL EXPLANATION, MOTIVATIONAL
EXPLANATION, AND HERMENEUTICAL
UNDERSTANDING. (REMARKS ON THE RECENT
STAGE OF THE EXPLANATION-UNDERSTANDING
CONTROVERSY.)

K-O. Apel

I. *Exposition: facing the third round of the
Explanation-Understanding Controversy*

CONSIDERING W. Dilthey's "Einleitung in die Geisteswissenschaften" (1883) as *starting point* of the *Explanation-Understanding* Controversy and considering the unified-science thesis of Neopositivism as it was based on Popper's and Hempel's DN-Model of explanation as *second stage* of the controversy one might speak of a *third stage* of the controversy initiated by the so called Neowittgensteinian phase of Analytic Philosophy, i.e. by the work of authors like P. Winch (1958), G. E. M. Anscombe (1957) W. Dray (1957), A. I. Melden (1961), and especially by G. H. von Wright's "Explanation and Understanding" (1971). Now, the special interest of this third stage, from the view-point of a continental observer, lies in the fact that in this context at least some concerns, motives and even arguments of the older "hermeneutic" tradition of a Philosophy of the "Geisteswissenschaften" (and even some motives of German Idealism) are taken up and defended with the aid of a highly sophisticated argumentation technique which seems to be far better suited for the problematic of modern philosophy of science than the old ways of arguing used by Dilthey and his continental followers.

It was in particular the careful analysis of the language-games or conceptual frameworks of scientific and metascientific arguments that provided new standards and criteria of dealing with the old questions. In this context the Neowittgensteinian device for a solution (or dissolution) of the intricate problems of the *explanation-understanding* controversy has been presented, it seems, by a distinction between the language-game of *things* and *events* presupposed by *causal explanations* of natural science, on the one hand, and the language-game of *persons* and their *actions* presupposed by *understanding* or

161

motivational-teleological explanations of the humanities on the other hand. Critical reflection on these language-game presuppositions of methodology seems to show that every attempt to reduce the methodology of *understanding* and *explaining actions* in terms of *aims, motives* or *reasons* to the methodology of *causal explanations of events* amounts to an illegitimate confounding of different conceptual frameworks and hence to a "category mistake", to speak along with G. Ryle (1938). Facing the idea of two different and mutually exclusive language-games the critics of Neowittgenstein-ianism have spoken of a "New Dualism" that replaces the Cartesian dualism of ontological substances by the dualism of categorical frameworks of possible coherent or semantically consistent world-interpretation (cf. Ch. Landesman 1965/66, A. Beckermann 1974 and 1975).

Now, from the point of view of a continental observer with a hermeneutical background it seems interesting to ask the following questions concerning the third stage of the explanation-understanding controversy :

1. First, may Neowittgensteinianists be considered as ideal advocates of all interests and motives of traditional *Hermeneutics* on the present level, so to speak, of philosophical argumentation?

2. Second, may it be said that Neowittgensteinianism has won the victory in the third round of the *explanation-understanding* controversy, such that on its presuppositions the question as to the relation between natural science and the humanities has been definitely settled?

In the present paper, I wish to deal with these questions in the inverse order by concentrating especially on the controversy between G. H. von Wright and his critics; and I will indicate in advance that I shall neither with respect to the first nor with respect to the second question arrive at a clear cut affirmative answer; instead I shall suggest the necessity of a new approach which, on the one hand, can uncover and delimit the *hermeneutical* truth-kernel of Neo-wittgensteinianism by purging it of illegitimate claims and false strategies; and, on the other hand, may also account for the undeni-able possibility of showing up a formal analogy between *motivational* and *causal explanation* without giving up the well understood autonomy claim of the humanities.

162

II. *An attempted reconstruction of the third round of the explanation-understanding controversy: The ambiguous and ambivalent strategy of Neowittgensteinianism in G. H. von Wright and its apparent partial refutation by his critics.*

Roughly speaking, the critics of von Wright's claim have two contentions in common : first, to show that the schema of "practical inference" used in teleological explanation may only then be rendered *logically conclusive* as a *theoretic explanatory argument* if further premises are incorporated into it and among them in any case a *general lawlike proposition;* second, to show that the *reasons* (i.e. *goal-intentions* and *means-beliefs*) presupposed in the practical inference, must be conceived of as *dispositions* as well as *effective reasons,* i.e. *causes,* of the behavior to be explained. Though, in their contentions to draw consequences from these postulates, in favour of the causalist covering law model the critics differ considerably.

One of them, A. Beckermann (1974 and 1975), who refers to von Wright's work only in connection with his contentions against Neowittgensteinianism as a whole, thinks the claim of a special status of *teleological explanation* (or "rational explanation" in the somewhat misleading terminology of W. Dray), and hence the methodological autonomy claim of the humanities, to be already refuted by the argument put (forward by C. G. Hempel, E. Nagel, and D. Davidson against W. Dray, Th. Mischel and others) that for any teleological explanation to have explanatory force it must *not only* show that the agent had *good reasons* for doing what he did but moreover that the agent in fact performed the action to be explained *because he had those reasons,* i.e. that the good reasons became *effective reasons,* i.e. *causes,* of the action (cf. Beckermann 1974, esp. II, 9).

Now, I think, that the demand for *effective reasons,* i.e. *causes,* is indeed justified under the condition that an explanation has to show that the *occurrence of an action was to be expected,* or, in other words, that an explanation must "provide information which constitutes good grounds for the belief that x did in fact occur" (C. G. Hempel 1963, p. 146), and, moreover, also under the slightly different presupposition that a *teleological explanation* should function as a *motivational explanation,* i.e. that it should ascertain *on which reasons* an agent, say a person standing on trial, in fact acted in a certain case. Nevertheless, the question whether this argument amounts to a restoration of the *covering law*-model of *causal explanation* may still be answered to the negative.

This shows itself when we consider the other claim of the critics of von Wright or Neowittgensteinianism, viz. that the schema of *practical inference* used in *teleological explanation* may only then be rendered *logically conclusive* as a *theoretic explanatory argument* if further premises are incorporated into it and among them in any case a *general lawlike proposition*. Must not this claim in fact lead to a restoration of the *subsumption-theoretic covering law model* of *causal explanation?* Let us here begin with an examination of R. Tuomela's critique of von Wright.

R. Tuomela takes as his point of departure von Wright's "final formulation" (1971, p. 107) of the *practical inference* (PI), which runs as follows (in Tuomela's formulation):

> (PI) (P1) From now on A intends to bring about X at time t
>   (P2) From now on A considers that unless he does Y no later than at time t', he cannot bring about X at time t.
>   (C) Therefore, no later than when he thinks time t' has arrived, A sets himself to do Y, unless he forgets about time or is prevented.

Tuomela now proposes an "amended version" of the practical inference, which runs as follows:

> (PI¹) (P_1) /as in von Wright's version/
>   (P_2) /as in von Wright's version/
>   (P_3) "Normal conditions" obtain between now and t'
>   (L) "For any agent A, intention X, action Y, and time t, if A from now on intends to realize X at t and considers the doing of Y no later than t' necessary for this, and if "normal conditions" obtain between now and t', then A will do Y not later than when he thinks the time t' has arrived.
>   (C') No later than he thinks time t' has arrived A does Y. (Tuomela 1975b, p. 22 f.)

What is the significance of the changes introduced by Tuomela? The additional premise (P3) should contain the "unless prevented"-clause of the conclusion (C) of the original version of the syllogism and besides that some *ceteris paribus*-assumptions the practical syllogism does not explicitly treat. Tuomela mentions the assumptions "that (1) A then had no other goal-intention X' which he preferred to X and (2) there was no other action Y', also necessary for X, such that A preferred Y' (or, rather, Y' together with its various consequences) to Y (with its consequences)" and beyond that a special assumption concerning the *rationality* of the agent "so that e.g. his present emotional state or his having an Oedipus complex or his miscalculations should not disturb his deliberations" (1975b, p. 21 f). These *ceteris paribus*-assumptions, however, packed into the third premise, get their special function only by the *quasi-law* (L) which Tuomela considers as the "interesting thing" about his amended version of the practical syllogism. The point of this generalization is said to consist in the fact that it makes the syllogistic inference "logically conclusive", i.e. transforms it into a "kind of covering 'law' explanation", if only in a "formal and pickwickian sense", for the law is "non-contingent" and therefore "not very interesting from the point of view of the empirical explanation of action", according to Tuomela (1975b, p. 23).

Now it is clear also for Tuomela, that the non-contingent character of the quasi-law (L) stems from the *conceptual* or *analytic* character of the *connection* between the premisses and the conclusion in *practical inferences* which made use of as *quasi-law* within the amended version of the *theoretical-argument* schema of so-called *teleological explanations*. Thus the point of the amended version, it seems to me, is only to ensure, especially by the included *rationality*-condition, that the *conceptual connection* between the antecedent-conditions and the conclusion, which makes the practical syllogism *logically conclusive* as a means of *understanding* actions, is turned into a *normative standard* (in the methodological sense of Hugo Dingler (1921, p. 148 f.) of *theoretical explanations* which as a standard, cannot be falsified. For, in Tuomela's amended version of the explanation-schema it is supposed that the "normal conditions"-clause be *exhausted* in cases where the pure schema wouldn't work as *prediction* device. In these cases one would have to assume that the "normal conditions"-condition (P_3), especially the included *rationality*-condition, was not fulfilled and thereby, I would like to emphasize, eventually the quest for a genuine causal covering law explanation would arise. This interpretation of the "logical conclusiveness" of the "amended version" implies, however, that still (as von Wright had claimed) the "normal conditions", supposed to obtain, cannot be affirmatively *specified ex ante*, like ingredients of a genuine *contingent natural law*, but can only be *postulated ex negatione*, so to speak, viz. by supposing the realization of the ratio of the practical syllogism as standard of the normal, i.e. nonpathological, function of the human psycho-biological system (cf. Tuomela 1975b, p. 80 f.). This is the reason why the quasi-law (L) is not very interesting from the point of view of the *empirical explanation* of action, as Tuomela states it. It in fact rather functions as an *ideal type* of human "competence" (to be compared with Chomsky's concept of "grammatical competence") which may serve as a standard for a *normative-reconstructive understanding* of human actions that still poses the task of *empirical causal explanations* of the "performances" that deviate from the ideal standard (cf. Tuomela 1975a). I shall come back to this point.

Nevertheless, the *quasi-law* (L) into which the *practical inference* is transformed within the frame of a *theoretical explanatory argument* is not simply *analytical* in the same sense as the inference schema itself is as a device of *understanding* actions as realizations of the practical inference; for it is not the naked inference schema, so to speak, that makes up the quasi-law but rather the inference schema together with a *quasi-empirical hypothesis* that might be formulated as follows : If normal conditions obtain then the schema of the practical inference may be used like (as if it were) a causal law within the theoretical frame of a *motivational explanation*, which could be understood as answer to the question *why necessarily* a certain action was to be *expected*.

This conclusion eventually seems to be reconfirmed, I think, by R. Tuomela insofar as he pleads for *empirically* relevant "liberalizations" of the "amended version" of the practical syllogism in order to account for the *factual behaviour* of people as it may be explained with regard to the different special psychological and socio-cultural (e.g. institutional) marginal conditions which more or less restrict the validity of the *ideal competence-standard* of *practical syllogism* as a standard for "normal conditions" of factual performances (cf. R. Tuomela 1975a and b, p. 26).

Thus it seems that von Wright's claim that his conception of "teleological explanation" as a "definite *alternative* to the subsumption-theoretic covering law model" has been refuted by his critics. For, if teleological explanation is to fulfill the function of a *theoretical explanatory argument*, then it must fulfill, it seems, at least the two following requirements of a *subsumption-theoretic causal explanation* : First, it must conceive of reasons as *effective* reasons, i.e. as *causes*; secondly, it must insert a *quasi-law* into the inference schema, be it a *quasi-analytical universal quasi-law* of *rational action*, be it a *contingent, non-universal regularity of behaviour* that can serve as a *quasi-law* concerning socio-cultural habits of action.

166

III. *Causal explanation, motivational explanation, and
hermeneutical understanding: a new approach suggested
from the view-point of our leading interests of knowledge.*

Now, looking at this situation from the point of view of the epistemological and metascientific-methodological relationship between
natural science and the social sciences or the humanities, respectively,
I think that the real problem of the *explanation-understanding*
controversy cannot be tackled, let alone solved, under the presuppositions of von Wright and his critics; that is to say, it cannot be raised
in a relevant form under the usual presupopsition that the *leading
questions* of research in all sciences, or in the sciences and in the
humanities, may be taken as essentially the same in as far as they
would require (at most *different types of*) *theoretical explanations*
as suitable answers. Not even the *theoretical subject-object-relation*,
as it is presupposed in "explanations" as answers to "why to be
expected"-questions, may be taken as a self-evident presupposition
in the case of the leading interest of *understanding* in the humanities.
Broadly speaking I would rather postulate that the problem concerning the relationship between natural science and the humanities
should be conceived of as a problem of *different leading questions*
and moreover of *different leading interests of knowledge.*

Thus it seems obvious that certain *why-questions*, as e.g. the
question *for what reasons* (i.e. intentions or beliefs) an agent is or
was acting, can only be asked in the social sciences, or more precisely :
in the *hermeneutical social sciences*, i.e. in the so called "humanities".
Within this context, however, these questions may be interwoven
with questions as to *understanding* the very *meaning* of actions,
speech, texts, works and institutions which are also questions exclusively of the humanities but interestingly *not* such questions as could
be answered by "explanations" in the sense of modern "logic of
science". Thus e.g. the question *what kind of action* a person is
performing may be answered by recourse to a *practical inference*
from supposed *reasons* (i.e. *goal-intentions* and *means-beliefs*) to the
given action; but in this context the *practical inference* is not an
explanatory argument at all; for it does not provide an answer to the
question *why the action was to be expected* which might eventually
be answered without *understanding* the action as performed for
good or bad reasons; nevertheless within the humanities we have
an *autonomous interest* in *understanding* what kind of human
actions we are confronted with by understanding the reasons behind
the actions. These *hermeneutic* questions of understanding actions

are no "why to be expected"-questions at all but have rather affinities to the problems of *meaning-explication* in both the *descriptive* and the *re-constructive* branch of *language-analytical* philosophy and logic of science. Thus an epistemological inquiry that reflects upon the different *questions* underlying natural sciences and the humanities may be led to the insight that the older dichotomy of "explanation" and "understanding", suggested by G. Droysen and W. Dilthey, was a more radical approach to the problem of the relationship of natural sciences and the humanities than the logical analysis of types of explanation.

Now, against this conjecture the following objection may be raised. *Explicative understanding* of *what* a thing is must be presupposed in every kind of prescientific and scientific knowledge; it is presupposed, it seems, for *describing the data* and hence for raising further questions to be answered by *explanations* in the natural sciences as well as in the social sciences; therefore, we must not look for a *methodological* difference between *explanation* and *understanding*, it could be said, but rather for *different types of explanation* corresponding to the *different types of prescientific understanding*. As von Wright puts it : "One could say that the intentional or nonintentional character of their objects marks the difference between two types of understanding and of explanation" (1971, p. 135). This clear cut distinction and parallelism between the ontological and epistemological foundations of natural science and hermeneutical social science seems to be very persuasive at first sight; and it obviously corresponds to the Neowittgensteinian dualism of of two different language-games and corresponding world interpretations. I think, however, that this type of New Dualism is too simple an architectonic to cope with the ontological and epistemological problems involved by the *explanation-understanding* controversy. Properly speaking, it seems to me to do justice neither to the special methodological features of the *humanities* as *hermeneutic sciences* nor to the fact that there are and must be *quasi-naturalistic social* or *behavioural sciences*. For, as far as I can see, there are two epistemologically and methodologically relevant facts that do not fit in with the parallellism of the two types of understanding and explanation, respectively.

The first is constituted by the circumstance that *understanding good reasons*, e.g. understanding the "practical inference" as good reason for actions, may be methodically elaborated without becoming at all a *theoretical explanatory argument*. This, so to speak, is a point of *Hermeneutics*, i.e. of the hermeneutical interest of knowledge. The other fact is constituted by the circumstance that there are in fact quasi-causal and even quasi-nomological *motivational explanations* in psychology and in the social sciences, i.e. explanations which cannot be sufficiently accounted for by the naked structure of the "practical syllogism" but only by its integration into the structure of a *theoretical explanatory argument* which, in a sense that we tried to approximate in the preceding discussion, corresponds to the structure of a *causal* (or *statistical*) *explanation*. These facts, I think, cannot be understood on the presupposition of von Wright's version of neowittgensteinian New Dualism; but this does not mean, in my opinion, that there is no truth-kernel in Neowittgensteinianism. I rather want to suggest that there is another version of Neowittgensteinian dualism which, in connection with the conception of the *different leading interests of knowledge*, may very well serve as a basis for understanding the above sketched fact of methodologically different types of social or human sciences. But let us try to elucidate these theses more closely.

First, there is the fact that *hermeneutic* i.e. *methodically interpretative understanding* in the humanities is not only a prescientific or protoscientific precondition for the stage of asking *why*-questions and setting up *explanatory* hypotheses but rather a *scientific continuation of the prescientific understanding* of symbolic and parasymbolic meanings or meaning-intentions. This means that even so called *teleological* or *rational explanations* of actions, centred around the rationality of practical inferences, are to be conceived of as means in the service of *methodical understanding* as long as they are not conceived of as *quasi-causal motivational explanations*. This remarkable continuum between *prescientific understanding* of the world ("Weltvorverständnis") and *methodically interpretative understanding* is, in my opinion, the reason for the famous (or notorious) "hermeneutic circle", i.e. for the fact that reciprocal presupposing and correcting of prescientific understanding of meaning and methodical interpretation of meaning, be it in the case of texts or be it in the case of intentional actions, must itself be considered as a methodological ingredient of Hermeneutics. This relationship of mutual correction between prescientific and scientific-hermeneutic understanding is rather different from the relationships between prescientific *explicative understanding* and *explanation* in the natural sciences. The latter, I think, normally escapes (precludes the function of) the "hermeneutic circle" just by the fact that *explanation* as an objective *theoretical argument* should not by itself extend the *explicative understanding* of the meaning of the data but should presuppose a definitive intersubjectively valid interpretation of the *explananda* so that at least in the case of "normal science" (Th. Kuhn) there is a sharp demarcation presupposed between *explanatory hypotheses*, on the one hand, and presupposed *explicative understanding* of the phenomena in the light of language-game paradigms on the other hand.

Now, the reason why the continuum of, and even a methodical circularity between, prescientific and scientific-hermeneutic understanding is characteristic for the humanities rather than a sharp demarcation between prescientific explicative understanding and explanation is provided, in my opinion, by the fact that the *humanities* or *hermeneutical social sciences* are not constituted in the same sense as the *explanatory natural sciences* by a transition from the *practical* to the *theoretical* relationship to the world. More precisely, one should say that *methodical understanding* in the *hermeneutic sciences*, and within their frame also *understanding of human actions in the light of "practical inferences"* (in the sense of von Wright), never springs from that theoretical *subject-object-relation* that is always already presupposed (without much reflection) in *scientific explanations*, including those "motivational explanations" that answer the question for *causally effective reasons* and make use of "practical inferences" within the frame of *theoretical explanatory arguments*. For a theoretical explanatory argument, which rests on a strict *objectification* of the world, *reenactive understanding of practical inferences* and hence *understanding of human reasons* (i.e. *goal-intentions* and *means-beliefs*) can in fact only have the function of a prescientific heuristic precondition or means, as was maintained by Hempel (1948). But this does not mean that the *humanities* could be made *sciences* by reducing their methodology to that of strictly *theoretical explanatory arguments*, for by this turn they lose their special *knowledge-interest*, as we had to notice in reconstructing the scientistical-minded critique or transformation of von Wright's approach.

The truth seems to be that *understanding of reasons as (good or bad) reasons* does not spring, as *causal analysis* in fact does, from an already presupposed theoretical (epistemological) *subject-object-relation* but rather from a—hermeneutically reflected—*subject-cosubject-relation*, i.e. from *communicative experience* of human interaction. Hence it is not enough to make the distinction, along with von Wright, between two different kinds of prescientific world-understanding (and hence data-description) corresponding to two different (viz. "intentional" and "non-intentional") types of "objects" in order to understand the difference between the language-games of natural *science* and *hermeneutics*. For the language-game underlying hermeneutics is *not* primarily one of *describing objects*, i.e. objectified data, *in the light of theories* which *a priori* necessitate the transition from *explicative understanding* to *explanation*; rather it is a language-game (of intersubjective communication) that is at the same time a *practical* pre-condition of the *theoretical objectifying sciences* as human institutions and a *metainstitution* of ultimate *metascientific* reflection upon the *truth-claims* and eventually the *meaning-claims* of the theoretical results of science. I cannot go into these problems in this context but may only state that in both regards the enterprise of describing *objectified* data in the light of theories must *presuppose* a communication-community of intersubjective *understanding* of symbols, intentions, reasons, etc.

Thus the relationship between the language-game of *scientific description and explanation of objectified data* and the language-game of *hermeneutic-understanding* is not one of a *parallelism of two frameworks of objectifying and virtually explanative science,* corresponding respectively to the nonintentional and intentional characters of their objects. Such a view, it seems to me, has always already tacitly absolutized the *scientistic* conception of man's relation to the world, i.e. the epistemology of the theoretical *subject-object-relation.* In contradistinction to this conception the relation between the language-games of science and hermeneutical understanding in my opinion may be characterized in a phenomenologically more adequate way by the category of "complementarity" (as it was used by N. Bohr). That is to say, the *leading interests of knowing,* corresponding to *objectifying science,* on the one hand, and *hermeneutic understanding,* on the other hand, at the same time exclude and complement each other. They exclude each other inasfar as it is not possible to *objectify scientifically* the *behaviour* of a human being in a strict sense so long as one maintains with regard to this human being the relationship of *communicative understanding between co-subjects.* One must suspend this relationship more or less when one tries to objectify human behaviour. But these mutually excluding attitudes and interests of knowing by this very fact also *complement* each other. This might be seen from the fact that objectifying science is only possible if the *explicative understanding of objectified data,* which is mediated by *propositional acts,* may presuppose, a *communicative understanding* between the members of a community of researchers, which is mediated through

171

performative speech acts. That is to say, one scientist alone cannot, in principle, objectify the whole world including all his virtual fellow-scientists.

I think that this *complementarity-situation* (cf. Apel 1972) contains also the key for understanding the truth kernel of the so called *New Dualism* of the Neowittgensteinians. To see this point one needs only to try, in a thought-experiment, to make a transition from asking one's communication-partner for the *reasons* of his opinions or his actions to asking him for the *effective reasons,* i.e. *causes,* of his opinions or actions in order to get a *quasi-causal motivational explanation.*

Let us suppose that both communication-partners are engaged in a psychological experiment about so-called "concept-transfer" in adult persons as regularly stimulated by certain schematic pictures, i.e. that they are both trying to bring about empirically testable *explanations of people's being motivated towards beliefs and actions by controllable environment-stimulations.* Then it seems clear that the communication-partners representing the communication community of scientific researchers may perform their tests upon the test-persons and eventually attain motivational explanations only when they also are able to *communicate about each other's good reasons for beliefs and planned actions.* (This is, by the way, not only an empirical prerequisite but a transcendental-logical one, for the beliefs and experimental actions of scientists presuppose, in principle, inter-subjective agreements about their meaning.) Now, the two fellow-scientists cannot replace their communication about *good reasons* for their beliefs and experimental actions by asking each other for the *effective reasons* of them (although they must take it as a matter of course that intelligible good reasons for beliefs and planned actions may also function as effective reasons in case of performance). For, if they seriously tried to substitute demands for *effective reasons* in the place of demands for *good reasons* they would in fact abolish their language-game of communication about motivational explanations; for they would treat each other like objectified test-persons and for doing so they would presuppose, both of them, a new language-game of communicating about good reasons of beliefs and experimental actions. That is to say, that psychologists *quâ* fellow-scientists *cannot* reduce their own inter-subjective communication about *good reasons* to a communication about the causally effective reasons (motives) of their test-persons or of themselves *quâ* test-persons because this would contradict the

172

situation of *complementarity* between *explanations* (as theoretical objectifying arguments) and *communicative understanding.*

Now, from this thought-experiment it becomes clear that the *complementarity*-situation is in fact the phenomenological basis for the *Neowittgensteinian Dualism,* i.e. for the mutual exclusion of the two different language-games of *reasons* and *causes* respectively. But at the same time it becomes also clear that this "New Dualism" must not be understood as excluding ontologically the function of good reasons as *effective reasons,* i.e. as "causes from freedom" (Kant) or even as causes within the framework of "statistical relevance-explanations" (Salmon, Suppes, Beckermann), which again does not exclude the determination of singular actions by causes from freedom, i.e. by "effective intentions" (Tuomela). From this latter conclusion it follows, however, *that the dualism of language-games corresponding to the complementarity-situation cannot be considered as a sufficient basis for distinguishing the methodology of all types of social science from that of natural science.* Such a "transfer" of the Neowittgensteinian key obviously amounts to a confusion of the point of view of the original *language-game complementarity* with the scientistically prejudiced point of view of *two parallel frameworks of world objectification and theoretical explanation.* It does not take into regard the fundamental epistemic point of view that methods of inquiry and even types of science (in a broad sense) are answers to human *questions* or types of questions and hence to *leading interests of knowledge,* and therefore it cannot take into account the remarkable fact that, whereas natural science, at least physics, clearly corresponds to one leading interest of knowledge, viz. the interest in nomological *explanatory theories,* human individuals and societies may become the topic (to avoid the term "object") of complementary leading interests of knowledge, viz, roughly speaking, *hermeneutic sciences* springing from the interest in reestablishing and/or improving *communicative understanding* of *reasons* (i.e. *intentions, beliefs* etc.) within the framework of a communication-community and, on the other hand, *quasi-nomological (empirical-analytic) social sciences* corresponding to the interest in *quasi-causal statistical relevance-explanations* as a basis for social engineering.

It has to be noticed, however, that the possibility of scientifically objectifying human beings and societies does not amount to simply reducing the methodology of these objectifying (empirical-analytic) sciences to that of the natural sciences. The epistemological and methodological basis situation may rather be characterized by the dialectical circumstance that man, being the *subject* of science,

173

remains a *subject-object* also in case he is scientifically objectified concerning his *habits of action* or *quasi-nature*. The most spectacular and notorious implication of this dialectical feature of the objectifying social sciences is exposed by Mertons's theorem of *selffulfilling or selfdestroying prophecy* in case of predictive applications of quasi-causal explanations.

I nevertheless have pleaded for the claim, defended by the critics of von Wright, that there are *quasi-causal explanations* in the empirical-analytic social sciences that may be treated along with *subsumption-theoretic covering law* explanations rather than with such "teleological explanations" that practically function as *good reasons essays* in the light of practical inferences.

My first reason for insisting on this point is provided by the fact that the usual explanations presented in such types of social science as are presupposed in social technology (including pedagogics based on learning theory) are in fact not primarily interested in expanding or deepening our *understanding* of human reasons, in order to critically compare these reasons as good or bad reasons with our own reasons in case of acting, but rather in *objectifying* and *disposing of* reasons as, at least statistically relevant, *effective conditions* of human behaviour to be supposed by *conditional predictions*. The fact that *intelligible reasons*, supposed as *effective* reasons, should be *good reasons* rather than *bad* ones is not the point of methodologically relevant interest in these quasi-causal explanations but rather taken for granted as a heuristical pre-condition; this is similar, i.e. inversely corresponding, to the fact that the *causal* function of *effective* reasons is taken for granted in case of successful *good reason essays*.

My second reason for pleading for the existence of *quasi-causal explanations* is provided by the fact that by abstraction from *history*, i.e. from epochal events in human life, the *empirical-analytic social sciences* may dispose of human *habits of action* as *quasi-laws* that are *contingent* and *falsifiable* by their deviation from the *ideal universal quasi-law of rational action*, such that the empirically conditioned deviation might itself become the topic of causal explanations. Now, in order to terminologically account for the special status of *quasi-causal explanations* which is different both from that of *naturalistic causal explanations* and from *teleological* (or *rational*) *explanations* in the sense of *good reason essays*, I have decided to call them "motivational explanations", facing the fact that in modern *psychology* this term is applied to a type of theoretical argument which usually comes closer to quasi-causal explanation than to a genuine *good reason essay*, as it is in the foreground of interest e.g. in *history of science*.

Let us now try to sum up the issue of our considerations with regard to the *explanation-understanding* controversy.

The constellation of the three key terms—causal explanation, motivational explanation, and hermeneutic-understanding—should already suggest that I do not think it useful to work with only one dichotomy, say that of *explanation versus understanding* or that of causal *explanation versus teleological* (or *rational* or *intentional*) explanation, in order to deal with the epistemological and methodological questions concerning the relation between *natural* science and the human or social science as a whole.

If one conceives of *social sciences* as the *humanities* (i.e. "Geisteswissenschaften" in German), then I would in fact focus on the old Droysen-Dilthey dichotomy of *explanation versus understanding*, stressing the methodologically relevant character of *understanding* by the attribute "hermeneutic". And I indeed hope to have shown in the present paper that the old dichotomy of *explanation versus (hermeneutic) understanding*, being founded by the *complementarity* between *theoretically objectifying* science and *communicative understanding*, corresponds to the truth-kernel of Neowittgensteinian *New Dualism* and therefore expresses the proper concern of Neowittgensteinians (especially of von Wright's recourse to "practical syllogism") much better than the dichotomy of *causal explanation versus teleological (or rational) explanation*. This latter distinction, at least in von Wright's version, seems to involve the hidden motive of a *scientistic parallelism of theoretically explanatory arguments* and therefore cannot be unambiguously defended against the scientistical-minded critics of Neowittgensteinianism. A special point in my suggestion of a *correspondence* between the truth-kernels of the Droysen-Dilthey dichotomy, Neowittgensteinianism and the complementarity thesis is, of course, made up by the claim that *communicative understanding* (and in its context understanding in the light of *practical inferences*) may and must become a topic of a *hermeneutic methodology* of *hermeneutical sciences* without being transformed into a *theoretical explanatory argument* but including the original version of von Wright's "teleological explanation" that needs no law like sentence as ingredient of its inference schema.

However, to show that a methodology of communicative *understanding*, in contradistinction to that of *theoretical explanation*, is required for dealing with the *humanities*, in accordance with their leading interest of knowing, was only *one* point of my contentions.

The *second* point, trying to do justice to the critics of von Wright and Neowittgensteinianism consists in the claim, that there *is* another type of social science, polar-opposite to the *humanities*, which cannot be adequately understood under the Neowittgensteinian presupposition of two mutually exclusive language games of *causes* and *events*, on the one hand, *reasons* and *actions*, on the other hand. The reason for this fact is provided, on my account, by the circumstance that the *complementarity* between the *leading interests in objectifying explanation* and in *communicative understanding* does not simply correspond to the *ontological* difference between the realm of *nature* and that of *humanity*, but may be brought to bear also *within* the realm of the human or social sciences. Human individuals and human societies may indeed be made the *objects of explanatory arguments and theories* not only concerning their physico-biological aspects but also, in a sense, concerning their historically and mentally mediated *habits of action*, i.e. concerning their historically developed quasi-nature, so to speak. This objectification of humanity must however be performed by the same humanity, which thus far, i.e. in its function as (transcendental) subject of knowledge, can indeed not be objectified by science owing to the complementarity-situation.

Professor Dr K-O. Apel
J. W. Goethe-University of Frankfurt
W. Germany

XIII

REASONS IN ETHICS

L. Bergström

It is often taken for granted that at least some ethical statements can be supported by reasons or evidence of a purely factual kind. In other words, it is assumed that some inferences from factual premises to an ethical conclusion are sound or reasonable, even if they are not deductively valid. This seems to be a very important assumption, both in moral philosophy and in everyday thinking. For all I know, it may be quite true. What bothers me, however, is that I am not sure that I understand it. More precisely, if E is an evaluative or normative ethical statement and F is a purely factual statement, what does it *mean* to say that "F is a reason for E" or that "F supports E" or that "F is a ground for E" or that "F justifies E" or that "F constitutes evidence for E"? This is the question that I propose to discuss in the present paper.

As far as I know, moral philosophers have not paid much attention to this question. I find this rather strange in view of the fact that so much energy has been devoted to the clarification of ethical language. The meaning of the expressions listed above does not seem to be less obscure than the meaning of so-called ethical terms such as "good", "right", and "ought". And the former expressions seem to be just as important in moral philosophy as the latter.

I

I shall begin by making a few preliminary remarks in order to prevent certain possible confusions or misunderstandings. First of all, it should be noticed that the fact that F is a reason for E, or that F constitutes evidence for E, is not identical with the fact that F is a reason for *accepting* E. Nor, of course, is it identical with the fact that F is a reason for *expressing* E in some situation. It is possible

177

that F is a reason for accepting E whenever F is a reason for E. But it does not follow that F is a reason for expressing or communicating E. And if F is a reason for accepting E, or for expressing E, it does not follow that F is also a reason for E. I am primarily interested here in the latter relation, the relation which holds between F and E when F supports E. I shall not be concerned with reasons for accepting or expressing ethical statements.

Secondly, I want to distinguish between reasons for ethical statements and reasons for *doing* something. If E is a norm to the effect that a certain action is right or ought to be done, and if F is a reason for E, then F is perhaps also a reason for doing the action mentioned in E. This seems rather plausible, but it might be doubted. As Sidgwick puts it, "the answer which we really want to the question 'Why should I do it?' is one which does not merely prove a certain action to be right, but also stirs in us a predominant inclination to do the action" (Sidgwick 1907, p. 5). If this is so, F may be a reason for E even though it is not a reason for doing the action mentioned in E, for F may prove this action to be right even though it does not stir any inclination in the agent to do the action. In any case, it seems that there may be reasons for doing a certain action which do not constitute evidence for the norm that this action is morally right or ought to be done. For example, the fact that I want to eat oysters is surely a reason for my ordering oysters in a restaurant, but it is hardly a reason for the statement that I ought to order oysters—especially if this statement is a moral one. Hence, since I am primarily interested in reasons for moral statements, I shall be concerned with reasons for acting only in so far as these also happen to support moral statements.

Thirdly, it might be held that a statement to the effect that F is a reason for E contains the statement that F is true. In particular, when we say, as we often do, that a certain *fact* is a reason for something, it is surely natural to suppose that we are implying that the statement which describes this fact is true. However, I shall pay no further attention to this, since I want to concentrate upon the relation between F and E. For the sake of simplicity, I shall assume that it is not part of the meaning of the expression "F is a reason for E" that F is true.

Fourthly, I shall assume that the *meaning* of "F is a reason for E" is independent of the answers to normative and evaluative questions. Thus, the proponents of different moral systems may use such terms as "reason" and "evidence" in the same sense even if they sometimes or always disagree as to whether a given factual statement *is* a reason for a given ethical statement. Let me try to illustrate this by an example.

Suppose that Jones says that a certain law ouht to be adopted by the society to which he belongs because a great majority of the members of that society wants the law to be adopted. In other words, Jones claims that the factual statement that a majority wants the law to be adopted is a reason for the normative statement that the law ought to be adopted. Smith agrees that a majority wants the law to be adopted, and he is also inclined to agree that the law ought to be adopted, but he does not regard the former statement as a reason for the latter. The point is not, then, that Smith believes that this reason is outweighed by other reasons. He holds that it is not a reason at all.

The case described here seems to be quite realistic, and I think that most of us would say that it involves a disagreement between Smith and Jones. This disagreement *might* be merely verbal; Smith and Jones might be using the term "reason" with different meanings, so that they are not really contradicting each other. In that case, both may of course be right. However, it is surely much more natural to suppose that they *are* contradicting each other; that their disagreement is a genuine one which probably reflects their different moral views, and that one of them is right and the other is wrong. This is indeed the case if they are using the term "reason" in the same sense. In Mill's terminology, they may be using it with the same connotation, but with different denotations. This is both possible and plausible.

In general, then, I wish to discuss the meaning of "reason", not its denotation. And I shall assume that the meaning of this term is morally neutral in a sense in which its denotation is presumably not morally neutral. It may be a moral question to decide whether F is a reason for E, but I shall assume that it is not a moral question to decide what it *means* for F to be a reason for E, and it is this latter question that I wish to discuss here.

II

In order to explain the meaning of a given expression one may try to find some other expression which satisfies the following conditions : (i) it has, at least roughly, the same meaning as the original expression, and (ii) it is, at least in some way, easier to understand than the original expression. This is what I shall try to do. In our case, the original expression is the following :

G

(1) *F* is a reason for *E*.

I shall assume that (1) has the same meaning as

(2) *F* constitutes evidence for *E*.

But (2) cannot be used to explain the meaning of (1), for it is just as difficult to understand (2) as it is to understand (1). The philosophical difficulty is the same in both cases. Hence, the assertion that (1) is synonymous with (2) has no philosophical value. Indeed, I could just as well regard (2) as my original expression.

What I have just said about (2) can also be said about certain other formulations, such as "*F* is a ground for *E*", "*F* supports *E*", "*F* justifies *E*", and so on. It seems that what is required here is some expression which is not *obviously* synonymous with (1) or with these formulations. For if an expression is obviously synonymous with these, it can hardly be more intelligible than they are, and hence it cannot be used to explain their meaning. We might then be inclined to try the following expression :

(3) If *F* is true, then *E* is true.

It might be suggested that the meaning of (1) can be identified with that of (3), and that (3) is more intelligible than (1).

However, (3) is ambiguous. The connective "if ... , then ..." can be interpreted in various ways. If it stands for material implication, then (3) is intelligible enough, but its meaning is different from that of (1). For (3) would then be true whenever *F* is false or *E* is true. And if the connective "if ... , then ..." is taken to express entailment or logical implication, then again (3) is intelligible enough, but it cannot be regarded as synonymous with (1). For it seems that (1), as well as (2), is typically used in cases where the speaker does *not* believe that *F* entails *E*; on the contrary, he is likely to believe (correctly, I should say) that *F* does not entail *E*.

There is one interpretation of (3), though, which seems to make (3) synonymous with (1). This may even be the most natural interpretation. Thus, in a discussion of the connective "if ... , then ...", P. F. Strawson says that "in general its employment in linking two clauses indicates that a statement made by the use of the first would be a *ground* or *reason* for a statement made by the use of the second (Strawson 1952, p. 37, my italics). With this interpretation (3) seems to have the same meaning as (1) and (2). But this does not take us anywhere near a solution of our problem. For if this interpretation is identified by the use of some expression like (1) or (2), it does not help us to clarify the meaning of these expressions. The statement expressed by (1) is not expressed in a more precise way by (3). At best, it is the other way round. Hence, (3) is useless for my purpose here.

At this point, it might be held that even if (1) does not express the statement that F entails E, it is possible to explain the meaning of (1) in terms of entailment. Thus, it might be held that (1) means that E is entailed by the conjunction of F and some "major premise" which is presupposed but not explicitly mentioned. Let us then consider the following formulation :

(4) There is a statement P such that $(P \& F)$ entails E.

As it stands, (4) is clearly not synonymous with (1). This is shown by the fact that (4) is always trivially true. In order to prevent this, certain restrictions have to be put upon P. For example, P should not be logically incompatible with F, and P should not by itself entail E. Moreover, we must require that P is true, for otherwise P could always be taken to be the material implication $(F \supset E)$, which would make (4) true by *modus ponens*. But even if (4) is modified by these restrictions on P, it is still not synonymous with (1). For it would still be true whenever F is false or E is true—in which case we could again let $P = (F \supset E)$. And F is hardly a reason for E simply because F is false or E is true. Hence, further qualifications are needed.

In particular, it is not sufficient that P is true. Hence, we may require that P is also "lawlike" or "necessarily true" in some sense. But neither logical necessity nor physical or natural necessity is suitable here. If it were required that P be a law of logic or a law of nature, most of us would presumably regard the corresponding version of (4) as false whether or not we regard (1) as true. It seems, rather, that the necessity in question would have to be the kind of "moral necessity" which could perhaps be ascribed to *moral principles*. Accordingly, it might be held that the following formulation is synonymous with (1) :

(5) There is a true moral principle P such that P is logically compatible with F, P does not entail E, and $(P \& F)$ entails E.

181

In fact, I am inclined to believe that this proposal would seem quite acceptable to many moral philosophers.

Now I do not wish to deny that (1) is synonymous with (5). But I think it is of some importance to point out that this is no real solution of my problem. For in order to understand (5) one must understand what it means for a statement to be a moral principle, and in order to understand this one has to understand the meaning of expressions like (1). This is so, roughly speaking, because a statement is not a "moral principle" in the relevant sense unless it says something about the reasons for moral statements. A moral principle does not merely say, for example, that every action which has a certain characteristic is morally right. It says something more than this, namely that actions are right *because* they have this characteristic—or, in other words, that a statement to the effect that an action has this characteristic is a *reason* for the statement that it is right. Hence, even if (5) is synonymous with (1), (5) does not provide us with a satisfactory explication of (1).

III

Let us now try another approach to our problem. It is sometimes suggested that there is merely a causal or psychological relation between F and E when F is a reason for E. For example, C. L. Stevenson holds that, in general, "ethical judgments are supported or attacked by reasons related to them psychologically, rather than logically" (Stevenson, 1944, p. 115). Accordingly, it might be held that (1) is synonymous with something like the following expression :

(6) The acceptance of F causes the acceptance of E.

One advantage with this interpretation is that the understanding of (6) does not seem to presuppose the understanding of (1) or (2). The notion of evidence is reduced here to other notions, namely to the notions of acceptance and causation. Hence, if (1) is synonymous with (6), then (6) could really be used to explain the meaning of (1).

But I am inclined to believe that (1) and (2) are very seldom used with the same meaning as (6). For example, the notion of evidence which is relevant in connection with moral principles (in the way indicated above) can hardly be the one expressed by (6). Moral principles do not involve any descriptions of our psychological habits. Moreover, we would surely insist, in general, that the question

182

of whether F is a reason for E is quite independent of the actual psychological effects of accepting F.

It would be more plausible to say that the psychological effects of accepting F *ought* to include the acceptance of E when F is a reason for E. And it might then be held that (1) has the same meaning as

(7) The acceptance of F ought to cause the acceptance of E.

This interpretation has the same advantage as (6) of reducing the notion of evidence to other notions; in this case, the notions of acceptance, causation, and obligation (or value). Unlike (6), however, it is not purely empirical. In this respect, it is similar to (5), and it seems that this is also an advantage, since I want to find an interpretation which is morally neutral in the sense explained in section I.

However, (7) can hardly be synonymous with (1), for it seems that (1) may be true even though (7) is false. From a moral point of view, it does not seem reasonable to maintain that the acceptance of F ought to cause the acceptance of E whenever F is a reason for E. The acceptance of E ought rather to be caused by the acceptance of two statements, namely F and the statement that F is a reason for E (or a corresponding moral principle). If a person does not believe that F is a reason for E—if he is strongly convinced, for example, that F is rather a reason *against* E—then, surely, his acceptance of F ought not to cause his acceptance of E. (Another thing is that it may still be true that he ought to accept E.)

If this argument can be shown to be mistaken, I would argue instead that (7) may be true while (1) is false. It seems quite possible that we ought, in some or most cases, to adopt a moral system which is not really correct. For example, even if utilitarianism is a correct moral system (a set of true moral principles), there may be good utilitarian reasons for adopting a non-utilitarian moral system in most situations of everyday life. If this is so, and if my first argument is incorrect, there are presumably cases in which the acceptance of a certain factual statement F ought to cause the acceptance of an ethical statement E even though F is not really a reason for E. In such cases, (7) would be true while (1) is false.

If both these arguments are mistaken, and if (1) and (7) always have the same truth-value, I would argue that this is because (1) is a reason for (7). And if (1) is a reason for (7), then of course (1) and (7) cannot have the same meaning. In either case, (7) is no solution to my problem.

Someone who accepts my view that (1) may be true even though (7) is false might be inclined to think that some weaker version of (7) is synonymous with (1). The following formulation might then be suggested :

(8) It ought to be the case that everyone who accepts F also accepts E.

It seems that (8) is weaker than (7) in the sense that (7) entails, but is not entailed by, (8). However, (8) is not synonymous with (1). For (8) is true whenever E is a statement which everyone ought to accept, and (1) is clearly not true in every such case. Everything is not a reason for a statement which everyone ought to accept.

Let us now try to exploit a definition which has been put forward in a more traditional epistemological context. According to R. M. Chisholm we may say that one proposition "justifies" another provided the two propositions are such that, for any subject and any time, if the former proposition is evident to that subject at that time, then the latter proposition is evident to that subject at that time (Chisholm 1966, p. 23). The connective "if ..., then ..." in this definition can hardly be taken to express mere material implication, for then every proposition which was never evident to anyone would justify any proposition. This seems absurd. Presumably, the connective should be taken to express some kind of subjunctive implication. If we follow Chisholm's suggestion with this qualification, we might say that (1) is synonymous with

(9) For every subject s and time t, if F were evident to s at t, then E would be evident to s at t.

It should be noticed here that a proposition may be evident to s at t even though it is never accepted, or even contemplated, by s. According to Chisholm, a proposition p is evident to s (at t) provided it satisfies the following conditions : (i) if s were a rational being with purely intellectual concerns, and if s were to choose between believing p and neither believing nor disbelieving p (at t), then he would choose to believe p, and (ii) there is no proposition q such that, if s were a rational being with purely intellectual concerns, and if s were to choose between believing p and believing q (at t), then he would

184

choose to believe q rather than p. In other words, the suggestion that (1) is synonymous with (9) connects the notion of evidence in ethics with the notion of rationality.

However, it seems that (1) may be true in cases where (9) is false. I am not very clear about the notion of rationality, but it seems to be generally believed that rationality is compatible with more than one moral system. Hence, even if F is a reason for E, there is probably some person to whom E would not be evident even if F were evident to him. If such a person were a rational being with purely intellectual concerns, he might nevertheless have certain moral convictions which would make him choose not to believe E even if he would choose to believe F. Hence, (9) can hardly be synonymous with (1).

IV

I shall not make any further attempt here to find a satisfactory explication of (1). In fact, I am inclined to believe that such an explication cannot be found. I suspect that the notion of evidence in ethics must be regarded as unanalysable or irreducible. Of course, I do not claim to have shown this conclusively. Neither have I shown that the notion in question is unintelligible. After all, we have somehow learnt to *use* expressions like (1) in everyday discourse. But we do not all use them in the same way, and there is no guarantee that we use them with the same meaning, or that we ever use them with a definite meaning.

Finally, it should be noticed that much of what I have said here applies primarily to the notion of a *sufficient* or *conclusive* reason. This is the notion which seems to be involved, for example, in the notion of a moral principle which does not admit of any exceptions. However, we often speak of reasons or evidence when we are thinking rather of statements which give *some* support to an ethical statement even though they are clearly or possibly inconclusive. For example, many people would say that the statement "You promised to do this" is a reason for the statement "You ought to do this", even if it is not a conclusive or sufficient reason. The notion of such genuine but possibly inconclusive support seems to be involved, for example, in the notion of a moral rule which states a mere *prima facie* obligation (as well as in the very notion of a *prima facie* obligation).

Now I am inclined to believe that it is at least as difficult to

185

understand this weaker notion as it is to understand the notion of a sufficient reason. In the case of the latter notion, we may perhaps provide at least a *partial* explication by postulating that the statement "*F* is a sufficient reason for *E*" always entails the material implication "*F* is true $\supset$ *E* is true". Obviously, this does not hold for the weaker notion. Moreover, the weaker notion is probably not definable in terms of the stronger. It might be thought that if (1) is merely taken to involve the weaker notion, it could be regarded as synonymous with something like the following formulation :

    (10) There is a factual statement *G* such that (i) *G* is not a sufficient reason for *E*, (ii) the conjunction (*F* & *G*) does not entail *E*, but (iii) the conjunction (*F* & *G*) is a sufficient reason for *E*.

However, (10) is unacceptable as an explication of (1) since, roughly speaking, (*F* & *G*) may contain parts which are quite irrelevant to *E*; in particular, *F* itself may be irrelevant to *E* if *G* has the form (*F* $\supset$ *H*) and *H* is a sufficient reason for *E*. Neither will it do to add the condition that no statement which is logically weaker than (*F* & *G*) is a sufficient reason for *E*. For even if *F* is a reason for *E*, this condition will not be satisfied in cases where there are two or more logically independent sufficient reasons for *E*. Such cases may be morally impossible, but they do not seem to be logically or empirically impossible.

On the other hand, the notion of a sufficient reason is perhaps definable in terms of the weaker notion. Thus, the statement that *F* is a sufficient or conclusive reason for *E* can perhaps also be expressed by the following formulation :

    (11) *F* is a reason for *E*, and every factual statement *G* which is empirically compatible with *F* and which is a reason against *E* (i.e., a reason for $\sim E$) is such that the conjunction (*F* & *G*) is also a reason for *E*.

But (11) can of course only be understood by someone who already understands the notion of a (possibly inconclusive) reason. And I am still not sure that I do.

Professor Lars Bergström
University of Uppsala, Sweden

L. BERGSTRÖM

REFERENCES

Chisholm, R. M. (1966) *Theory of Knowledge*, Englewood Cliffs: Prentice-Hall, Inc.
Sidgwick, H. (1907) *The Methods of Ethics*, London: Macmillan & Co., Ltd.
Stevenson, C. L. (1944) *Ethics and Language*, New Haven: Yale University Press.
Strawson, P. F. (1952) *Introduction to Logical Theory*, London: Methuen & Co., Ltd.

XIV

CONFORMITY AS A CONDITION FOR HUMAN INTENTION

A. W. Müller

I

IN HIS BOOK *Thought and Action* (1959), Stuart Hampshire suggests "that there is no limit to what a man can try to do; he can try to do anything that he chooses, provided that he has some idea of how it might possibly be done" (p. 170). Taken one way, this is the affirmation of a truism : Any expression which is of a *form* that will combine with "So-and-so has tried to—" will, of necessity, mention something a man can try to do, or be, if he has an idea of how to achieve it. (Hampshire's point, by the way, is one about the difference between trying and achieving). What I have quoted can, however, be taken in a much more controvertible way. It can be taken to mean, or to imply, that there are no *a priori* limitations on the possibilities of conjoining into a *story* of a man's trying and doing any *series* of expressions which, singly, are coherent ascriptions to a man of an action or an attempt at an action, and jointly, do not imply any physical impossibility. I have no reason to think that Hampshire wishes what he says to be interpreted in this way. I do think that philosophers of an empiricist persuasion would tend to hold a view of the will which allowed of no limitations of the kind in question. Whether or not I am right about this, it is worth asking *what* makes the second way of taking Hampshire's words controvertible and *what* might be said against the view of the human will which it represents.

There may be different routes by which we might hope to arrive at an answer to these questions. One promising route seems to me to be an argument to the effect that the members of a linguistic community must agree, to some extent, in their aims, interests and intentions, if their behaviour is to be describable in terms of aims, interests and intentions at all. If there must be a minimum amount of such conformity in a man's life, this means that his ability to decide for himself what to aim at presupposes a certain sharing of aims, interests and intentions, though it may not mean a limitation on his liberty to set himself ever so uncommon an objective at any given time.

I am going to be concerned with the conditions of application of a whole family of related concepts which all characterize a man's behaviour by relating actions of his to something that he *wants* and in terms of which he can give an *account* of them. What a man tries to do, or to be, is his aim in what he actually does; the concept of an aim largely coincides with those of end, purpose and goal; when I (seriously) try to X, I intend to X; my aims, ends, goals are things I intend; my intending to X accounts for what I do in three ways : I may do what I do in order to X, or my intention to X (e.g. : not to take any steps in a certain matter) may dispose me *not* to do certain things or just to express that intention, or what I do may be what I intend to do—my X-ing is intentional; the somewhat vague notion of interest indicates relevance to a goal or intention. Among aims I shall include conditional aims, i.e. tendencies to intend this or that under given conditions. I shall try to steer clear of an account of how, precisely, all these concepts interrelate, and hope that nothing in my arguments depends on differences that I do not make explicit. I.e. I believe that my minimum conformity thesis holds, indiscriminately, of human intentions, ends, goals, aims, purposes and interests.

What gives rise to the supposition that these are not subject to any condition of conformity? A human, it might be urged, is essentially free to decide what he will go for. He may be driven by diverse desires and he may give in to custom and conventions, but he can, in principle, make up his own mind whichever way he likes. There are, no doubt, all sorts of factors to account for the fact that people do not come up with totally exotic intentions and interests, but this is an empirical issue which in no way affects the range of possible applications of the *concepts* of intention and interest. Any state, activity or act of mine which I can conceive of myself as contributing towards or performing can be the object of an intention of mine, and if the *nature* of a content of intention is delimited in this way, there will be no further limits on the contents of a number of simultaneous or successive intentions, except that simultaneous or successive conceivability of the corresponding fulfilments is demanded.

189

I am going to assume, not to argue, that the concept of intention requires the possibility of ascribing intentions to a man, on the whole correctly, on the basis of his verbal and non-verbal behaviour. This may seem a large assumption to some. Maybe it will itself gain some plausibility as I approach my more modest aim of drawing consequences for the possible range of a man's objectives from that assumption. Three types of basis for ascribing intentions to a human being seem to be constitutive of the concept of intention : (1) Observing what a man is doing, I am able, in general, to name intentional actions and activities of his and thereby ascribe to him intentions to do these things. (2) On the basis of the same kind of observation, together with knowledge or assumptions about his beliefs, I very frequently form a judgment as to the (further) intention with which he does what he is doing. (3) There are expressions of intention in language (including gestures) which, on the one hand, supplement the evidence in both of the two preceding types of case ("I am doing—", and "I am doing this in order to—", respectively), and, on the other hand, are the decisive evidence for very general policies and for intentions for the future, which do not in any direct way show up in, or affect, a person's present observable behaviour ("I intend to—"). It is the fact that any human intention can find expression in words, which seems to give further support to the idea that there are no limits to the originality of a man's intentions : There are no limits to the originality of meaningful combinations of words, and any such combination which is of the form of an expression of intention will be a possible *prima facie* ground for attributing the corresponding intention. I do not think that I have conclusive arguments to establish, against this kind of claim, my minimum conformity thesis. But I shall now try to make it plausible by considering more closely, from various points of view, the conditions under which we are justified in ascribing an intention to somebody.

II

Let us start from the kind of case where someone, A, does X in order to Y. How can the intention be known? We see him do X, let us suppose, and he tells us that Y-ing is his objective in doing it. The description of someone as engaged in an activity or action X is itself a topic that invites philosophical questions in the area of our topic : the X-ing must be intentional. At present, however, I want to ask : What are the conditions that enable us to understand him as expressing an intention to Y? His utterance would not be such an expression unless his X-ing could, at least in his opinion, contribute to his Y-ing. He may, of course, express such an opinion. But again, he could not be meaning what he means by his utterance unless certain conditions were satisfied.

It might be said that it is pretty easy to decide whether a person is using a language that one understands and that the supposition that he is using coherent sentences of this language without their usual meaning is on the whole, ridiculous. But is this observation to the point? It is indeed true that we should be extremely puzzled if we were presented with a substantial sequence of marks, or of sounds, that, by itself, *could* be interpreted in such a way as to present a meaningful series of connected sentences of a language but, to all appearances, lacked any appropriateness or relevance to a context, or could not even be traced back to a language user. So we do not hesitate to take an utterance of a sequence of English assertoric sentences as expressing judgments of the utterer—though we should not forget that lunatics as well as children and foreigners who have not mastered the language do produce English sentences that do not express the judgments they are, by the rules of English, designed to express. Now we can ask for an *account* of what it is to take an utterance as expressing a judgment, even if it were inexplicable or, in some sense, impossible that apparent assertions should not really be assertions. So we can ask for the conditions under which something expresses a belief even if, for whatever reasons, we are entirely certain that the conditions are satisfied. For *what is it* that we are then certain of? What gives the noises or marks in question the quality of an assertion if it is not the mere fact that they conform to a syntactical pattern? How is that meaning which we attribute to sentences out of context, to be described? If we are asked to give an account of what a typewriter is, our answer must explain how it works and what it is used for. We cannot confine ourselves to a description of its construction, even though we may safely assume that the universe does not contain an object that looks like a typewriter but has not come to exist in the context of a production which was geared to the characteristic employment of typewriters. In a similar way we can ask ourselves what goes into an account of assertoric sentences (and of expressions of intention). What is involved in someone's speaking a language in which intentions can be communicated, and what is involved in someone's using this language to speak about his intentions on a particular occasion?

191

A partial answer to this question will involve us in considerations of goals and interests and thus, I hope, throw light on our topic.

If my investigation concentrates on conditions for *assertoric* discourse, this is because, on the one hand, the communication of intentions heavily relies on it : Assertoric sentences express a person's beliefs about the situation to be affected, and his expectations about the situation to be effected, by what he is up to, as well as his ideas about the way his action would contribute towards a change from the one to the other. Unless this type of utterance is at his disposal, declarations of intention cannot be attributed to him, even though "I am X-ing (with a view to Y-ing)" and "I am going to X" are not, themselves, typical forms of *assertoric* sentences. A second reason for concentrating on assertoric discourse is the fact that *its* dependence on aims and interests is, from a certain, perhaps plausible, point of view, particularly unexpected, and an account of this dependence, therefore, I hope, will be all the more illuminating.

III

In our example A says something which means that his X-ing contributes to his Y-ing. The conditions under which A's utterance means this do not just relate to its relationship with the immediate context. They are, rather, a matter of how his utterances are and have been related to his preceding observations and operations, to subsequent behaviour and, in particular, to other utterances, both his own and other people's. We may, I think, take this much for granted without investigating the intriguing details of a theory of the meaning of assertoric sentences. It is important to see that a correlation between a sentence and the kind of surroundings that its utterer is typically aware of will not do as a basis for explaining the meaning even of the most fundamental sort of assertoric sentence. I will only hint at some of the reasons why an account on these lines is insufficient for just these sentences, which, following Quine, we may call observation sentences, and whose meanings are presupposed in those of a more complex nature, like ones of the form "X-ing is a means to Y-ing".

(1) What gives rule-governed reactions to different types of situations the character of assertions? The concept of verification does not get us any further here; for how do we recognize a procedure as an attempt at *verification*? Consider a man who plays a piano sonata in accordance with a score, and is prompted by what he

perceives to play what he plays. Why are the sounds he makes *not* part of a language and, in particular, not assertions warranted, verified and corrected by looking at the score?

(2) Apart from the learning stage, sentences are *not* normally used when correlated situations (by reference to which they would be conclusively verified) are observable. Can we then give an account of their meaning by merely attending to those correlations?

(3) The relevance of such a correlation to the meaning of a sentence consists in the fact that questions of the justification for uttering a sentence are partly questions of the occurrence (or possibility) of characteristic perceptions and observations. But this raises the question : What—apart from, possibly, an utterance of the very sentence in question—is decisive evidence for the utterer's being aware of a situation?

(4) A sentence might be correlated with a situation in virtue of any number of aspects of that situation, and a repetition of one and the same sentence on a number of occasions does not essentially alter this state of affairs. Reality is not structured for us independently of our use of language. But *how* is *language* supposed to mark out features of our surroundings?

All the questions I have raised in giving reasons against a correlation theory of sentence meaning, point in one direction. They must all be answered by invoking the interests, goals and intentions with which the members of a linguistic community make use of assertoric language in general, of particular sentences on particular occasions, and, more fundamentally, of the reality with which occasion sentences are correlated.

Thus, the concepts by which we pick out objects, properties, events and so forth are formed, largely, in accordance with the practical interests we take in our surroundings. It is in connexion with manipulating things, being acted upon, preparing for either, and so on, that we come to distinguish unities in our experience, isolate kinds of changes, raise questions of identity and difference, understand the pointing gesture, etc., and no use of language can be completely cut off from its role in the service of those interests, without which the concepts which structure our experience would lose their interest and cease to be recognizable in the occurrence of their verbal expressions. (Remember that a language must be learnable!) The interest of an assertoric sentence is, in part, the interest we take in the situation which it describes (or purports to describe). The rule-governed utterance of a sentence—unlike the piano performance—

is what it is (viz. an assertion) in virtue of the differences it tends to make to subsequent behaviour, i.e., in the case of observation sentences, in virtue of its function, very roughly speaking, as a proxy for an experience of what it describes. With this is, of course, connected the fact that a sentence will *not* normally be used in a situation which would allow its immediate verification or falsification. Further, the relevance of speakers' perceptions, or awareness conditions, to determining what their sentences mean, is, *in part*, cancelled by the fact that perception and awareness are exhibited in acting and refraining from action, i.e. in the very same phenomena by which the role of those sentences is recognized, Characteristic awareness conditions do not, therefore, make a contribution to sentence meaning quite independently from characteristic behavioural consequences, and this seems to be a further difficulty for a correlation theory.

IV

Now behaviour and interest can be relevant, in the ways suggested, to the existence of sentence meaning and of communication about our surroundings only if these surroundings are not entirely neutral with respect to the goals that guide attention and intention in our dealings with them; or, rather : only if our goals are not neutral with respect to the surroundings. Some features of our experience must have for us a *"meaning"* different from that which others have and "mean", in a practical sense, this rather than that. The users of the language must share a set of goals and interests as well as non-goals and non-interests in virtue of which there are limits to and convergences in the ways in which they would treat certain objects, properties, situations and occurrences, in the ordinary course of events. We may think, here, of primitive actions and responses, like taking, warding off, looking at, going towards, and so on, in connexion with which we learn to recognize, and to talk about, different elements of our environment, respectively; but also of what we think worth talking about or knowing, of how we treat children and old people, of what is done in public and what is not, and of a host of more or less complex patterns of behaviour tendencies which form the background to our understanding of a man's words and deeds on almost any given occasion.

Such considerations may, by the way, throw some light on an aspect of the so-called "principle of charity", which David Lewis, in an article on *Radical Interpretation*, puts forward in this form (p. 336) : "Karl should be represented as believing what he ought to believe and as desiring what he ought to desire. And what is that? In our opinion, he ought to believe what we believe and he ought to desire what we desire, or perhaps what we would have desired in his place." Unless something like this attitude (which does not seem to bear a very close resemblance to charity) were, *conceptually*, presupposed in any hope that a linguist might have of identifying and understanding the foreign language, it would be sheer provincialism, and the principle had better be called one of self-love.

It might be said that such actions as the taking, and the warding off, of appropriate things are essential for survival, so why have recourse to conditions for linguistic communication in order to show the need for shared aims? Well, it is true enough that without having certain specifiable goals, humans would not survive, and that, *therefore*, on evolutionary grounds, so to speak, members of a human community will, on the whole, share these goals. Their connexion with survival and, hence, with the concept of a human life may not be a contingent one, but it would not yield a basis for limiting the applicability of the *concept* of intention. It is this kind of limitation which I claim has to be granted because expressions of intention, and therefore human intentions, are embedded in a language, and that means : in a rule-governed communal activity which cannot get off the ground, or continue to exist, unless tendencies to treat one's environment in certain standard ways, are shared. It is of no interest to our enquiry whether such conformity is guaranteed by natural selection or anything else. Shared aims may in fact be *learnt* together with the acquisition of language. (The behaviour constitutive of the learning would not itself then be a pursuit of such aims, to begin with!)

An attempt to visualize a *human* life whose interests, goals and intentions showed no conformity with its social environment would have to result in a picture of a man, or human organism (I will suppose him to be kept alive, somehow), whose behaviour would not provide a background which gave sense to his "utterances", among which expressions of intention were to be found. Non-conformity is, of course, a matter of degrees, and there are transitions of a quantitative as well as of a qualitative nature between styles of life from autonomous *via* original, funny and deviant to incomprehensible (in some literal sense). But it might be sensible to distinguish, for example, two kinds of madness from the point of view of an

195

ascription of intentions : Some lunatics can be said to behave and talk in a manner that reveals *out of the way* intentions, and this provides one sense in which we may not understand what a man is up to in various situations. But could not someone's lunacy consist in a manner of behaving and talking which allowed, or perhaps demanded, a refusal to describe him as expressing intentions at all? Here, we would not understand what he was up to in a different sense : we would give up trying to square his words with his behaviour by assuming misperceptions, extraordinary beliefs, misunderstanding of information, faults of memory, changes of mind, etc., *and uncommon interests and aims*; we would not have, in his verbal and non-verbal behaviour, the criteria by which to draw the required distinctions, so we would not recognize any utterance or gesture or writing of his as expressing an intention since, *if* we did, we should not know how to choose between all sorts of different and mutually exclusive interpretations to be put on the whole context (e.g. : misuse of a word—lie—interfering policy—thinking the intended thing impossible . . .). In a sense, such a man would not *be* "up to" anything.

V

Why, we may ask, can we not imagine a man whose behaviour showed no conformity with standard goals and interests but did bear out the presence of such intentions as were, to all appearances, expressed in his utterances? This, I admit, is a natural question to ask. It also seems difficult to answer because, if I am right, we cannot have an idea of what we are being asked to imagine and, yet, we seem to have an intuitive understanding of the alleged description. The best I can do by way of a tentative reply is to make a number of observations on some aspects of the connexion between language, behaviour and intention.

(1) Remember that my claim is not that a sane man cannot play the fool once in a while or have a number of idiosyncracies. My claim is that there must be a level of conformity, which I am unable to determine any further, below which a man's behaviour cannot drop without ceasing to exhibit human intentions.

(2) Can behaviour "bear out" the presence of intentions expressed in a man's utterances? To some extent : yes. But (a) the question of a man's intentions often cannot be settled by observing his movements : Is he aware of what he is doing, and is he doing it on

purpose? And which descriptions of what he is doing will the answers to these two questions relate to? Is his action a means to a further end, and to which end? Is it this or rather that aspect of his activity that he is interested in? What are his plans for tomorrow? for the future? for the organization of the factory? Was there an intention which he has failed to carry out? Answers to questions like these will have to rely on what the man says; his behaviour can contradict, but scarcely provide a warrant for, such answers. And (b), although what he says cannot be "borne out" more than partially by his behaviour, the fact *that* he says something, and that, *inter alia*, he expresses particular intentions, has to be borne out by an overall correspondence between the words and sentences he utters and the rest of his behaviour.

(3) Would it be possible to describe, as a first move, those of a man's intentions, aims, interests etc. which we could identify without depending on his utterances, and, as a second move, those, if any, which were expressed in, or inferable from, his utterances? If so, we might be able to recognize a man as speaking and understanding our language, although the behaviour that went with his hearing and uttering pieces of that language in no way conformed to ours; for we could then see, e.g., his reaction to something he was told in the light of *his* interests in what was being talked about. Once assured, in this way, of his mastery of the language, we could gather from what he said whatever further odd goals might govern his life. For a number of reasons, that I shan't discuss here, I do not believe in that division of human aims and interests into those that are, and those that are not, tied to the use of language. Let me just say a few things in reply to the argument drawn from this division.

First, it seems very doubtful to me that we can conceive of a pattern of (non-verbal) behaviour which we would treat as embodying interests, aims and intentions none of which we shared. If we try to do it we find that, e.g., the recurring result of various sequences of movements cannot, *as such*, be called a goal. If we cannot see it as the point of anything or as having a point, if it is no part of a context resembling a human or even animal life, why call it a goal rather than just a freak of nature? Why, indeed, assume that the type of result we have picked out corresponds to one type of situation in the scheme of his supposed intentions?

Secondly, the language required for the existence of human intentions is itself, to some extent, a matter of shared goals. Communication demands readiness to inform, a specific channelling of attention, considerations of relevance, and so on—all of which involve a sharing of aims and interests. Where we cannot take an overall conformity in a man's aims and interests for granted, and have to get clearer about these before we can even hope to understand the significance of his utterances and actions, language cannot serve its function as usual; so in making the supposition of a totally "non-conformist" life (with intentions expressed in language), we should in any case be envisaging a use for language, if such there be, that differed substantially from its actual role in our lives. The use of language, especially in communication, serves common interests, but to do this it also has to rely on the *presumption* of a huge background of interests and non-interests of the participants that cannot be *revealed* in either words or deeds on a given occasion, which will, after all, be delimited in respect of time and possibilities of enquiry. But what should we say if someone did not conform with any of our interests and aims but uttered sentences which, by the rules of our language, seemed to express (non-conforming) intentions on which his behaviour did not, on the whole, cast any doubt? Well, what should we say if an oak tree took to producing noises which, by the rules of our language, seemed to give true reports on its constitution and its environment? I mean to say that the question whether someone speaks our language or not would have to be decided not just on the strength of a narrowly delimited kind of employment of words but by taking into account his behaviour in the context of all sorts of occurrences of those same words and his use of them in all sorts of surroundings. He cannot, for example, have grasped the point of basic assertoric sentences without an awareness of standard goals and interests of the people who use them; and it is hard to see how he could show any such awareness without, to some extent, sharing them and cooperating the way we do. A similar point could be made about the conditions for his ability to identify *actions* the way we do within the chaos of our bodily movements.

VI

Let me, once more, pick up the topic of assertoric sentences. It is difficult to give an accurate account of how intentions, aims and interests contribute to the meanings of such sentences. This is so for the following reason : An understanding of any *particular* sentence S can, in general, be based on an overall mastery of assertoric discourse and an acquaintance with the contribution made by the constituents of S to the use of other sentences. It is that overall mastery of a language which involves attitudes of a practical sort. To use a picture : The meanings of the assertoric sentences of a language form, as it were, a structure supported, by *inter alia*, standard intentions, aims and interests in such a way that supporting elements (a) relate to different sentences in different degrees of directness and (b) can be withdrawn, at least temporarily, at a limited number of points at any time without the structure collapsing. (So that, by a familiar fallacy, the impression can arise that *no* such supporting elements are needed and that each part of the structure is held in its place just by being linked to others.) As a result, an account of the meaning of a sentence S will, typically, be complicated by its reference to an open set of different aims etc. that are, by themselves and in relation to indefinitely many circumstances, appropriate, in varying degrees, (a) to an utterance of, and (b) to a reaction to, S. However, a general argument concerning the role of aims etc. as indispensable supports of the structure of assertoric sentence meanings as a whole seems to me to present less of a problem.

Suppose that intentions are not constitutive of the functioning of assertoric discourse. This means that the connexion between what users of the language say and what they do can be completely random. We can, therefore, suppose that people drop truths (and perhaps some falsehoods as well) about the location of telephone directories, imminent thunderstorms and the decidability of theories, whatever the environment of their utterances—whatever, in particular, the activities that surround and do not surround them. This, it might seem, would just be a very odd and unlikely use of language, but an imaginable one. I think it is clearly not imaginable. No use of language has been specified in the alleged supposition. If any such use had been specified, it would, as I have hinted before, have to be learnable by someone watching it. The meanings of sentences of that language—as specified, e.g., in a translation—would have to be determined by the circumstances of their occurrence. But, *ex hypothesi*, there are no circumstances characteristic of particular types of utterance and, *a fortiori*, no circumstances revealing rules of employment.

Although this kind of argument does not say anything about a specific practical significance constitutive of particular parts of speech, it may be possible to trace down to certain kinds of expression part of the support which, in a language like English, sentence meaning receives from standard aims and interests. I am, primarily, thinking of words relating to elements of our surroundings which have a set significance for our lives. This significance may be due to their natural disposition to affect us favourably or adversely—as is the case, e.g., with milk, the weather and human character traits; or to a function men have given the thing in working on, or producing, it for that purpose, or in setting it apart for the job by a convention—fields, machines and human symbols are cases in point. The use of our expressions for such things reflects the direction of our interests in them. This means not that every occurrence of them is somehow connected with a characteristic interaction of speakers or hearers with their surroundings, but that a person has not grasped the rules of their use unless he is aware of the interests that we characteristically take in the objects, events etc., which they signify. And this awareness cannot, in turn, show up just in what he *says*: otherwise we should be going round in a circle, since what he says will, itself, have to belong to the kind of language whose mastery is under discussion. It is, moreover, clear that there can be such expressions only because a lack, in any given instance, of the characteristic interest is the exception rather than the rule among the people who use them.

I think the meaning of so-called functional terms and others of the kind I have been speaking about, and the evaluative language that goes with them, might, profitably, be discussed on the assumption that the use of such terms, along with those parts of language that are concerned with pain, comfort and a lot of other things, reveals *points of concentration* of a general dependence of assertoric discourse, and of language generally, on interests and aims that give point and meaning to it. The amount of practical agreement on which language rests and which it reflects carries over, as a kind of prior limitation, or minimum conformity, to what is going to be describable as a history of a person's intentions. For intentions do not exist apart from that language, and they relate to a reality our conceptualization of which is incompatible with its indifference to them. If this is right, the concepts of human intention and also, therefore, of free will seem to be incompatible with assumptions of arbitrariness, indifference, and complete independence from accepted goals, which have, at times, been associated with them.

Dr Anselm W. Müller
Universität Trier

A. W. MÜLLER

WORKS REFERRED TO

Hampshire, Stuart (1959, ³1965): *Thought and Action*. London: Chatto and Windus.
Lewis, David (1974) *Synthese* 27, 331–344.

XV

"TWO DOGMAS" REVISITED

H. Putnam

I BELIEVE that the time has come to take another look at Quine's celebrated article[1] "Two Dogmas of Empiricism". The analysis of this article that is usually offered in philosophy seminars is very simple : Quine was attacking the analytic-synthetic distinction. His argument was simply that all attempts to define the distinction are *circular*. I think that this is much too simple a view of what was going on. (The continuing recognition of the great importance of "Two Dogmas" shows that at some level *many* readers must be aware that something deep and momentous for philosophy was going on.)

I shall argue that what was importantly going on in Quine's paper was also more subtle and more complicated than Quine and his defenders (and not just the critics) perceived. Some of Quine's arguments were directed against one notion of analyticity, some against another. Moreover, Quine's arguments were of unequal merit. One of the several notions of analyticity that Quine attacked in "Two Dogmas of Empiricism" was close to one of Kant's accounts of analyticity (namely, that an analytic judgement is one whose negation reduces to a contradiction), or, rather, to a "linguistic" version of Kant's account : a sentence is analytic if it can be obtained from a truth of logic by putting synonyms for synonyms. Let us call this the *linguistic* notion of analyticity. Against this notion, Quine's argument is little more than that Quine cannot think how to define "synonymy". But Quine also considers a very different notion—the notion of an analytic truth as one that is *confirmed no matter what*. I shall contend that this is the traditional notion of aprioricity, or rather, *one* of the traditional notions of aprioricity. This notion, or variants thereof, has played a central role in all of philosophy since the ancients, and in all the different branches of philosophy. More-over, I think that Quine's attack on this notion was correct. And

202

Quine's argument against *this* notion was not at all concerned with circularity of definitions.

If I am right, Quine is a philosopher of historic importance. He is of historic importance because he was the first philosopher of the top rank both to reject the notion of aprioricity and at least to sketch an intelligible conception of methodology without aprioricity. Of course, if I am wrong and there is such a thing as *a priori* truth, then I am doubtless overestimating Quine's importance in the history of philosophy. There are some philosophers in the history of philosophy whose importance does not very much depend upon their being *right*. But Quine's importance does, I think, depend to a large measure upon his being right in one central claim, a claim which he expressed by saying that there is no sensible distinction between analytic and synthetic truths but which he should have expressed by saying that there is no sensible distinction between *a priori* and *a posteriori* truths.

Review of Quine's arguments. At a superficial level, what is going on in "Two Dogmas of Empiricism" looks quite simple, as we remarked above. Quine is going to show us that there is no sense to be made of the notion of analyticity by showing that all of the suggested definitions lead in circles. But (as Grice and Strawson long ago pointed out[2]) it is puzzling why this is supposed to be a good argument. Could it not, after all, just be the case that the various members of the family of linguistic notions to which the notion of analyticity belongs are not definable in terms of or reducible to other, non-linguistic notions? If this is the case, then something more doubtless needs to be said about the status of such linguistic notions and, perhaps, about the status of linguistic theory; but a mere demonstration of definitional circularity would hardly seem to be enough to overthrow as widely accepted and used a notion as the notion of analyticity.

It is as Quine begins to carry out his program of showing that the various suggested definitions of analyticity are not satisfactory that things get more interesting. For it is not hard to see that the definitions Quine assembles for attack could not possibly be definitions of one and the same notion, however vague.

Thus, the first major notion of analyticity that Quine considered in his paper was the traditional notion of a statement that is "true by definition". Quine suggested that this notion might be clarified, given the notion of *synonymy*, in the following way : a statement is analytic if it can be turned into a truth of formal logic by substituting synonyms for synonyms. But, Quine argued, the notion of *synonymy* is hopelessly vague. The only evidence that Quine produced to support this remarkable claim was that he, Quine, could not clarify the notion in a few pages. Given that the even more basic linguistic notion of *grammaticality* has not been satisfactorily clarified in many pages by many authors to the present day, and that no one proposes to do linguistics without the notion, it is clear that Quine presented a bad argument against this particular notion of analyticity.[3]

In saying that Quine's argument was a bad argument, I am not proposing to present a theory of synonymy here, and, in any case, I do not possess a complete and satisfactory theory. But, in a paper I wrote many years ago[4] I outlined a theory that does explain the analyticity of such statements as "All bachelors are unmarried", "All vixens are foxes", etc. The idea, in a nutshell, is that there is an exceptionless "law" associated with the noun "bachelor", viz. that someone is a bachelor *if and only if* he has never been married; an exceptionless law associated with the noun "vixen", viz. that something is a vixen *if and only if* it is a female fox; etc. Moreover, this exceptionless law has, in each case, two important characteristics : (1) that no other exceptionless "if and only if" statement is associated with the noun by speakers; and (2) that the exceptionless "if and only if" statement in question is a *criterion*, that is, speakers can and do tell whether or not something is a bachelor by seeing whether or not it is an unmarried man; whether or not something is a vixen by seeing whether or not it is a female fox; etc. (An operational procedure for telling whether or not such an "if and only if" statement is functioning as a criterion was suggested in my paper. I contended that only a few hundred words in a natural language have this "one-criterion" character—most words are either associated with *no* exceptionless criterion, or with more than one. And I further suggested that all clear cases of analyticity involve these special few hundred words).

In a more recent publication,[5] I also present the beginnings of a theory of meaning, in terms of a "causal" theory of reference and a theory of what I call *stereotypes*, which can, I hope, provide an account of synonymy for the natural kind words, at least. It is on the basis of this research that I feel optimistic about the legitimacy and linguistic usefulness of the notion of synonymy, whether we have a good "definition" or not.

In the section of his paper entitled "The Verification Theory and Reductionism", Quine moves after a different target, and it is here that the style of his argument becomes quite different. In this section of his paper, Quine first sketches the view of the Vienna Circle. On this view (as Quine explains it), statements have a meaning by being reducible to statements about sense experience. This view went well with the view that each meaningful statement has its own individual range of confirming and disconfirming experiences. Analytical truths are simply those statements which have the universal range of confirming experiences, that is, which are confirmed no matter what.

But why should this concept, the concept of a statement which is confirmed no matter what, be considered a concept of *analyticity*? Confirmation, in the Positivist sense, has something to do with rational belief. A statement which is highly confirmed is a statement which it is rational to believe, or rational to believe to a high degree. If there are indeed statements which have the maximum degree of confirmation in all circumstances, then these are simply truths which it is *always rational to believe*, nay, more, truths which it is never rational to even begin to doubt. Many philosophers have believed that there are such truths. Perhaps this is what Aristotle thought a *first principle* was like; more likely it is what Descartes thought a *clear and distinct* idea was like. On the face of it, then, the concept of a truth which is confirmed no matter what is not a concept of *analyticity* but a concept of *aprioricity*. Yet both Quine and the Positivists did take this to be a concept of *analyticity*. Why they did is a question to which I shall return.

Quine's argument against the notion of a truth which is *confirmed no matter what*, is not an argument from the circularity of definitions. Quine's argument is an argument from what is clearly a normative description of the history of modern science. Let me quote it in full :[6] "Any statement can be held true come what may if we make drastic enough adjustments elsewhere in the system. Even a statement very close to the periphery can be held true in the face of recalcitrant experience by pleading hallucination or by amending certain statements of the kind called logical laws. Conversely, by the same token, no statement is immune to revision. Revision even of the logical law of the excluded middle has been proposed as a means of simplifying quantum mechanics; and what difference is there in principle between such a shift and a shift whereby Keppler superceded Ptolemy, or Einstein Newton, or Darwin Aristotle?"

Notice what Quine is saying here. First he is saying that proposals to use nonstandard logics in quantum mechanics cannot be ruled out by any legitimate principle of scientific method. He is saying that the fallibilism which Peirce recognized as contributing essentially to the success of modern science extends also to the laws of logic. He is not just making a sociological remark to the effect that some scientists and some philosophers of science are willing to consider revision of logical laws for the sake of simplifying physical theory as a whole; he clearly thinks that it is right, fitting, and proper that they should be willing to allow such a possibility. Open-mindedness even to the extent of being prepared to revise logical laws is necessary in the scientific enterprise. If this is right, then the laws of logic are not principles that a rational man is *forbidden* to revise. They are not *clear and distinct ideas*. They are not *a priori* truths.

Secondly, Quine is pointing out that previous revolutions have required us to give up principles that were once regarded as *a priori*. And thirdly, in this trenchant paragraph, he is suggesting that the proposal to use a non-standard logic in quantum mechanics is not fundamentally *different* from the proposal to use non-Euclidean geometry in the theory of space-time, which has been accepted since Einstein's General Theory of Relativity.

In short, Quine is saying that the history of science, properly understood, leaves no room for *this* notion of an "analytic" statement, that is, for the notion of an *a priori* or *unrevisable* statement.

Quine strikes the same note in other papers, although always with unfortunate brevity. In "The Scope and Language of Science"[7] he writes, "We have reached the present stage in our characterization of the scientific framework not by reasoning *a priori* from the nature of science qua science, but rather by seizing upon traits of the science of our day. Special traits thus exploited include the notion of physical object, the four-dimensional concept of space-time, the classical mold of modern classical mathematics, the true-false orientation of standard logic, and indeed extensionality itself. One or another of these traits may change as science advances. Already the notion of a physical object, as an intrinsically determinate portion of the space-time continuum, squares dubiously with modern developments in quantum mechanics. Savants there are who even suggest that the findings of quantum mechanics might best be accommodated by a revision of the true-false dichotomy itself." And in "Carnap and Logical Truth" Quine attacks the disinterpretation of non-Euclidean geometry, writing "the status of an interpreted non-Euclidean geometry differs in no basic way from the original status of Euclidean geometry."[8] I believe that Quine's methodological argument against aprioricity is a correct one, and I shall try to spell it out below. But first let me deal with the question I raised above : Why did Quine think that being-confirmed-no-matter-what is a notion of *analyticity*?

He thought so because the Positivists, whom he was attacking, held that to fix a statement's range of confirming experiences is to fix its *meaning*, and that this meaning-fixing is done by *stipulation*. As a part of their view, the Positivists held that *a priori* statements (statements with the universal range of confirming experiences) are *true by meaning alone*. And since truth by virtue of meaning is analyticity, it followed (for the Positivists) that the aprioricity is analyticity.

Another way to put the same point is this : the Positivists believed that what determines the range of confirming instances is a set of *conventions*. They believed not only that there are *a priori* truths, but that these truths are simply statements true by stipulation or convention.

In "Two Dogmas of Empiricism", Quine alludes only briefly to the idea of truth by convention, but in an earlier paper,[9] published in 1936, Quine dealt at length with this position of the Positivists, and argued that once we refute the idea that logical truth *arises* from conventions which are explicit, or could in principle *arise* in this way, then all that is left of the claim that logical truths are true by convention is the assertion that these are statements which, as a matter of sheer behavioristic fact, we would never give up. And in "Two Dogmas of Empiricism" he has advanced to the point of denying that there are (or ought to be) such statements.

Curiously enough, then, Quine *confused* analyticity and aprioricity because of Positivist assumptions (assumptions he was attacking) ! But, fortunately, this confusion does not invalidate his argument against aprioricity.

The "historical" argument. I want to explain why I think Quine's very sketchy "historical" argument against the existence of *a priori* (unrevisable) statements is correct.[10]

First of all, let me say a word about the esoteric subject of quantum logic.[11] What I claim is that the "weirdness" of the quantum mechanical universe can be understood in the following way : Just perform the thought-experiment of asking yourself : What experiences would we have if the world obeyed "quantum logic" instead of Boolean logic? (Of course, a certain minimal logic, a common part of Boolean logic and the proposed quantum logic, has to be used as the meta-logic.) If one allows this question as a meaningful question at all, one finds that *all* of the "anomalies" of quantum mechanics are explained by a few simple differences in the logic, just as the apparent anomalies of general relativity are explained by the peculiarities of the space-time. Unless one has some good argument that logic *cannot* be explanatory in the way geometry can, there is, then, a *prima facie* case for considering the hypothesis that we live in a *non-Boolean world*, as, at least, an admissible hypothesis (which is all Quine would need).

Now, what do philosophers of quantum mechanics who *reject* quantum logic reply? There are those, e.g. van Frassen, who see *all* scientific theories strictly from an instrumentalist point of view. From their perspective, there is no need for quantum logic, of course. But what of realist philosophers of quantum mechanics? They all, without exception, seem to count on quantum mechanics being proved *false* in certain particular ways.[12] No doubt, quantum mechanics *will* prove false in *some* (probably unforeseen) ways. But what if future successor theories to quantum mechanics *retain* just the features that make quantum mechanics philosophically *puzzling*? I think that I can honestly claim that the quantum logic interpretation of quantum mechanics is the *only* realistic interpretation of quantum mechanics in the following sense : It is the only realist interpretation of the *present* theory. If the present theory is true, or, subjunctively, if it *were* true, or if the true theory retains certain key features of the present theory, however much it may differ from present quantum mechanics in other respects, then the interpretation I defend *is* an interpretation of the true theory, and no other realist interpretation *has ever been proposed*—only *wishes* for a different physical universe!

If I am right in the foregoing, then anyone who concedes that the present theory *could* be true should concede that there is a strong "case" for the possibility of a quantum logical universe.

'Now, back to Quine's "historical" argument. The obvious way to try to counter Quine's oblique reference to the fact that scientific revolutions have overthrown propositions once *thought* to be *a priori* is to say that the seeming *a prioricity* of *those* propositions was "merely psychological". But the stunning case is *geometry*. Unless one accepts the ridiculous claim that what seemed *a priori* was *only* the *conditional* statement that *if* Euclid's axioms, then Euclid's theorems, (I think that this is what Quine calls "disinterpreting" geometry in "Carnap and Logical Truth"); then one must admit that the key propositions of Euclidean geometry *interpreted* propositions ("about form and void", as Quine says), and these interpreted propositions were *methodologically* immune from revision

208

(prior to the invention of rival theory) as Boolean logic was prior to the proposal of the quantum logical interpretation of quantum mechanics. The correct moral—the one Quine draws—is that some statements can only be overthrown by rival *theory*; but there is no such thing as an absolutely unrevisable statement.

Quine's "linguistic" definition of analyticity. The definition of analyticity that Quine proposes (but only for the purpose of knocking it down) in the section of his essay on "truth by definition" is, let us recall, that a statement is analytic if it can be obtained from (or, equivalently, turned into) a truth of logic by substituting synonyms for synonyms. This is a *linguistic* definition, because the operative notion is *synonymy*, and this is a notion (and a legitimate notion) from the discipline of *linguistics*. Accepting the notions of "logical truth" (in the sense of "truth in which the only words that occur essentially are words from the restricted vocabulary of *formal logic*") and "synonymy" only commits one to accepting this definition of analyticity as (sufficiently) *clear*. But does this notion of analyticity have any *usefulness*?

One sort of usefulness that *this* notion of analyticity does not have is this : it does not explain why such a special epistemological status was traditionally accorded to so-called Logical Laws. Although the truths of logic are "analytic", on this definition of analyticity, they are, so to speak, *analytically* analytic. Any truth of logic comes from a truth of logic, namely itself, by a substitution of synonyms for synonyms (e.g., the *identity* substitution—the substitution that puts each non-logical term for itself). This makes the truths of logic analytic—by the definition of "analytic"—but it says nothing whatsoever about how we *know* a statement is a truth of logic, or about the revisability or unrevisability of such (putative) knowledge. That logic is analytic is now an illustration of how we have decided to use the noise "analytic", not a substantive thesis about logic.

This "linguistic" notion of analyticity might possess a second sort of usefulness, however, but only if the notion of *logical truth* were very much restricted. It might clarify Kant's notion of a judgment whose negation reduces to a contradiction, provided we took a "logical truth" to be a substitution instance of a theorem of *monadic* logic (i.e., logic up to but *not* including the undecidable logic of relations). The statements obtainable from the theorems of monadic logic and their substitution instances by putting synonyms for synonyms are probably more or less the class Kant had in mind. But if "logic" is extended to mean all of set theory, then the class of "analytic" truths, on this definition, becomes so artificial that it is hard to see why one would feel motivated to introduce a technical term to designate it.

If the special epistemological status traditionally accorded the Logical Laws cannot be explained by the "analyticity" of those laws, that does not mean that we have to simply decide to accept it as inexplicable, however. I urged above that there are statements in science which can only be overthrown by a new theory—sometimes by a revolutionary new theory—and not by observation alone. Such statements *have* a sort of "a prioricity" prior to the invention of the new theory which challenges or replaces them : they are *contextually a priori*. Giving up the idea that there are any absolutely *a priori* statements requires us to also give up the correlative idea (at least it was correlative for the Empiricists) that *a posteriori* statements (and to Empiricists this meant all revisable statements and also meant all synthetic statements, all statements "about the world") are always and at all times "empirical" in the sense that they have specifiable confirming experiences and specifiable disconfirming experiences. Euclidean geometry was always revisable in the sense that no justifiable canon of scientific inquiry *forbade* the construction of an alternative geometry; but it was not always "empirical" in the sense of having an alternative that good scientists could actually conceive. The special status of Logical Laws is similar, in my view; they are contextually *a priori* (or were, prior to quantum logic).

Even if analyticity cannot explain the special status of Logical Laws (insofar as it is real), that special status, that contextual aprioricity, *and* certain very strong synonymy relations *can* explain the status of such statements as "All bachelors are unmarried", "All vixens are foxes", etc. And it is important to explain the special status, the contextual aprioricity of these in-themselves-uninteresting statements, because otherwise a really important thesis—the thesis that no statement is totally immune from revision—might be cast into doubt. So the notion of "analyticity", when properly hedged (by restricting the meaning of "logical truth" as suggested above) can be of limited but real philosophical significance.

Let me close by considering one final question : can one agree with Quine's "historical" argument and still reject Quine's "circularity" argument? Can one hold that there are *no a priori* truths, but there *are* analytic truths (in the "linguistic" sense)?

The answer is plainly that one *can*. If one accepts the distributive laws of the standard (Boolean) propositional calculus, for example, then one will accept any statement of the form

$$p(q\text{v}r) \equiv pq \text{ v } pr$$

as logically true (and *a fortiori* as analytic). But in quantum logic there are statements of the form $p(q \text{ v } r) \equiv pq \text{ v } pr$ which are *not* regarded as logically true ($p(q \text{ v } r) \equiv pq \text{ v } pr$ is not a "tautology" in quantum logic). So if we change our minds about what Logical Laws are correct by going over to quantum logic, we will change our minds about the "analyticity" of these statements.

This does not mean that there are no analytic statements, if quantum logic is correct. Such familiar Logical Laws as $p \text{ v } -p$, the implication of p by $p.q$, the implication of $p \text{ v } q$ by p alone and by q alone, all are correct according to quantum logic. But it does mean that, since the logic is revisable for empirical reasons, our decision as to *which* statements are analytic can be changed for empirical reasons. Even a statement that really is analytic is not immune from revision—for even if a statement is *in fact* a Law of Logic, or comes from a Law of Logic by synonymous substitution, we are not *prohibited* by any methodological canon from revising it—we will just be making a mistake if we do. (Compare this case with the situation in geometry : even if we arrive at the *correct* geometry for space-time, still our geometry will not be *unrevisable*. It is just that we will—as a matter of *fact*—be making a *mistake* if we revise it. "Fallibilism" does not become an incorrect doctrine when one reaches the truth in a scientific inquiry.)

In sum : (1) a putatively analytic statement may not really be analytic, not because we were confused about meanings, or confused about logic, but because the *logic of the world* may be different from what we suppose it to be, *as a matter of empirical fact*. (2) A really analytic statement is not *a priori*, because even when we happen to be *right* about logic, fallibilism still holds good. We never have an absolute guarantee that we are right, even when we are.

Notice how different the situation would be if the Laws of Logic *were* immune from revision. If that were the case, one could only give up an analytic statement (or the sentence which expressed an analytic statement), without an actual logical *blunder*, by altering the meaning of the words and thereby changing the language. Analytic statements would be as unrevisable as if they were true by convention. It would be as if there were truths by language alone. But on the view advanced here, there are *no* truths by language alone. There are analytic truths—truths by *logic and language*. But analytic truths

211

are not *unrevisable* (no truth is). They are only unrevisable *unless we revise the logic or the language,* which is a very different matter.

Professor Hilary Putnam
Harvard University

NOTES

[1] Listed as Quine (1951) in the References at the end of this paper.

[2] In Grice and Strawson (1956).

[3] This is probably too harsh on my part. The notion of analyticity and the notion of a "Meaning Postulate" had become so overworked in philosophy (not to mention such notions as "analysis" of a concept, "conceptually necessary", etc.) that synonymy and analyticity had, indeed, have become unclear notions *as used by philosophers.* And even if synonymy *is* a reasonably clear notion as used in *linguistics,* any *theory* of synonymy which we are likely to see will look "Quinian" to this extent (I predict): most words will *not* be synonymous with any descriptions whatsoever, and most of the truths philosophers class as "conceptually necessary" will not be "analytic" in the sense discussed here. Pointing out the "circularity" of the definitions of synonymy and analyticity offered by philosophers was Quine's way of calling attention to the alarming looseness of the *use* these philosophers were making of the notions, and to their exaggerated confidence in the clarity of the notion of *meaning,* which was Quine's real target.

[4] Putnam (1962).

[5] Putnam (1975).

[6] Quine (1951), p. 40.

[7] Quine (1957), p. 16.

[8] Quine (1960), p. 359.

[9] Quine (1936).

[10] In recent years Quine appears to have changed his position on logic. Thus in Quine (1970) he argues *against* the possibility of revising Boolean logic without losing simplicity (however, he makes the error of considering only the simplicity of the logic in isolation, not the simplicity of the total system, which is what is relevant), and also argues that to abandon Boolean logic would be to "change the meaning" of the logical particles. (For a reply to this argument, see Putnam (1968).) I am ignoring this "backsliding" on Quine's part (as I view it), because my interest is in bringing out what Quine's *best* argument was.

[11] See Putnam (1968).

[12] For example, Arthur Fine tells me that his proposed interpretation of quantum mechanics would have the consequence that one *can* simultaneously measure some non-commuting observables.

REFERENCES

Grice, H. P. and Strawson, P. F. (1956) "In Defense of a Dogma", *Phil. Review* 65, 141–58.

Putnam, H. (1962) "The Analytic and the Synthetic", in *Minnesota Studies in the Philosophy of Science*, III, pp. 358–97, ed. Feigl, H. and Maxwell, G. Minneapolis: U. of Minnesota.

Putnam, H. (1968) "Is Logic Empirical", in *Boston Studies in the Philosophy of Science*, V, pp. 216–41, ed. Cohen, R. and Wartofsky, M. Dordrecht, Holland: D. Reidel.

Putnam, H. (1975) "The Meaning of 'Meaning' ", in *Minnesota Studies in the Philosophy of Science*, VII, pp. 131–93, ed. Gunderson, K. Minneapolis: U. of Minnesota. (Putnam (1962, 1968, and 1975) are also reprinted in Putnam's *Philosophical Papers*, 1975, Cambridge University Press. Putnam (1962) and (1975) are in vol. II; Putnam (1968) is in vol. I under the title "The Logic of Quantum Mechanics".)

Quine, W. V. (1936) "Truth by Convention", in *Philosophical Essays for A. N. Whitehead*, ed. Green, O. H. New York: Longmans, Green, and Co. Reprinted in *Philosophy of Mathematics*, pp. 322–45, ed. Benacerraf, P. and Putnam, H. Englewood Cliffs, New Jersey: Prentice-Hall, 1964.

Quine, W. V. (1951) "Two Dogmas of Empiricism", *Phil. Review* 60, 20–43.

Quine, W. V. (1957) "The Scope and Language of Science", *British J. for Phil. of Science* 8, 1–17.

Quine, W. V. (1960) "Carnap and Logical Truth", *Synthese* 12, 350–374.

XVI

ANALYTIC VERSUS CATEGORIAL THOUGHT

K. Hartmann

THE LAST decade has seen a revived interest, in England and America, in Kant's theoretical philosophy, more specifically an interest in Kant's transcendental argumentation. We may mention Professor Strawson's *The Bounds of Sense*, Jonathan Bennett's two books on Kant's *First Critique, Kant's Analytic* and *Kant's Dialectic*, or refer to a host of articles, among which R. Rorty's proposal to amend Strawson's stand strikes us as the most important. Kant's argument, if it is permissible to speak of an argument rather than of a full-fledged theory, is supposed to account for conditions of epistemic possibility : for there to be objectivity of things experienced, there has to be conceptualization of items given, and this in turn requires a unity of the experiencing subject. In fact, the latter condition is coincident with the conceptualizing required by the former condition : Kant adduces a synthesis which conceptualizes intuitional data (or, in *a priori* terms, a matrix of data) and, at the same time, secures the unity of consciousness having those conceptualized data as an object. Thus the inference of certain *a priori* concepts of objects of experience, as underpinnings of objectivity, is tied to the establishment of a subject having the experience and to various types of its self-synthesizing. (In the *Critique of Pure Reason*, this general argument is divided into two steps, that of the *Analytic of Concepts* and that of the *Analytic of Principles*. We cannot here enlarge on this complication).

The Analytic Reconstruction of Kant's Central Argument
An analytic scrutiny of transcendental procedure in the *First Critique* will focus on the stringency of the inference of both the objectivity and the subjectivity of experience, or on the mutual implication between the objectivity of the experienced and the experiencing

subject. In this context, it will have to come to terms with the dual foundation of Kant's epistemology—intuition and concept; it will wonder on what grounds experience must go beyond coloured patches in order to qualify as experience. In a somewhat uneasy collaboration, spatial intuition affords particulars, temporal intuition lets us have routes of experience of particulars, while conceptualization pins down particulars as other than mere mental states. In analytic translation, to say that one experiences patches raises the problem whether this does not already require substantives (some-things) to be predicated adjectivally, a translation which, in this case, is quite close to Kant's insistence on judgment, although in a weaker, language-oriented version. The weakness shows in the defence against objections : skeptical claims for a language game undercutting the objectivity game must bear the onus of proof that the skeptic's is a playable game at all. If we ask whether there might be experience just of mental states (the imagining of which possibility Strawson, in a much commented passage—*The Bounds of Sense*, p. 109, *cf.* p. 99—allows), how could we be shown that we must go beyond such states? The language game idea suggests that the language game, if any, would be another one, in all probability one not permitting of discourse (*cf.* Rorty, *Review of Metaphysics* (RM) 24, pp. 221–223). The case can therefore be made that only if a person uses objectivity concepts (involving, on Strawson's view, a physical object) can he also have experience. Two language games— about objects and about the experiencing subject—are mutually implicative : this is the analytic rephrasing of the central idea of Kant's transcendental deduction.

What emerges is analytic consent to a basic idea of Kant's, that there is a mutual implication of subjectivity and experienced object-ivity. The mutual implication—non-strict in view of improbable but not demonstrably impossible alternative language games—can be phrased in terms of concepts mutually implying each other or, more cautiously, as cases of mutually implicative *possessions* or *uses*, on the part of the subject, of certain concepts. On this rephrasing, Kant's transcendental deduction is acceptable to analytic philoso-phers, or at least to some of them.[1]

There are niceties : e.g., whether Strawson can legitimately accept Kant's doctrine about the necessary unification of the subject under the motto of a "self-ascription" of mental states. A re-interpretation of Kant seems to serve his purpose : objectivity requires a contrast of "is" and "seems", thus making the subject the receptacle and sum-total of all "seemings" of which it must be aware to maintain the

215

contrast. Rorty has stressed this line of argument which replaces Kant's synthesis by something more acceptable analytically (*cf*. RM 24, pp. 231–233). We ignore a further point, *viz.*, Strawson's suggestion that the subject requires, for purposes of self-identification, a foothold in an intersubjective world which in turn requires spatial ordering. Quite generally, let us put in a reservation to the effect that we cannot go into the detail of Strawson's or Bennett's or Rorty's retracing of Kant's argument. We simply wish to discuss a methodological point concerning the vehicle of analytic reconstruction, *viz.*, *concept* in its analytic acceptation.

We should remind ourselves that the analytic reconstruction of Kant's theory covers only a central piece, the transcendental deduction. Further Kantian claims concerning substance and causality have to be judged on their merits; an analytic appraisal of these claims tends to be skeptical (*cf*. Bennett's conventionalistic treatment of substance and his logical criticism of Kant's *a priori* argument for causality).

What matters in our context is that the analytic reconstruction of the transcendental argument constitutes a transformation of Kant's dual (intuitional and conceptual) foundation to an *intra-conceptual* one, however mediated by a subject credited with the possession or use of concepts concerning physical objects and concepts, or a concept, concerning itself. As Rorty says, "intuitions drop out" (RM 24, p. 227). We cannot treat them as something which in view of its being so-and-so merits certain conceptualizations. If we did, we would presuppose determinateness and thus conceptualization as a condition for conceptualization (*cf*. Rorty, RM, pp. 225–227). Intuitions cannot figure in the analytic reconstruction of Kant's transcendental argument. As Rorty sums it up, "All that transcendental arguments—*a priori* arguments about what sort of experience is possible—can show is that if you have certain concepts you must have certain other concepts also" (RM 24, p. 231).

Mental States and the Deficiency Argument

It is obvious that the analytic transformation of the transcendental argument is a step towards rationality in matters of transcendental philosophy. In other words, Kant's reliance on what *occurs in*, and *to*, a subject when experiencing, its having of mental states and performing of syntheses, however transcendental, is replaced by an account in terms of concepts. Strawson, if we are to believe Rorty, has not quite made this step. Still, the drift of the analytic reconstruction of the transcendental argument is one in the direction of *conceptual reconstruction,* and, accordingly, it must object to Kant's own formulation in terms of synthesis as a vehicle of theory.

Part of the problem could be said to be that, to formulate the transcendental argument in terms of a synthesis of data so as to result in objective experience and subjective unity, is to invoke mental states which, according to the theory, must not "be" if it is true that awareness is conceptualization (*cf.* Strawson, *The Bounds of Sense,* p. 110; Rorty, RM 24, pp. 216, 239 f.). Unless mental states—representations of the concept type and of the intuition type—are already ingredients in a synthesis, they are unconscious. But maybe we should not say this without qualification since Kant wanted to maintain a "having" of an inner sense. So we might give the criticism another twist : if mental states are acceptable as presences (within a unity of temporally extended self-ascription), then there is no way to infer, except by external teleological argument, anything from their very deficiency over against experience. But this seems to be what Kant tries to do. We would argue that, in the *Analytic of Principles,* he uses fictive mental states—unordered in point of temporal mode—as a starting point for an inference to the effect that we must transcend these states in favour of objective experience : subjective time requires a determination to save it from randomness; the determination afforded, we have objective, conceptually supported temporal predicates : the house which calls for categorial determination as substance to conform to simultaneity, the ship which calls for causality to conform to process (*cf.* K.H., RM 20, pp. 223–249, esp. 229–234; K.H., *Proceedings of the Third International Kant Congress,* pp. 47–62, esp. 50–52). Clearly, such use of a fictive premise, triggering the argument for a conceptual complement condemning the very premiss, is unacceptable; it can be seen to be due to a mixture of stances, a phenomenological one and a logico-transcendental one, a mixture designed to yield the desired categorial extrapolation. Surely, relations of conceptual implication must not be based on phenomenological inspection impoverished for purposes of transcendental argument. There never "are" unordered subjective times in need of conceptual redress.[2] This reflection casts a doubt on Kant's *Analogies* concurring with certain analytic conclusions; persistent substance and causality will, if at all, have to be secured without reference to the inner sense.

Analytic versus Categorial Reconstruction of the Transcendental Argument
Our brief review of part of the intuitional problem in Kant, *i.e.,* its temporal aspect in the *Analytic of Principles,* suggests a favourable

view of the *conceptual* reconstruction of the transcendental argument. But questions arise as to whether we must have an *analytic* reconstruction, whether it is only "when the Wittgensteinian interpretation of concepts is adopted that we are able to give arguments for one concept presupposing another", as Rorty has it (RM 24, p. 237).

There are in fact difficulties attaching to the analytic reconstruction. (1) This reconstruction does manage to concur with an argument for a mutual implication of concept uses (*physical object, experiencing subject; is, seems*) to the extent that the onus of proof that there are alternative language games can be laid to the door of the skeptic; but it can account for the determination "physical object" only by pointing to a particular which, in order to qualify for one, must feature the familiar spatial and temporal characteristics. The object disclosed by transcendental argument remains theoretically *underdetermined*, indebted to plausibility. The various features or categories that may be implicated cannot be shown on a view which takes the transcendental argument to be an argument mainly about a very basic and abstract implication. (2) Viewing things from another angle, we cannot obtain a *completeness proof* of objective determinations the way Kant envisaged, however imperfect his attempt may have been, resting his case on the "metaphysical deduction'. Such a proof may be a *desideratum* rather than a feasibility, but one can try to see how far one can go. (3) A final consideration is that analytic philosophy discusses link-ups between concepts as the joint *possession* or *use* of words or language games by a subject. It is *not*, after all, a *theory of the mutual implication of concepts.*

Now, while a conceptual reconstruction of the transcendental argument may be called for (also in view of the miscarriage of the deficiency argument), it is not true that only on Wittgensteinian terms can mutual implications of concepts (and *a fortiori* of concept use) be defended. The very different approach of what we call a *categorial position* is another option; an option, incidentally, which is alive to Kant's concern with categorial concepts establishing, and refining upon, what is meant by objectivity. Of course, we need not think that, simply because Kant wanted to account for a complete set of categories, we must be able to prove him right. Still, there is, over against Kant and the analytic reconstruction of his position, an alternative scheme to account for conceptual implications, and it may be worthwhile to inspect it briefly.[3]

The Categorial Scheme
The scheme we have in mind shares with analytic philosophy its

reliance on concepts rather than intuitions and syntheses : on this scheme, too, intuitions and syntheses appear as irrational vehicles of theory, jarring with conceptual implications and committed to a view involving the Cartesian "mental eye" (Rorty) or evidential "glow" (Bennett). But the categorial scheme differs from analytic philosophy in several ways. (1) It transcends the indebtedness of analytic philosophy to a *particular* subject experiencing a *particular* object, an indebtedness foreign to conceptual implication as such. Possession and use of concepts X and Y leaves it to the particular subject to urge the conceptual implications in question, however much the case may be strengthened by intersubjective assumptions. Ontological relevance of concepts cannot be claimed. By contrast, the scheme advocated here can conceptualize the very relationship between subject and object at issue in Kant's transcendental deduction; it can say in general terms what the conceptualization of the real must be for the subject to be conceptualized as a subject, *i.e.*, as conceptualizing, and *vice versa*. The scheme can handle interdependences or mutual implications or presuppositions that Rorty claims can only be dealt with on a Wittgensteinian interpretation. All that is needed is a theory of conceptual relations as such.

(2) The envisaged rationalization of concepts will bear in mind that concepts are entertained as true of being. It goes without saying that a theory of conceptual determinateness has to consider the germane character of concepts, *viz.*, to be graspings of what is, appropriatings of being by thought. Accordingly, to the extent that an *a priori* account of them can be given, concepts are treated as *categories*.[4]

(3) The position we advocate is that of *universal conceptual explication*; it is not restricted to an immediate mutual implication of subjectivity and objectivity. Objectivity, e.g., is not sufficiently accounted for by relating it to substantive terms matched by a spatialized particular; more is involved in calling a referent a "physical object", and still more in other types of objectivity. Subjectivity is more than the sum-total of "seemings" : on an abstract level, it "is" concept. However, subject-object-relationships feature a wide range of cases, depending on whether the subject stands over against a physical object, another subject, or a community. The concept of subject will have to be enriched accordingly. Here conceptual, in the sense of "categorial", analysis can be of use.

We realize that we are drifting beyond a reconstruction of Kant towards another philosophy. Our scheme is basically Hegelian. It is a conceptual appraisal of categorial *unities*. Judging from its vantage point, we can see that a Kantian approach (or an analytic

219

reconstruction of it) is theoretically imperfect : it focusses on an epistemological notion of the subject which keeps it separate from its referent, *picturing*, as it were, the configuration of subject and referent rather than considering their unity expressible in categorial terms. What beginning there is in Section 16 B edition of the *First Critique* in the direction of a conceptual grasping of the transcendental unity of apperception as general concept, as concept as such, is not brought to fruition by Kant himself, and the analytic reconstruction does not follow the lead either. The contrast of "is-seems" is not itself a conceptualized unity.

(4) What matters on the view proposed is that an argument can be provided for the *completeness* of categories of the real, including the subject. Such an argument can be given (5) in a *dialectical logic*. This treats of different types and degrees of unity in a concatenation ranging from deficiency (or immediacy) to perfection or absolute unity. Intuition can thus be conceptualized as a certain deficient, or finite, stage of subjectivity. Such finitude can be pursued to its "logical" conclusion, *i.e.*, we are asked, in terms of a calculus of negations threatening contradiction, to disclose more rational solutions. We have an explanatory sequence of concepts, treating rationally of what otherwise would have to be left to mixtures of intuitions and concept or to *bona fide* language games. (Incidentally, in Hegel, we have two theoretical variants of dialectical logic : a conceptual approach to the subject as confronting all manner of objects, and a conceptual approach to all manner of ontological unities, of which the subject is one. The former is implemented in the *Phenomenology of Spirit*, the latter in the *Logic* and the *Encyclopedia*. The subtlety of this complication cannot be discussed here).

There are obvious felicities to the scheme : it features conceptualization of concept, completeness proof of categories, intraconceptual (transcendental, speculative, dialectical) explanation or hermeneutic rationality, inclusion of non-epistemic subjective stances, pure *a priori* status, a non-picturing approach. It is a *pure* theory.[5]

Conversely, the analytic reconstruction of Kant's transcendental argument and, indeed, analytic philosophy generally emerges as a position built on heterogeneous foundations as it analyzes conceptual implications in conjunction with subjective inspection. It is committed to an epistemological first-person orientation which, *pace* Rorty, matches Hume's and Kant's commitment to the Cartesian tradition. It is still a picturing position which, in opposing subject and object, cannot achieve any assurance that its concepts have ontological relevance. Concepts are seen as elements of language games. In many ways, then, the analytic approach shares Kant's imperfections although its insistence on concepts goes beyond Kant in the right direction.

Conclusion

Admittedly, the categorial (transcendental, speculative, dialectical) theory will saddle us with questions as to its validity, particularly as concerns its full Hegelian version. These questions cannot be examined here. Suffice it to say that there is a reading of Hegel's philosophy which exonerates it from metaphysical commitments.[6] It does not oblige us to accept otherworldly ghosts—all that is needed is a theoretical subject of the theory : the *absolute idea*, or *philosophy*, nor does it—which is the more interesting point—urge us to accept existential inferences of the type, "all nature is causally ordered", "all nature is a collection of substances", and the like. Epistemological proof of metaphysical tenets is replaced by conceptual, *i.e.*, ontological, analysis of what there is. The position is more modest than the Kantian one.

In conclusion, let us submit that there is a changing attitude in both "camps" as to what can be expected of philosophy : just as analytic philosophy—in spite of its recent concern with the transcendental argument—lessens our expectations as to what can be done by way of argument or proof, leaving as it does problems in the charge of language games, so does the advocated categorial scheme, which is in fact a *catalogue raisonné* of determinations of the real not aspiring to the epistemological proof of anything. All it claims is the non-emptiness of categorial concepts. Rigorously controlled *understanding*, or *systematic hermeneutics*, in a global conceptual scheme modelled on the Hegelian, may be worth having in these days of philosophical caution and prove an interesting rival to analytic analysis.

Professor Klaus Hartmann,
University of Tübingen
Germany

NOTES

[1] In Bennett's reconstruction of the argument, the transcendental deduction does not suffice as an argument for the desired interdependence of subjectivity and objectivity; it remains for the *Analytic of Principles* to try and succeed (which again

is denied). Bennett has however admitted a lack of appreciation of the transcendental deduction in his review of Strawson's *The Bounds of Sense*. *Cf. Philosophical Review*, July 1968, p. 342; "What Strawson primarily seeks to salvage from the Transcendental Deduction (*TD*) is an argument from (1) "A self-conscious being must apply concepts" to (2) "A self-conscious being must apply objectivity-concepts." There is such an argument in the *TD*, and Strawson has satisfied me that I have erred in seeing the *TD*'s value as wholly residing in Kant's arguments *for* (1)."

[2] Husserl will be right with his contention that there are noetic syntheses of the stream of consciousness—retentions and protentions—different from noematic—objective—syntheses, if syntheses, and transcendental ones at that, there are to be.

[3] A problem not to be treated here is to what extent Neo-Kantianism is an option within the said alternative. H. Cohen certainly is a case in point, but so is H. Wagner's *Philosophie und Reflexion*.

[4] Connoisseurs of Hegel will protest that Hegel uses "category" only for what he calls "objective logic", using "Begriff" (concept) for his "subjective logic". In our context, this terminological distinction does not seem relevant.

[5] For the distinction of "pure theory" and "mixed theory" (*i.e.*, a theory involving irrational elements supposedly incapable of conceptualization) see K.H., RM 20, 229 ff., 235 ff.

[6] *Cf.* K.H., "Hegel: A Non-Metaphysical View" in *Hegel*. A Collection of Critical Essays, ed. by A. MacIntyre, New York 1972, pp. 101–124.

XVII

THE USE AND ABUSE OF HEGEL

H. S. Harris

In two successive issues of *The New York Review of Books* there appeared recently an article by Anthony Quinton entitled "Spreading Hegel's Wings" (29 May and 12 June 1975). On the cover of the earlier issue the article was given the more catchy headline "The Hegel Craze"; and in the second instalment Quinton can fairly be said to have justified this initial billing. In the first instalment he restrains himself, and writes in general as if there was nothing particularly crazy about the revival of interest in Hegel: "There are good reasons why Hegel's metaphysics, for all the obscurity of its presentation and the elusiveness of the general picture of the world it seeks to convey, should exert a continuing fascination" (1975a, p. 37). The second instalment concludes much more trenchantly: "I keep hearing of young colleagues who have developed an interest in Hegel, but nothing audible or visible seems to come out of it. Some strong spirit should address itself to the cryptogram of Hegel's metaphysics, with Ivan Soll's clarity and concision, but at a greater critical distance. If it turns out, as I am inclined to expect, that Hegel's metaphysics is composed of all the dross in Kant, carefully purged of all his insights, that will at least ease the conscience of those who confine themselves to Hegel as a theorist of society and culture" (1975b, p. 42).

Perhaps the "strong spirit" of Quinton's hopes has now appeared in Charles Taylor (1975). Certainly, since I have remarked on it myself in print (1972) I am not going to quarrel with Quinton's claim that Hegel is one of a fairly small group of thinkers who seems to *obsess* those who study him seriously to the point where they lose their critical balance. Himself an extremely sober individual, as coldly ironical in his attitude towards all forms of "enthusiasm" as ever Hume was, Hegel seems to generate transports of enthusiasm

223

in friend and foe alike. There *are* "Hegel crazes" (and "anti-Hegel crazes" too); and a great part of Hegel's influence in the history of culture is of the "crazy" variety. I do not think this situation is likely to change much. But I do think that a critical decision that Hegel's system is "no more than a dense incrustation of baroque ornament" (Quinton, 1975b, p. 40) would be likely to make it worse; for as I see it, it is the uncontrolled use of all that baroque equipment in cultural interpretation that represents the worst form of "Hegel craze". So, if the machinery is in principle uncontrollable, the outlook is bleak. That Hegel is a modern "prophet" is an awkward, but inescapable, historical fact; I have no faith that he can be turned into an interesting and useful social philosopher if his "system" is what Quinton believes it to be.

Such evidence as I have seen of a recent revival of interest in Hegel in the English-speaking world actually has very little of the "craze" about it. This is clear enough from Quinton's review—where the craziest item dealt with is unquestionably Popper's attack in the *Open Society and Its Enemies* (1945). This marked the nadir of Hegel's reputation before the revival began. But the case for the revival could be made more strongly than Quinton makes it; and his final sceptical outburst might then begin to appear a bit overdone. Thus, a case where interest in Hegel has produced an "audible and visible" contribution to contemporary discussion is offered by R. J. Bernstein's *Praxis and Action* (1971). Here Marxism, Existentialism and Pragmatism are first set in a Hegelian context and then brought into a fruitful relation with "analytical" controversies about the concept of "action". But then a book that is subtitled "Contemporary Philosophies of Human Activity" is not likely to be considered for inclusion in a Hegel survey.

Bernstein's return to Hegel exemplifies the normal *use* that philosophers make of their predecessors. Hegel has not been useful in this way very often to the English speaking world, because most serious students have been too much impressed by the *systematic* character of his original enterprise to feel that the fragmentation of his thought was justifiable or even possible. But in those who were influenced by him respect for his systematic ideals was accompanied by a deep distrust of his methods. The "dialectic" has seemed too confidently rationalistic in its pure form (i.e. in the *Logic*) and too hopelessly impressionistic in its historical exemplifications to be acceptable to the Anglo-Saxon mind in either shape; and its extraordinarily rapid demise in its "systematic" application (at least so far as "scientific" subjects like physics, biology and psychology were

224

concerned) appeared to many sympathetic minds as a conclusive empirical proof that the distrust was well founded. What was accepted from Hegel—where he was influential at all—was therefore some of the regulative ideals of his *Logic*—and so far as any work of his was seriously studied in England and the U.S.A. it was the *Logic*. But the kinship between the historic Hegel and most of what was called "Anglo-Hegelianism", because it was regulated by these ideals, was distant.

Politics represents the exception. The kinship between the *Philosophy of Right* and Bradley's essay on "My Station and its Duties" (1878) is far from distant. Beginning from there we can observe the development of a tradition in English (and even in American) political theory that is genuinely "Hegelian". But here we encounter another paradox. For as Marx—a "Hegelian" who accepted the "method"—was the first to point out (1844), and as Findlay—who seems to accept both the systematic ideal and the method—has confirmed (1958, p. 327), many of the crucial positions of the *Philosophy of Right* are laid down without arguments of any kind. Marx assumed that the unstated argument was a straightforward appeal to historical fact; and there is no stick with which Hegel has been more often beaten than his supposed acceptance of the principle that whatever historically and socially *is*, is right. The Anglo-Saxons sought rather to provide their own theoretical arguments. As they did so, the conservatism of Bradley—far too distinguished for the "backbencher" to whom Findlay contemptuously assigns it—became the near-Socialist inspiration of T. H. Green and the liberalism of Royce and Bosanquet; and we may note that it arrived on the Liberal *front* bench in the person of an outstanding Minister for War, Lord Haldane.

The one thing that all parties have so far agreed on is that the "Secret of Hegel" remains a secret. This does not surprise me, because I don't believe that Hegel's "secret" is a philosophical one at all. One thing that I seem to have learned from Hegel is that there are no "secrets" in philosophy. What makes it appear that there is one in Hegel's own work is just a set of historical conditions which combined with his own historically determined perspective regarding the principal problem of philosophy to create the impression that he was trying to think in a way in which no one can possibly think about questions that have no determinate sense. This impression is not correct, but there is no denying that Hegel used language in a way that is not at all natural. If he is to become part of the history of western philosophy in the ordinary sense, if he is to be used and abused as other thinkers are, instead of being reverenced or damned as a new Christ or Antichrist, (and more frequently just ignored because prophets, true or false, are not generally of much interest to philosophers), two things are necessary. First, a patient and often painful effort to comprehend the historical and cultural conditions out of which his philosophy emerged; and secondly the placing of his conception of the task of philosophy in its historical perspective, that is to say the comprehension of *his* perspective within the perspective in which we ourselves now operate. For several years I have been working as an under-labourer among those who are struggling with the first task. Here and now I propose to make a sighting shot at the second. Anything more than an attempt to get the range and direction for this larger task of putting Hegel's philosophy into current perspective would be premature—at least for me. I hope the result will not be just another "Hegelian" mirage. But I am certainly in no position at the moment to demonstrate that the prospect before me is a solid reality in four dimensions.

What then, in Hegel's view, is the task of philosophy? He continually reiterates an answer which sounds so simplistic as to be trivial, whether we take it to be true or false; and as soon as we recognize its non-trivial sense it begins to appear shockingly dogmatic. Philosophy, he says, has as its goal, "the scientific knowledge of the truth" (Nicolin and Pöggeler, p. 3). This particular formulation (of 1830) is quite obviously mistaken to our ears. The formula of 1812 "the interest in what the *true*, what the *absolute ground* of everything is" (Lasson, 1923, p. 51; Miller, p. 67) sounds less trivially absurd, but the prejudgement of the two vital questions— whether there is any "absolute ground", and if so whether we can ever know what it is—seems patent. In the still earlier form that he gives in the *Phenomenology* "the actual knowledge of what truly is" (Hoffmeister, p. 63; Baillie, p. 131) the absurdity and the arrogance come together in such a way as to justify Quinton's comment that instead of imitating Aristotle, the Hegelian philosopher is supposed to imitate Aristotle's God. We can see, however, that we ought to substitute Thomas Aquinas in the place of Aristotle since it is by no means clear that Aristotle's God *has* "the scientific knowledge of the truth".

My fundamental thesis is that Hegel's apparent "dogmatism"— in the Kantian sense—is *only* apparent. The *appearance* arises from the confluence in his mind of two concerns which we are apt to regard as irreconcilable, so that we have given one of them up for lost. In the first place Hegel thinks Kant was not critical enough—

that his division between the phenomenal and the noumenal will not work. This is a concern which we can appreciate readily enough, because, by and large, we share it; but unfortunately it is combined with a determination on Hegel's part to rescue from the noumenal realm all of the religious experience, the matters of "faith", for which Kant made a home there. Those of us who have the feeling that there is a lot of "metaphysical dross" in Kant find *this* concern quite incomprehensible. There are enough of us who think that "the scientific knowledge of the truth" is what philosophy is *about* (not, of course, what it *is*) to guarantee that the general project of criticizing Kant's *Critiques* will retain its interest for us. But when Hegel asserts, as an obvious commonplace, that "philosophy has its objects in common with religion, to be sure" (*Encyclopaedia*, section 1), he puts himself firmly into the historic past for a large group of us for whom Kant's *Critique of Pure Reason* marks the European dawn of *our* philosophic present, in the matter of the dissociation of philosophy from theology. This is—we would say—the point at which Europe finally got in step with the United Kingdom—as well as enabling all parties to take an enormous step forward. And any post-Kantian thinker who insists on returning to the past in *this* respect must arouse in us a healthy suspicion that we need not bother about him.

When we look carefully, however, we discover that Hegel's concern is to discover just what significance the older philosophical theology retains in a *radically* critical theory. Kant claimed to have "made room for faith", and Hegel objected to this—just as we do when we virtually ignore most of the second *Critique*. I think it may eventually be shown that Hegel objected *too* violently, and that his distrust of *all* "postulated" entities led him into some demonstrable mistakes in his philosophy of science. But his distrust of the "postulates of Practical Reason" ought to endear him to Anglo-Saxon thinkers who can speak confidently of "the dross in Kant"—for our study habits with respect to Kant show very plainly where we believe the "dross" to be. We do not like Kant's development of "practical faith" as a way of exploring the "noumenal" realm any better than Hegel did. I think, too, that we agree with Hegel that the older traditions of metaphysical rationalism, both classical and modern, must have *some* interpretation as philosophers of experience. We cannot—we *do* not—simply draw a line at 1781 and forget about continental speculation before that date. In the present strictly philosophical context I propose to set aside Hegel's whole attempt to give a philosophical interpretation of revealed religion as irrelevant to the main issue. This endeavour has done much to gain him his reputation as an interpreter of culture; but it has been a great stumbling block to what Hegel would have called the "scientific" comprehension of his work. For Hegel personally the philosophical interpretation of religious experience was a matter of the most urgent import. He was educated in a theological seminary, in a world in which religious teaching and practice was the most important *symbolic* form for the exercise of social authority and the development of communal consciousness. He saw a great social revolution, of which he was an enthusiastic partisan, come close to shipwreck, for the lack of an ideology adequate to maintain the communal sense of identity; and he became a philosopher himself as a direct result of his efforts to create an ideology that would be adequate for the post-revolutionary society which he thought he could see on the horizon. But none of this has any "scientific" significance (as he would have said). Philosophy is above all that practical strife. It is true that all through his professional career he loved to appeal to some of the principal dogmas of the Christian faith— the Creation, the Incarnation, the Trinity—to support his positions and explicate his arguments. But of Christian *philosophy* he knew very little, and he had an unduly low opinion of the little that he did know. Of the philosophers who were particularly important to him—Heracleitus, Parmenides, Plato, Aristotle, Spinoza and Kant— only the last was a Christian and it was exactly the "Christianity" of Kant that Hegel rejected. As far as his appeals to the common faith are concerned it is vital to realize that in one respect at least Hegel always remained faithful to the revolutionary commitment of his youth. It is philosophy that must decide the true interpretation of the faith, not the faith that determines the bounds of philosophy.

Kant's *philosophy*—the critical theory of the mind as determining how "what is" shall appear—becomes for Hegel the foundation of the thesis that *knowledge* itself—the structure and order of appearance—is what absolutely *is*. Within the critical philosophy itself we become aware of the reasons why we cannot have knowledge of any "being-as-such" that is completely independent of possible experience. To postulate any such being is to postulate the ultimate unintelligibility of reality. Such a postulate is not sensible, because the primary fact, from which the Critical Philosophy begins, is the reality of finite intelligence. The one unproblematic ontological certainty is that there is, in the world, an activity that knows the world piecemeal; and the nature and structure of this activity is something that the knowing activity itself can determine absolutely.

228

When this is done properly we shall have before us "absolute knowledge"—the knowledge of the knowing activity as it absolutely *is*.

The difficulty in carrying out this programme is that the knowing activity is necessarily directed upon the world as what is *other* than itself. The *assumption* that its ultimate concern is an object other than itself appears to be inescapable. Thus Kant could recognize in the *Critique of Judgement* that we must *postulate* the ultimate intelligibility of reality in order to organize our finite cognition of it. But at the same time he could not avoid writing in the *Critique of Pure Reason as if* it were ultimately unintelligible. For he shows there that the attempt to treat ultimate reality as directly intelligible only gives rise to an endless dialectic of which the history of pre-critical philosophy is the visible result.

Hegel set out, therefore, to see whether the history of philosophy could be viewed as a validation of the postulate of ultimate intelligibility. The moral of the Critical Philosophy for him was that critical philosophy must take its own pre-critical history as its object. The history of philosophy must from henceforth be viewed as the struggle of man to gain absolute knowledge—i.e. to know the nature and structure of his own cognitive experience; and similarly, general history must be viewed as his struggle to *realize* his rational capacities *practically*, i.e. to achieve rational freedom. The achievements of the decade between 1780 and 1790—the decade of Hegel's adolescence and passage to manhood—were for Hegel convincing phenomenal evidence that the freedom of man and the intelligibility of the world were not mere "postulates" but realities just as solid and potent as Newtonian physics. The Critical Philosophy and the French Revolution have the same sort of significance for Hegel that Newton's *Principia* has for Kant.

Hegel does not hold that either history generally or the history of thought in particular is progressive in any simple way. Indeed he saw both of them as dialectical in a far more radical sense than Kant dreamed of. Both in the schools and in life, men are continually occupied in doing the opposite of what they believe themselves to be doing. The philosophers, engaged as they thought in determining man's place in the order of nature and the relation of that order to an Author quite other than themselves, were actually laying out the conceptual structure of their communal interpretation of experience; and the historic communities, striving to declare and make effective the will of their rulers and their Gods, were actually creating the institutional structures which would finally make the exercise of social authority into an autonomously *human* function, i.e. a

229

function that is consciously regulated by the use of reason, and justified by appeal to reason.

I have said that I do not want to deal with Hegel's general philosophy of culture. But the lesson of the *Philosophy of History* is very easy to see when we put it in its Kantian context. This lecture-series was given for a "general" audience. It has always been the most popular, and for that very reason the most misunderstood of Hegel's works. With the publication of G. D. O'Brien's *Hegel on Reason and History* (1975) we can have some confidence that those bad old days are over. But even he does not go quite as far as I would like. Pre-critical history—i.e. the history of man before the emergence of a properly historical consciousness—is the story of the necessary rise and fall of the "divine right of kings" (and/or priests and prophets). This is because the maintenance of a community of individuals with wills of their own initially *requires* the existence of authority in a visibly objective form. The law *is* objective, but only what comes to us through external sense is initially recognized as objective. Once the law of the community has achieved true (i.e. *conceptual*) objectivity, the historical consciousness can assume its mature form, and begin to ask how the law came to be, who really made it, and what it is for. When the historian examines the answers to these questions he makes his first philosophical discovery : the existence of "Providence" or the operation of Reason in disguise, the "cunning of Reason". But this discovery, be it noted, is implicitly the abolition of Providence, the outlawing of God as a direct agent in history, and—at least in principle—the unmasking of Reason. God and Providence are really done for when we understand how the operation of our own subjective passions has generated the objective structure of our institutions. But the cunning of Reason remains the abiding concern of the historian, for the very meaning of "hindsight" as an ordinary phenomenon of practical experience is that a pattern of events recalled from the past has a different aspect from what the events had when they were projected as objectives for the future, or when they were acts and policies being contended about in the present. The historian must *always* look for a "rationality" that the agents themselves were not aware of, in order to comprehend why leadership was accepted or rejected, and why policies succeeded or failed. But the critical historian *knows* that he is observing and seeking to comprehend the struggles of men in their world, and that "God's" agency in the business is entirely a function of *their* faith and *his* reason.

In our present perspective we cannot help agreeing with Marx that for the historian to speak of God *at all* in these circumstances is a "mystification". To us it seems better to speak of "ideals" and "ideology" on one side and "real explanation" or "truth" on the other. But Hegel was speaking to an audience of educated Lutherans, and he wanted to show what the *real* relation of the supposedly *separate* worlds of noumena and phenomena was. For his audience (and for him) "God" was the natural name for "absolute being" (on the side of *faith*) and for "absolute truth" (on the side of *knowledge*). From our post-theological point of view there is "mystification" involved here, but we ought to admit that Marx himself was more a victim of it than those he sought to enlighten. It is certainly misguided for the historian to see himself as "justifying the ways of God to man". But it is a *greater* mistake to give the "noumenal" role of "God" to the "economic process" (or any *finite* aspect of the historical situation).

Understanding Hegel's socialization of Providence in history will help us to comprehend the kind of objectivity that he discovers in philosophical speculation. The philosopher who knows what he is doing must think for himself about his world. But he must also think about it as the world that belongs to him in common with all his fellows. He must strive to articulate just those aspects of it that belong to "science"—i.e., they belong to its structure as a world that *knows* itself. In order to avoid being trapped by the subject/object structure of finite knowing (and ending up with a separation of the noumenal from the phenomenal), he must think from the point of view of the world as a whole. But further he must show that this is what the history of philosophy was always leading up to. Just as the dialectic of passions and ideals in political history is revealed by the historian to be the expression of human rationality, so the dialectic of theoretical reason in its history must be shown to evolve in and of itself towards a self-conscious totality that maintains its own equilibrium through the restless self-criticism of pure thought.

I believe we all find Kant's undertaking in the *Critique of Pure Reason* both intelligible and intellectually respectable, though I suppose we all agree that it could not be perfectly successful, if only because it was too closely connected with a particular state of mathematics and physics. Hegel's system seems to me to be connected in much the same way with a particular condition of the life sciences —a condition which was destined to be overthrown very dramatically and very soon by the quite unphilosophical Charles Darwin. Just as Newtonian physics is the science which Kant's concept of "Nature" is constructed to fit, so Aristotelian biology is the paradigm of Hegel's logic of the "true infinite". Living nature is conceived by Hegel as a stable equilibrium of generational cycles—so the structure of "absolute knowledge" will have this kind of stability (if it has any). For if the world is intelligible at all, it cannot be an accident that thought is the prerogative of a particular type of living organism.

If nature is—as this biology takes it to be—a closed system in which there is living spontaneity without essential novelty, then "absolute knowledge" can express the structure of a *free* consciousness of it, not finally, but perfectly. There can be no *final* expression of it, for to imagine such a thing involves a violation both of the structure of experience and of the nature of language. All language—including Hegel's *Logic*—is the utterance of some particular individual, and it gets its significance from the collective experience of the community whose historic and cultural tradition materially constitute the speaker/writer's memory, and whose institutions constitute his active personality. Philosophy is possible because one can speak *for* this community, and a philosopher must speak in the first instance to it. Only within it, and to its members can he offer his philosophic demonstrations. A later culture, or a culture with a different tradition and institutions, will need a new (or different) demonstration. But if the totality of Nature in which free consciousness is begotten is an absolute constant, the *identity* of what is demonstrated in all such culturally conditioned efforts at self-understanding will always be evident, and the degree of evidence (both intensive and extensive—i.e. both its probative *force* and the range of recipients for whom it is probative) will increase with the range of conscious experience that is successfully "inwardized" (whether through speculative recall of what is past, or through thoughtful appreciation of what is present).

It is the constancy of Nature as the objective foundation and background of human history, that justifies the *separation* of the *Logic*—Hegel's equivalent of the Platonic χωρισμός. Like Plato Hegel uses the "myth" of Creation as a way of expressing the absolute *difference* between the logical and the empirical aspects of experience. (We should note that he does not use this sort of language when he comes to the *speculative* transition from Logic to Nature, for at that point it is the *identity* of thought and being that matters.) It makes sense to speak of the *Logic* as "the exposition of God *before* the Creation" (Lasson, p. 31; Miller, p. 50) only because if Nature itself is completely determinate, then all speculative thought has the same determinate goal. This goal was expressed by Spinoza in language that was still valid for Hegel, although the meaning of

232

the key word had changed, as "the union of the mind with the whole of Nature".

Hegel's concept of "Nature" was different from Spinoza's—he could not have fought his lifelong battle against Newton without being very clearly aware that the "idea of Nature" is one that has a *history*. But he thought that this history was one that could and must be philosophically "comprehended". It was for that that a "philosophy of nature" was necessary, and necessarily *prior* to any "philosophy of science". And he thought further that in his return from Newton to Aristotle, or, to put it more dialectically, his integration of Newtonian mechanics into a synthesis inspired by Aristotle, the cycle of the "true infinite" had completed itself. That his understanding both of the empirical data and of the scientific theories was imperfect he well knew. Hence he foresaw that the advance of knowledge would make revisions in the *argument* of his *Logic* necessary. The improvement of his *Logic* even in the existing state of knowledge was a very real possibility in his mind (Lasson, p. 36; Miller, p. 54). But the conceptual ideal of Nature as a continuous *logical* development, leading up to Spirit and providing, because of its perfect determinacy, a fixed reference point to which Spirit would always *return* and so close the cycle of its own *free* (or historical) development, this was for Hegel an "intellectual intuition".

Of course the *fact* of biological and natural evolution is not practically important. The idea that the earth itself has a history, and that life *may* have evolved during this history, was quite familiar to Hegel. He considers the hypothesis and dismisses it as philosophically irrelevant. The abysses of geological time are no more significant for our human task of self-comprehension than the abysses of astronomical space. Yet both of these "bad infinites" make Hegel uncomfortable, and it is clear that this is because they are a threat to his return to the great tradition of speculative theology. One cannot think of the world as "created" (in a logically harmless or strictly mythical sense) if it is evolving in a non-cyclic way. For one will not then be dealing with a God who merely symbolizes intelligibility.

We may well think that this barring of the return to speculative theology is a *gain*, not a loss, and that Hegel's stoutly maintained affectation of indifference about the hypothesis of evolution was wise. The whole project of a "return" to speculative theology in which the philosopher is consciously unified with his God strikes us as absurd. But if Nature is really a non-cyclic temporal process then it cannot be comprehended as a self-grounding whole. The "idea of Nature" now becomes a *free* function of the evolution of Spirit, not a fixed reference point in terms of which the cycle of Spirit's evolution can be charted and comprehended. It was not an accident, I think, that the Darwinian revolution in biology proved to be the precursor of a more radical conceptual revolution in physics. Certainly it was no accident that that later revolution went hand in hand with the development of an instrumentalist philosophy of science.

We know what Hegel would say about instrumentalism, for Fichte was a consistent instrumentalist with respect to natural science, and Hegel recognized him as one. To read Hegel's critiques of Fichte for not having a proper philosophy of nature (Hegel, 1801), is to be made vividly aware of how desperately *we* need a philosophy of nature. For we are now in Fichte's position of regarding nature simply as the system of real possibilities for action, without a vestige of Fichte's "philosophical faith" to guide our active choices. For us, therefore, it is a *practical* necessity to understand how we *can* be safely "at home" in the world, not—as it was for Hegel—a *theoretical* need to know how we *are* "at home" in it. Of course all "needs" are practical in a sense : but there is a great difference between satisfying the need for knowledge in order to perfect our happiness and understanding the conditions of our own survival.

As a result of *our* scientific revolution Hegel's two circles of Nature and Spirit must, for the future, be conceived as one. If this circle can be formulated *systematically* at all, then Hegel's philosophical system will retain some philosophical interest. But the "separation" of the *Logic* will have to be given up; and with it we must surrender all possibility of a theological interpretation of experience that is critically rational. Hegel's God is not a "separate" intelligence until we separate Him by "expounding his essence before the Creation". But if there is nothing absolute to think about except the historical evolution of our own consciousness, then *only* "the procession of the Spirit"—the process of "inwardizing", taking possession of our own experience and of the experience of others, dead or elsewhere—only the structure of this process remains as the content of "absolute knowledge".

Even within his own "separated" *Logic* Hegel recognized that the process of rational communication itself is in a special category. He presents it—in its "separated" form as the "knowing of knowing"—as the ultimate essence of his "absolute knowledge". This is the point, I think, where the *general* and abiding interest of his philosophy must lie. Few of us will want to emulate Hegel's systematic

attempt to interpret his time to itself—his success was highly doubtful, and it is even more doubtful whether the same degree of com-
prehensiveness is achievable by one man in our world. But all of
us face the problem of communicating with others whose frame
of reference, and/or standpoint and goals, differ widely from our
own. We also face the problem of comprehending a past which is
a continuous texture of conceptual frameworks in dialectical conflict and interaction. I am not here using the word "dialectical" in
any technical sense, and I do not think that the *general* interest of
Hegel's work lies in any *technical* theory of the dialectic proposed
by Hegel. Hegel's purpose in all of his technical statements was the
"speculative" one that I have tried to sketch. He wanted to show
how all the possible frameworks are connected, each in its appropriate way, with one *absolute* framework. The problems that we
all have are first to make ourselves *aware* of the frameworks that
we use; secondly to *reconcile* the plurality of frames that we personally use and need with one another; and thirdly to construct
effective lines of communication with those whose lives are now—or
were long ago—organized in and by different frames. Hegel's whole
life was devoted to an immensely painstaking investigation of
exactly these problems. Himself a child of the Enlightenment, he
rebelled against the comfortable conviction that it is really quite easy
to see things in the light of Reason, and that only one frame of
reference is used by all honest and intelligent men at all times. We
may think that he was simply mistaken in his own speculative return
to this ideal in the *Logic*. But in any event we should not overlook
the value of his rebellion. We should examine his work to discover
all the *different* ways in which he sees different types of conceptual
conflict as being resolved. If we find the Hegelian dialectic difficult
to follow—and who does not?—we should *not* go for enlightenment
to formal theoretical statements about the dialectic, whether Hegel's
or those of someone else who does *not* find it difficult. We must go
rather back to the data, back to the concrete cases and situations
that Hegel was trying to interpret; and we must try out whatever
we discover on such half-way Hegelisms as Kuhn's (1962) theory of
"scientific revolution" or Collingwood's (1940) conception of metaphysics as the "science of absolute presuppositions".

We shall never be in a position to evaluate Hegel's philosophical
system and its method properly, until we recognize him as the greatest
philosopher of *history* that the world has so far produced. Only
Vico is worthy to be compared with him, and perhaps only Vico
and he are worthy of the title "philosopher of history" at all. Most

analytical philosophers of history are content either to use historical data as laboratory material for their own researches in the philosophy of mind, or to illustrate for historians the value of such researches. If they stumble into a genuinely historical problem—say the problem of the "causation" of a major event such as a war—they fail to recognize its historical dimension (the fact that we see the event in a different perspective now that it is *historic*, and so are conscious or at least *want* to be conscious of what Hegel called "the cunning of Reason") and they begin to do philosophy of social science. The real problems of the average historian, which are the problems first of how to get back into a lost thought-perspective, and secondly of how to reconcile that perspective with his own, and present it within the compass of his own perspective so that his audience is spared as much as possible of the conceptual struggle that he has had—these problems the philosophers generally leave untouched.

Hegel was a philosopher of history because he faced these problems in a uniquely philosophical way. He wanted to present all perspectives in their relation to the absolute perspective. Since the finite point of view, whether past or present, had to be uniformly suppressed (or preserved only in a sublimated form) Hegel was an historian of a peculiar kind—often a peculiarly *bad* historian by any ordinary standards. But we ought to recognize that his *Aesthetics*, his *Philosophy of Religion* and his *History of Philosophy* are all of them notable contributions to the philosophy of history. Each of them is more noteworthy, probably, than the official lectures on the *Philosophy of World History*, since the symbolic and conceptual modes in which a whole society perceives itself are more important to the historian than the understanding of any singular agents.

The greatest of all Hegel's contributions to the subject, and probably the work of his that is of the most general and abiding significance, is the *Phenomenology of Spirit*. This book was deliberately composed in order to lead us to the absolute standpoint from which the *Logic* would be written, by repossessing historically all the finite or immature points of view which marked important moments in the evolution of the absolute standpoint. Thus it is a work which retains its *systematic* relevance for us, because the concept of Nature is viewed in its evolution, and Absolute Knowledge itself has the role of a regulative ideal, not a reality; it is a goal, not an achieved system. But the *Phenomenology* has also proved perennially interesting as a collection of distinct loci, especially those chapters in which *personal* standpoints of the kind familiar to us in ourselves or our history books are developed. Like Plato, however, Hegel holds our interest because of the amount of work he makes us do for ourselves. To discover what he means, he forces us to do the historical labour over again. In the *Phenomenology* he even tells us that we must do it, and then fails to supply most of the specific historical indications that an ordinary historian (whether of the World Spirit or of anything else) would supply. If the *Logic* is the "thought of God", then the *Phenomenology* is the tongues of angels. It is my belief that a proper explanatory commentary on the *Phenomenology* would reveal to us a work that can teach us more about the kind of social beings that we are, and the kind of historical world that we necessarily create and inhabit than any other so far penned. But now the Bacchanalian revel has no doubt begun to make *me* drunk. My only excuse is that one *has* to believe something of this kind if one is going to write more than a grandiloquent programmatic statement. Essays like this present one are all too easy to write, but with the angel one must wrestle all night for one's life.

Professor H. S. Harris
Glendon College
York University
Toronto
Canada

BIBLIOGRAPHY

Bernstein, Richard J.: *Praxis and Action*, Philadelphia, University of Pennsylvania Press, 1971.
Bradley, Francis H. (1878) *Ethical Studies*, Oxford, Clarendon Press, 1927.
Collingwood, Robin G.: *Essays on Metaphysics*, Oxford, Clarendon Press, 1940
Findlay, John N.: *Hegel; A Re-Examination*, London, Allen and Unwin, 1958.
Harris, Henry S.: *Hegel's Development*, Oxford, Clarendon Press, 1972.
Hegel, Georg W. F. (1801) *Differenz des Fichte'schen und Schelling'schen Systems der Philosophie* in *Gesammelte Werke*, volume 4, Hamburg, F. Meiner, 1968.
Hegel (1807) *Phänomenologie des Geistes*, edited by J. Hoffmeister, Hamburg, F. Meiner, 1952; *Phenomenology of Mind*, translated by J. B. Baillie, London, Allen and Unwin, 1949.
Hegel (1812) *Wissenschaft der Logik*, edited by G. Lasson, Leipzig, F. Meiner, 1923; *Science of Logic*, translated by A. V. Miller, London, Allen and Unwin, 1969.
Hegel (1821) *Philosophy of Right*, translated by T. M. Knox, Oxford, Clarendon Press, 1942.
Hegel (1830) *Enzyklopädie*, edited by F. Nicolin and O. Pöggeler, Hamburg, F. Meiner, 1959.
Hegel: *Aesthetics*, translated by T. M. Knox, Oxford, Clarendon Press, 1975.

Hegel: *History of Philosophy*, translated by E. S. Haldane and F. H. Simpson, London, Routledge and Kegan Paul, 1955.

Hegel: *Philosophy of History*, translated by J. Sibree, New York, Willey Book Company, 1944.

Hegel: *Philosophy of Religion*, translated by E. B. Spiers and J. B. Sanderson, London, Routledge and Kegan Paul, 1962.

Kant, Immanuel: *Critique of Pure Reason*, translated by N. Kemp Smith, London, Macmillan, 1958.

Kant: *Critique of Practical Reason*, translated by L. W. Beck, Indianapolis, Liberal Arts Press, 1956.

Kant: *Critique of Judgement*, 2 vols., translated by J. C. Meredith, Oxford, Clarendon Press, 1911 and 1928.

Kuhn, Thomas S. (1962) *The Structure of Scientific Revolutions*, second edition, enlarged, Chicago, University of Chicago Press, 1970.

Marx, Karl: *Critique of Hegel's Philosophy of Right*, translated by J. O'Malley, Cambridge University Press, 1970.

O'Brien, George D.: *Hegel on Reason and History*, Chicago, University of Chicago Press, 1975.

Popper, Karl R.: *The Open Society and its Enemies*, 2 vols., Princeton, N.J. Princeton University Press, 1963.

Quinton, Anthony M. (1975a) "Spreading Hegel's Wings I", *The New York Review of Books*, 29 May 1975, 34–37.

Quinton (1975b) "Spreading Hegel's Wings II", *The New York Review of Books*, 12 June 1975, 39–42.

Taylor, Charles: *Hegel*, Cambridge University Press, 1975.

XVIII

HISTORY AND CLASS CONSCIOUSNESS*

G. Petrović

HISTORY and class consciousness are apparently two "phenomena" or "things" of an entirely different scope and significance, so that they should not be mutually "compared" or "measured". History seems to be a necessary form of human life, the only possible space of social development, and class consciousness merely one "aspect" or "quality" of those transient social "groups" we call "classes". The relationship between history and class consciousness appears thus as a relationship between a whole and one of its passing parts.

However, at least one important thinker, György Lukács, insisted on the essential connection between history and class consciousness, and even between history and class consciousness of a special class, the proletariat. In his conception the class consciousness of the proletariat was regarded not merely as an aspect or insignificant part of history, but as an essential precondition for establishing a truly human society and true history. Defining in this way the relationship between history, society and class consciousness, he claimed no originality but insisted that he was giving an orthodox interpretation of Marx and Marxism.

Lukács's book *History and Class Consciousness* is not limited to the discussion of the question indicated by its title. As we are interested here specifically in that question, and not in the book as

---

* Having received the invitation to the Oxford International Symposium with considerable delay, the author was not able to prepare a paper especially for the symposium. That is why this paper, already published in Serbo-Croatian in the Yugoslav edition of *Praxis* (No. 3–4/1974) has been translated into English and slightly revised. In addition to a number of inconveniences, this solution may have also two "conveniences": (1) it may show what topics are sometimes discussed among Yugoslav Marxist philosophers in their own language and how they are discussed; and (2) it may stimulate further discussion of a topic which has already been discussed in English, although not so much in Oxford or among philosophers.

such, we shall leave aside all other questions in it, and we shall take into account some other writings by Lukács, and some writers other than Lukács.

If the question about the relationship between history and class consciousness is typically Lukácsean, it is by no means only his, or at all purely technical (philosophical, sociological, or historical). The relationship between class consciousness (and consciousness in general) and history has also been discussed outside the province of pure theory. Thus in recent years in Yugoslavia the idea of the role of class consciousness in history has been sharply criticized from two seemingly opposite viewpoints : according to one strong national attitude consciousness is a much more important condition and component of the meaningful shaping of history and according to the other history needs no "committed", "ideological" consciousness, but only a "neutral", and "objective", one resulting from the development of science and technology. Now we are undergoing a phase in which the Lukácsean thesis about the key role of class consciousness in history is being revived and affirmed impetuously, though without Lukács's thoughtfulness (and without his sincerity).

Regardless of whether we agree with Lukács's view of history and class consciousness, in this question he is unavoidable. Thus we shall begin by a brief reminder of his ideas.

I

First of all, it should be noted that the conception of the relationship between history and class consciousness which was to be elaborated in *History and Class Consciousness* had already been sketched in Lukács's earlier and smaller work *Tactics and Ethics* (in Hungarian, Budapest 1919).

Already in this work Lukács pointed out that the class struggle of the proletariat cannot be equated with the class struggle of other classes, that it is not a particular phenomenon, but has a broader significance, as "a means for liberating mankind, a means for the true beginning of *human* history."[1]

However, Lukács also stressed that this "means" is not an automatic mechanism bringing salvation to mankind regardless of the will and the activity of individuals. The realization of socialism is impossible without the historico-philosophical understanding of the meaning of historical process, and without the ethical decision of individuals to struggle for the realization of this possible historical

240

goal. And morally right action presupposes not only an abstract philosophy of history, but also a developed class consciousness.

Class consciousness, which is a precondition for morally right (socialist) action, is defined by Lukács by the help of class interest, as a consciousness which, expressing the class interest, rises above its mere givenness. Class interest as a correlate of class consciousness thus conceived is described as a world-historical calling, something different both (1) from the sum total of the personal interests of individuals belonging to the class, and also (2) from momentary interests of the class as a collective unity.[2]

In opposing those who demand that in socialism the leading role in society should be conferred upon the so-called "intellectual workers", Lukács maintains that in order to solve the question about the possibility of meaningful and directive inclusion of human consciousness into the social development one should start from "some important statements which—themselves no further provable and also in no need of proof—form the basis of existence and knowability of society—just as much as do the fundamental principles of geometry in the science of space."[3]

These statements of axiomatic character according to Lukács are :

1. "The development of society is determined exclusively by forces which exist inside society (according to the Marxist view the class struggle and transformation of the relations of production)."

2. "The development of society has an univocally determinable, although still insufficiently known, direction."

3. "This direction should be brought into a determinate, though still insufficiently known, connection with human purposes; this connection is knowable and can be made conscious, and the process of making it conscious has a positive influence upon the development itself."

4. "This connection, of which we have already spoken, is possible because the motive powers of the society are, to be sure, independent of every *individual* human consciousness, from its will and purpose, but their existence can be thought only in the form of human consciousness, human will and human purpose."[4]

If we consider these four axioms which are, it is true, given only as "examples", the question of their consistency naturally arises. The first two maintain that the development of society—which is determined by the class struggle and transformation of the relations

241

of production—has its universally determinable, although still insufficiently known, direction, which, accordingly has to be independent of knowledge. In the third thesis we are told that by making this process conscious we can influence the development itself, and in the fourth that the motive powers of society can exist merely in the form of human consciousness. The latter, in contrast to the initial mechanistically materialistic statements already sounds entirely "idealistic". But let us leave aside these "details" and have a look at what Lukács derives from his axioms.

According to Lukács, from the four axioms an unambiguous Marxist reply to the question about spiritual leadership follows : " 'Spiritual leadership' cannot be anything but making conscious the development of the society, a clear knowledge of the essential in contrast to disguised and falsified formulas, hence the knowledge that the 'lawlikeness' of the development of society, its full independence of human consciousness, its similarity to the play of blind forces of nature, is mere appearance which can exist only so long as the blind forces of nature are not awakened by knowledge to consciousness."[5])

Spiritual leadership of society can, accordingly, consist only in making its development conscious; however this does not mean discovering necessary social laws, but coming to see that social laws independent of human consciousness are merely appearance. This view may easily give rise to some doubts : First of all, if spiritual leadership consists merely in making social development conscious, this may suggest that social development is independent of consciousness; but if "making conscious" consists in discovering that laws of social development are *not* independent of consciousness, it should follow that "making conscious" can not mean knowing something independent of knowledge.

The "awakening by knowledge to consciousness" may also provoke confusion, because knowledge is sometimes regarded as a specific form of consciousness. In order to guard against a possible misunderstanding, Lukács in a footnote explains that, in the traditions of German classical philosophy, he on the contrary understands consciousness as a form of knowledge, "that special stage of knowledge, in which subject and the known object are in their substance homogeneous, where, consequently, knowledge develops from *inside*, not *from outside*."[6] And he adds : *"The main importance of this method of knowledge consists in the fact that the mere fact of knowledge provokes an essential change in the known objective: That tendency which already existed earlier in it becomes—provoked by making it*

242

conscious—due to knowledge more firm and powerful than it was earlier and than it without knowledge could be."[7]

This description of consciousness and knowledge shows once more the basic weakness of Lukács's view, his oscillation between a contemplative and passivistic theory of knowledge and Marx's thinking of praxis and revolution. On the one hand, Lukács stresses the active role of consciousness and knowledge, maintaining that already "the mere fact of knowledge provokes an essential change in the known objective". On the other hand, when making more precise the character of this essential change, he seems inclined to reduce it to the fact that due to knowledge a tendency "which already existed earlier" becomes "more firm and powerful".

It seems that from this viewpoint one would not be allowed to speak of a revolutionary or subversive role of consciousness, but merely of auxiliary, or accelerant. However Lukács is concerned with the world-overthrowing role of Marxism : "The world-overthrowing power of Marxism stems from the fact that *Marx discovered the class struggle as the motive power of the development of society and the laws of the class struggle as laws of social development in general.* In this way he brought to consciousness the real motive power of world history, the class struggle, which until then operated blindly, without consciousness. The class consciousness of the proletariat developed by Marx's teaching shows for the first time in the history of mankind that true motive factors of history do not operate as component parts of a machine without consciousness (or on the basis of imagined motives, which comes to the same thing), but have awakened to consciousness that they are the true motive powers of history. The spirit, and even the meaning of the social development of mankind came—in the class consciousness created by Marxism—out of the state of unconsciousness. In this way the laws of social development ceased to be blind, catastrophic and fatal forces : they awaken to self-reflection, to consciousness."[8])

According to this, the class struggle was even before Marx the motive power of history, but Marx made this motive power conscious. However, it is not quite clear what emerged through this "making conscious" and what was the relation of this "class consciousness of the proletariat developed by Marx's teaching" and the consciousness of the proletariat *not yet* developed by Marx's teaching.

An answer to this question is given by an attempt to clarify the concept of class consciousness : "But the class consciousness of the proletariat in itself is merely a step to this consciousness. Becaue class consciousness in its mere givenness establishes only the relation-

243

ship of immediate interests of the proletariat toward the laws of social development. Final goals of development for the class consciousness of the proletariat are merely abstract ideals in a—new—Utopian remoteness. For the true *becoming conscious of oneself* (Sich-Bewusstwerden) of society one further step is necessary : *becoming conscious of the class consciousness of the proletariat* (das Bewusstwerden des Klassenbewusstseins des Proletariats). This necessary step means transcending direct class consciousness and immediate oppositions of class interests and coming to know that world-historical process which through class interests and the class struggles leads to the goal : *classless society, emancipation from every economic dependence.* However, mere class consciousness (exclusive recognition of immediate economic interests, which is expressed in the so-called social-democratic Realpolitik) can help this knowledge only by giving a measure for the rightness of *immediate steps.*"[9]

However, there are historical situations, such as moments of world crisis in which steps guided by immediate interests, like mere pattering in the night, are not sufficient. "In these moments there is necessary what I called the making conscious of the class consciousness of the proletarians : *the consciousness of the world-historical calling (Berufung) of the class struggle of the proletariat.* This consciousness enabled Marx to create a new philosophy revolutionizing the world and building it anew. This consciousness makes Lenin the leader of the revolution of the proletariat. This consciousness solely . . . is called to become the spiritual leader of society."[10]

In this way, only class consciousness can take the spiritual lead in society; it makes possible the undertakings of such individuals as are Marx and Lenin, be it the theoretical undertaking of creating a "new philosophy", or the "practical" undertaking of leading a revolution. But this class consciousness is not the class consciousness of the proletarians in its factual givenness, but the class consciousness of the proletariat which has become conscious, the consciousness of the world-historical process and of the world-historical calling of the class struggle of the proletariat. The class consciousness which has become conscious is thus a presupposition for Marx's and Lenin's achievements, and Marx's work is in its turn the presupposition for making conscious the class consciousness of the proletariat—a circle which is perhaps not so vicious as it at first might seem.

However, what is the relation between the individual proletarian and the class consciousness of the proletariat? In one of the papers in the collection *Ethics and Tactics* Lukács writes about that : "Every proletarian is in accordance with his class membership an

244

orthodox Marxist. What the theoreticians can arrive at only by the hard work of thinking, is always already given to the proletarian in accordance with his belonging to the proletariat—under the condition that he reflects on his true class membership and on all consequences which follow from it."[11]

In other words, every proletarian is potentially a Marxist, but the transformation of this potentiality into actuality presupposes reflection about one's class membership and about the consequences which stem from it. In his early articles Lukács thus outlined the theory of history and class consciousness which he was to elaborate in his main work. Although there are a lot of unclarities and things left unsaid, nearly all important elements of the conception which was to be elaborated in *History and Class Consciousness* are already contained here.

No doubt, *History and Class Consciousness* contributed a number of smaller precisions to this conception, and also two rather important : (1) the thesis that only the proletariat as a class can transform the whole of society *because* it is likewise a totality and (2) the thesis about the party as the guardian of the class consciousness of the proletariat.

The first thesis can be partly illustrated by the following quotation : "The totality of the object can only be posited if the positing subject is itself a totality; hence in order to think itself, the subject *must* think of the object as a totality. In modern society only and exclusively *classes* represent this viewpoint of totality as subject."[12]

The second thesis is expressed, for example, in the following passage : "However, in the dialectical unity of theory and praxis, which was found and made conscious by Marx in the emancipatory struggle of the proletariat, there can be no pure consciousness, either as a "pure" theory or as a mere demand, a mere "ought", a mere norm of action. The demand, too, has here its reality. That is to say, the stand of the historical process which gives the character of demand to the class consciousness of the proletariat, a "latent and theoretical" character, must be shaped as a corresponding reality and as such intervene actively in the totality of the process. This form of the proletarian class consciousness is the *party*."[13]

The above outline of Lukács's view on history and class consciousness is certainly very incomplete. However, for our purpose it may be quite sufficient, because our goal is not an evaluation of Lukács, but a discussion of a question which, although first sharply raised by him, has been treated by many others since.

245

II

Discussion of the theses outlined above has been very extended; thus it cannot be summarized here. Instead, we shall consider only two critiques of Lukács's theses, made from two opposite viewpoints in two recent essays by two contemporary Marxists, the Polish philosopher Adam Schaff, and the English sociologist Thomas Bottomore.

In his paper "The Consciousness of a Class and Class Consciousness" Adam Schaff reminds us that the term "class consciousness" is ambiguous, because it means, first, "the consciousness (characteristic) of a class", i.e. "that consciousness which a given class actually has under given conditions", and second "the consciousness of class interests", i.e. "the realization of what those interests are, and the resulting guidelines for a given class's activities under given conditions". Class consciousness in the second meaning manifests itself in two forms : (a) "as a theory, which consists of the total knowledge of a given class's position within a specified social structure (which always presupposes a more or less explicitly formulated theory of social structure and social development") and (b) "as an ideology, which consists of the totality of human convictions and attitudes (in the sense of readiness to act), combined with an active behaviour intended to put into effect a specified goal for social development, accepted within a given system of values."[14]

The two basic meanings, according to Schaff, are entirely different, and history knows many cases of discrepancy, chasm, and even direct opposition between the two. Such gaps arise when a class does not realize its actual interests and acts in disagreement with, or in opposition to, them. This occurs most frequently with nascent classes, which have not yet attained the consciousness of their interests, but it can also happen with developed classes, if the ruling classes succeed in preventing the members of the ruled class from widely developing their social consciousness.

According to Schaff Lukács saw the difference between the two meanings of "class consciousness", but using the term in two different meanings he came to paradoxical statements like the one that class consciousness meant the class-determined *un*consciousness of one's social situation.

In order to avoid such paradoxes Schaff suggests that the two meanings of "class consciousness" mentioned should be used as two different terms, and in such a way that the term "class consciousness" should be preserved as the term for class consciousness in the psychological sense, and the "class ideology" for class consciousness in the second sense. According to this proposal "class ideology" would stand for class interests (as the founders of a given ideology see them), whereas "class consciousness" would stand for those opinions and beliefs which the members of a given class actually share.[15]

To make this distinction, according to Schaff, is not to require that the two phenomena should be completely separated. On the contrary, when we have drawn the distinction we can clearly express the task, that the class consciousness should be raised to the level of class ideology, i.e. that the "well-shaped theory and ideology of the labour movement in the form of Marxism" should be brought "to the consciousness of the masses".[16] The experiences of revolutionary movement, according to Schaff, "make us sensitive to the importance of watching what the actual consciousness of the working class is and to the importance of shaping that consciousness in the spirit of revolutionary ideology."[17]

From this point of view it is the basic deficiency of Lukács's conception that he *does not* conceive the *possible* class consciousness of the proletariat as a class ideology which should be brought to the factual consciousness of the proletariat from outside (by ideologists).

The objection raised against Lukács by Thomas Bottomore is directly opposite. According to his view it is the basic difficulty in Lukács that he conceives Marxism as a theory of class ideologies which at the same time is itself a class ideology. And it is a basic shortcoming of Lukács that his conception is neither theoretical nor empirical, but ideological, that he is concerned with "how Marxism should be conceived in order to be an effective instrument of the revolutionary proletariat."[18] Lukács's distinction between the empirical, factual consciousness of the working class and its possible consciousness which it factually does not possess, according to Bottomore, leads of necessity to the idea of Party and its ideologists as the embodiment of the true class consciousness : "In practice, the meeting place of the working class, with its undeveloped consciousness, and the intellectuals, is the *party*; but the meeting is one-sided, for the party embodies above all a correct theory of the world, and it is therefore dominated by the ideologists."[19]

According to Bottomore this view diverges widely from Marx's idea of class consciousness : "Marx states quite plainly that the working class will, through its own efforts and experiences, attain a fully developed consciousness of its class situation and aims. Indeed he considered that this process had already advanced some way, in the form of the various socialist movements, before he undertook his own studies."[20]

After having given two quotations from Marx (one from the *Poverty of Philosophy*, and another from the introductory note to the *Enquête Ouvriére* of 1880), Bottomore comments : "According to Marx, then, the working class was able to become a *class for itself* and to assume responsibility for its destiny. What part would be played in the process by intellectuals, by political parties and movements Marx did not examine, but it seems clear that these would in any case be subordinate to the general development of the working class. At the other extreme, Lukács subordinates the working class to the "rational consciousness" expounded by party ideologists, and thus provides an intellectual justification for the unrestrained dictatorship of the party, which has characterized all the Soviet-type societies since 1917."[21]

III

Which of the two is right : Schaff reproaching Lukács for not having fully grasped the need for introducing class ideology into the class consciousness, or Bottomore criticizing Lukács for subordinating the working class to the party ideologists and to the dictatorship of the party?

I am afraid that neither of them is quite right, although they may be wrong in rather different ways. Bottomore may underestimate the role of intellectuals, but he is right when criticizing the subordination of the working class to the party ideologists. However he is unjust in regarding Lukács as a univocal advocate of such a subordination. Lukács, it is true, speaks of the party as a guardian of the class consciousness of the proletariat and such formulations are full of danger. But for Lukács the criteria of class consciousness are not the views of party bodies or party ideologists, but the class interests of the proletariat.

In contradistinction to Bottomore Schaff is wrong both in his interpretation of Lukács and (what is more important) in the way in which he wants to correct him. Like Bottomore he is inclined to reduce Lukács to one part of his thinking, but contrary to Bottomore, who energetically opposes every tendency to interpret Marxism as an ideology, Schaff tries to correct Lukács by elaborating Marxism as a theory of ideological indoctrination. Schaff's interpretation of Marxism as a "well-shaped theory and ideology" is rather far from

248

the essence of Marx's thinking of praxis and freedom, his insistence on the importance of shaping the consciousness of the working class "in the spirit of revolutionary ideology" is not only a terminological departure from Marx (for Marx, ideology being the false consciousness, "revolutionary ideology" is a contradiction in terms) but also a programme of social change in which there is not much room for unshaped, free and creative activity of social groups and individuals.

Despite all its weaknesses Lukács's authentic views are superior to views of critics such as Schaff. However, do not even Lukács's authentic views contain certain difficulties?

I think that the greatest difficulties and deficiencies of Lukács's position are due to the fact that he failed to think over more carefully his key concept, the concept of "history", and that he rather uncritically operated both with the concept of "history" and its derivatives "pre-history" and the "true history".

According to Lukács the class consciousness of the proletariat is the decisive condition and means for the revolutionary transition from the pre-history of mankind to its true history. This fundamental thesis remains a mere phrase, if we are not able to clarify what is meant by "history", "pre-history" and "true history". However, in his *History and Class Consciousness* Lukács systematically discusses class consciousness, reification, totality, orthodox Marxism etc., but he makes only occasional remarks on the essence of history. These remarks can be interesting and stimulating, but they are far from exhausting the basic question. Thus we learn that history is no longer "an enigmatic process *to which* man and things are subjected and which ought to be explained by the intervention of transcendent powers or made meaningful by reference to values which are transcendent in relation to history. History, on the contrary, is, on the one hand the product—unconscious until now, of course—of the activity of human beings themselves, and on the other hand, a succession of those processes in which the forms of that activity, these relations of man to himself (to nature and to other people) are reversed."[22] In other words "*history is exactly the history of the unceasing overthrow (Umwälzung) of the forms of objectivity, which shape the existence of man.*"[23]

However instructive these and similar remarks may be, they do not solve the problem of history, nor in particular the relation between the non-authentic pre-history and true history.

In my view, it is inadequate to define history simply as a continuous series of transformations in the relations of man to himself, to nature and to other people. The essence of history is the free creative activity through which man creates his world and himself. We can agree with Lukács that history cannot be explained or made meaningful by the operation of some transcendent powers. However no outside transcendent powers are needed here, not because there is no transcending in history, but because man himself is a transcendence. As a natural being developing within the limits of nature man is of necessity subordinated to general natural laws. However, insofar as he remains exclusively determined by the operation of natural laws, he is merely an alienated man, an animal endowed with intellect. Man's essence lies in the transcendence of the mere naturalness, so that a man is really man, and human society really human, in the measure in which man develops as a free creative being of praxis, and human society as free community of free persons. In other words : "Exactly the *transcending of the natural, the overcoming of the opposition between blind necessity and blind chance by free conscious activity makes up the essence of the historical.*"[24]

This essence of the historical has been only insufficiently realized in previous history. Marx and Engels have shown that previous history has happened basically according to laws which were independent from human will. This is not to say that history up to now developed without the conscious will and efforts of people. However by their efforts people have achieved results which were sometimes even contrary to those intended. This does not mean that until now human beings were merely the blind toys of impersonal forces. History up to now was only pre-history, but even pre-history, as a self-alienated form of human history, is immensely different from purely natural process, and in its brightest moments—in the moments of spiritual and social revolutions—it testifies to the possibility of the true human history.

Some—naive or vulgar—Marxists have been highly enthusiastic about Marx's discovery of the laws of historical process, believing that by this discovery history has been brought to the level of a natural process, and thus gained in value. In this belief they have been partly right, only that the bringing of previous history to the level of natural process was not an exaltation of that history, but a criticism of it as self-alienated history.

Marx and Engels, and in their footsteps Lukács, have seen that the transition from pre-history to true history cannot be an automatic, evolutionary, continuous process, that such a transition is possible only by a revolutionary transformation of inhuman social relations, by establishing an essentially different society and man.

Marx, Engels and Lukács have also seen that a revolutionary

transformation of man and society is not possible as a reorganization or reform carried out by a small number of individuals, wise rulers and their even wiser advisors, not even as a broader activity of propaganda, enlightenment and reconstruction, carried out by ruling groups, but only as a revolutionary deed, as the praxis of a "class with *radical chains*, a class of civil society which is not a class of civil society, an estate which is the dissolution of all estates, a sphere which has a universal character by its universal suffering and claims no *particular right* because no *particular wrong* but *wrong generally* is perpetrated against it; which can invoke no *historical* but only its *human* title, which does not stand in any one-sided opposition to the consequences but in all-round opposition to the presuppositions of the German political system; a sphere, finally, which cannot emancipate itself without emancipating itself from all other spheres of society, which, in a word, is the *complete loss* of man, and hence can win itself only through the *complete re-winning of man*. This dissolution of society as a particular estate is the *proletariat*."[25]

Following Marx and Engels Lukács believed that the proletariat cannot fulfil its historical role, if it does not become a class in itself, if it does not develop its class consciousness, the consciousness of its class interests and of possibilities of realizing them.

Kautsky and Lenin, and after them many others, have seen the difficulties in the assumption that the proletariat can spontaneously develop its class consciousness. As a way out of this difficulty they developed the theory according to which class consciousness like a kind of industrial product is manufactured by scientists, people who stand on the level of contemporary science, and who introduce class consciousness ready-made into the working class.

In contrast to the theory of conveying class consciousness to the working class from the outside, some have advocated the view that such a conveying is not only impossible, but also unnecessary, because the working class can and even lawfully must develop the consciousness of its class interests on the basis of its objective conditions of life. Such an idea of spontaneity was rightly criticized by Lukács as a theoretical failure and as a basis of political opportunism. Leaving aside the question about the ways of the development of class consciousness, Lukács however formulates the thesis about the party as a carrier and guardian of the class consciousness. In his later foreword (of 1967) Lukács interpreted his theory about the attributed class consciousness as an imperfect form of Lenin's theory of introducing class consciousness from the outside.[26] Is not this self-criticism to be understood as an indirect warning that his conception should not be identified with the too simple theory of Lenin?

The theory of bringing class consciousness to the working class from the outside and the one according to which the very conditions of its existence force upon the proletariat the right class consciousness are seemingly contrary. In fact they are basically identical, because both assume that consciousness is something ready made which can be enforced (by ideologists or by "objective conditions"). In opposition to such a view I think that only false consciousness can be forced from the outside. True consciousness can only be fought out by one's own thinking.

The factual raising of the working class to the level of its possible consciousness is not realizable apart from individual consciousnesses of individual proletarians; and individual proletarians cannot become conscious apart from their own activity. In addition to that the becoming class conscious of the proletarians (in the sense of Marx and Lukács) is the becoming conscious of the members of the working class not merely as members of the working class but also as potential founders of a free community of free human persons. Marx proclaimed as his ideal the realization of a society in which the free development of every individual would be the condition for the free development of all. However such a society cannot be realized by the harmonious operation of an army (even a proletarian army) commanded by a wise leadership (or forced to act by the objective conditions). It can be achieved only by the conscious struggle of freely associated fighters who constitute themselves as a community of free human personalities and who in the common struggle for the same basic goals and against the same enemies develop to the full their personal creative potentialities. Not even the most disciplined army of slaves, servants, or officials, regardless of how well it may be organized and led, can realize something which is contrary to its nature—a free human community.

What, then, is the relation between history and class consciousness? The class consciousness of the proletariat is indeed a necessary precondition of true human history, however under the condition that it is not the consciousness of the proletarians fighting to preserve their positions, but the consciousness of the necessity to negate the proletariat as a class and to realize a classless community of free personalities. The class consciousness of the proletariat in this sense is the consciousness of the possibility and ways of achieving universal human emancipation.

Is it identical with what I previously[27] called "the thinking of

252

G. PETROVIĆ

revolution"? The question is not that easy. At this place I may merely indicate : The existence of the proletariat with its at least partly developed consciousness is a precondition for the thinking of revolution, the thinking of revolution is a precondition for the full development of class consciousness.

The development of the class consciousness of the proletariat is not an automatic consequence of social development or of the proletariat's special position in that development. Its criterion is not the belonging to this or that stratum or class, and certainly not the membership card of an organization. Its possibility is laid down in the essence of man, its reality can be brought about only by one's own act, its criterion is the revolutionary deed itself.

Gajo Petrović
Zagreb
Yugoslavia

NOTES

[1] Georg Lukács, *Schriften zur Ideologie und Politik*. Werkauswahl, Band 2, Ausgewählt und eingeleitet von Peter Ludz, Luchterhand, Neuwied und Berlin 1967, p. 5.
[2] *Op. cit.*, p. 9.
[3] *Op. cit.*, p. 14.
[4] *Op. cit.*, p. 15.
[5] *Op. cit.*, p. 15.
[6] *Op. cit.*, p. 15.
[7] *Op. cit.*, pp. 15–16.
[8] *Op. cit.*, pp. 17–18.
[9] *Op. cit.*, p. 18.
[10] *Op. cit.*, p. 19.
[11] *Op. cit.*, p. 38.
[12] Georg Lukács, *Geschichte und Klassenbewusstsein*, Studien über marxistische Dialektik, Sammlung Luchterhand 11, Luchterhand, Neuwied und Berlin 1970, p. 96.
[13] *Op. cit.*, pp. 113–114.
[14] Adam Schaff, "The Consciousness of a Class and Class Consciousness", *The Philosophical Forum*, Vol. III, No. 3–4/1972, p. 342.
[15] *Op. cit.*, p. 348.
[16] *Op. cit.*, p. 352.
[17] *Op. cit.*, p. 357.
[18] T. B. Bottomore, *Sociology as Social Criticism*, George Allen & Unwin, London 1975, p. 97 (in the paper "Class Structure and Social Consciousness", reprinted from István Mészáros (ed.), *Aspects of History and Class Consciousness*, London, 1971).
[19] *Op. cit.*, p. 102.
[20] *Op. cit.*, p. 103.
[21] *Op. cit.*, p. 103.

[22] G. Lukács, *Geschichte und Klassenbewusstsein*, Luchterhand 1970, p. 321.

[23] *Op. cit.*, p. 321.

[24] G. Petrović, *Philosophie und Revolution*, Rowohlt, Reinbek 1971, p. 61.

[25] K. Marx and F. Engels, *Basic Writings on Politics and Philosophy*, edited by Lewis S. Feuer, Anchor Books, Doubleday, Garden City, New York, 1959, pp. 264–265.

[27] See G. Lukács, *Geschichte und Klassenbewusstsein*, Luchterhand 1970, p. 18.

[26] For example in the book *Philosophie und Revolution*, Rowohlt, 1971.

XIX

ON THE ONTOLOGICAL ARGUMENT WITH
SPECIAL REFERENCE TO JACQUES PALIARD

F. T. Kingston

DESPITE what are often regarded as devastating criticisms of the ontological argument offered by St Thomas Aquinas and by Kant, the interest in the argument continues. Indeed the number of convinced supporters of the argument seems to be more numerous than ever and certainly there is a lively interest in it among English-speaking philosophers. Norman Malcolm and Charles Hartshorne are the best-known supporters, but also the critical works by Alvin Plantinga and Jonathan Barnes in addition to numerous articles in various journals are evidence of this. Possibly the most complete volume on the topic is *The Many Faced Argument*—Recent Studies in the Ontological Argument for the Existence of God—edited by John Hick and Arthur McGill.

The main criticism of St Thomas and Kant centred on the contention that existence is not a concept, nor is it part of the essence of a thing. Thus in the *Summa Theologiae* (I, II 1, 2), St Thomas presents the argument under consideration of the question "Whether the Existence of God is self-evident?" in the form "that which exists actually and mentally is greater than that which exists only mentally. Therefore, as soon as the name God is understood, it exists mentally, it also follows that it exists actually." In reply to this argument, St Thomas states that "it does not therefore follow that he understands that what the name signifies exists actually but only that it exists mentally." "Nor can it be argued that it actually exists unless it be admitted that there actually exists something than which nothing greater can be thought and this precisely is not admitted by those who hold that God does not exist."

In *The Critique of Pure Reason*, in the Transcendental Dialectic, Kant presents his criticisms of the proofs for the existence of God. Here, the argument is first called *ontological* and Kant feels that this argument is the basic one to which all the others may be reduced.

However, his criticisms seem to follow the pattern of St Thomas Aquinas in stating that there is no contradiction in admitting the non-existence of a triangle with its three angles, and there is no contradiction in denying the existence of a necessary being. Being is not part of the concept of a thing and the real contains no more than the possible. "A hundred real dollars do not contain a penny more than a hundred possible dollars."

The criticisms of the argument presented by St Thomas and Kant are those which are generally presented by philosophers. A good example of this is A. J. Ayer's *The Central Questions of Philosophy* : "Even if we allow to St Anselm that to conceive of a greatest imaginable being is to conceive of him as existing, it will not follow that there is anything to which this concept applies."

The general consensus of those who continue to support the ontological argument seems to be that the criticisms of St Thomas and of Kant are quite valid based on their premises, but they are not dealing with the ontological argument in its true form. What then is the true form of the argument?

A considerable impetus was given to the interest in the argument by the late Professor Karl Barth, the theologian. In one of his earliest works, Professor Barth wrote about St Anselm's Proof (*Anselm: Fides Quaerens Intellectum.*) He states that Anselm was writing as a theologian, not as a philosopher, and consequently "the aim of theology cannot be to lead men to faith, nor to confirm them in the faith, nor even to deliver their faith from doubt." One begins from faith and therefore, *credo ut intelligam* means : "It is my very faith itself that summons me to knowledge." No wonder then that the fool has not understood what the word "God" means because one has to be a believer to know what Anselm is talking about. Barth believes that the discussion about the fool's lack of understanding of God is only a preamble to Anselm's explanation which follows about the nature of God as revealed by faith. God is seen to be a necessary Being, and therefore the knowledge of God's existence is quite a different matter from the knowledge of other things. "God exists— and he alone—in such a way that it is impossible even to conceive the possibility of his non-existence. That is the thesis of *Proslogion 3*. And that is not a repetition but a vital narrowing of the result of *Proslogion 2*." Thus, according to Barth, what St Anselm was doing was not proving the existence of God but giving an exposition of the significance of necessary Being, which is God.

It is the analysis of the significance of necessary being in *Proslogion 3* that has had a great influence on both Charles Hartshorne and Norman Malcolm. They stress that a necessary being must be regarded as quite different from contingent beings whose possible destruction may be easily conceived. To an extent, thought, in distinguishing the impossible from the possible, seems to bear on existence. We cannot conceive of the impossible to exist—i.e. a squared circle. Does this also apply to a necessary being which cannot be thought as non-existent? As E. L. Mascall states in *The Openness of Being*, one must distinguish between logical and metaphysical necessity, and it seems to be widely recognized that such an approach does not offer a proof but a clarification of the uniqueness of the idea of God.

Anselm wrote the *Proslogion* at Bec in Normandy, and it was the French philosopher Descartes who revived the argument for modern philosophy. Relevant to the topic also is the famous wager of Pascal. It is appropriate that some of the keenest contemporary supporters of the argument are French philosophers, whose interpretation sheds more light on the nature of man than on God.

One of the problems which critics repeatedly encounter in St Anselm is whether Anselm is writing philosophy or theology. On the one hand Anselm is concerned to offer a proof to the fool who says that there is no God; but on the other hand he clearly affirms that he would not have known God if God had not revealed himself. Professor Barth's belief that Anselm was writing pure theology is generally regarded as unsatisfactory, and E. Gilson and E. L. Mascall both affirm that in the Augustinian tradition in which Anselm found himself there was no dichotomy between theology and philosophy. There is no inconsistency in someone philosophizing from faith as long as he understands that his arguments to be philosophically acceptable must have universal appeal.

One point that is clear about St Anselm's *Proslogion* is that it was written as a kind of prayer, at least in the spirit of prayer. Is it possible that St Anselm was implying a natural faith, common to both believer and unbeliever? The natural faith would be based on the common element of the human situation. Though Gabriel Marcel was very critical of the ontological argument as usually presented in a form of philosophical idealism, yet he seemed to have an appreciation of the argument as seen in this light. In his *Metaphysical Journal* (1952), Marcel notes the merit of the ontological argument in showing that God's existence cannot possibly be denied on empirical grounds. The appeal must be to a personal Being—"I believe in You, Who are my sole recourse."

Among a group of deeply spiritual French philosophers who write in the tradition of Maine de Biran are such distinguished names as Jules Lachelier, Jean Nabert, Maurice Blondel, Maurice Nédoncelle, Louis Lavelle, Ferdinand Alquié and Michel Henry. Another one of this group who has written a good deal on the ontological argument is Jacques Paliard. Professor Aimé Forest, writing of the French reflexive philosophers, which he calls "the most remarkable feature of contemporary philosophy," says : "It is indeed remarkable that several of these directions of thought lead us to the doctrine of St Anselm. They wish to rediscover the meaning and value of the argument of the *Proslogion* and to give us a renewed understanding of it." Forest goes on to say that the unique idea of Jacques Paliard is that the mystical life is itself the concrete expression of the ontological argument.

According to Paliard the concrete realities of human experience seem to involve a natural necessity to assume the reality of God. Every human being has a natural belief that his life and the world in which he lives make some kind of sense and this is expressed in the search for knowledge and in moral activity. This natural belief is what Paliard calls implicit thought, or feeling or intuition. In seeking an understanding of the significance of this, Paliard adopts the distinction of Maine de Biran between objective knowledge and metaphysical knowledge. The objective approach, which is necessary and which is that of the natural sciences and of other disciplines, inevitably involves a separation between subject and object. By means of the metaphysical or reflexive approach he seeks to recover the original unity, not by fitting all into an undifferentiated mould, but by holding to nature and other people and the self in all richness and diversity. Reflexion is not introspection but it involves a search for the significance of the self active in the world. This is no easy matter, but according to Paliard, there is an endless quest to discover the ultimate meaning of the universe—"that than which nothing greater can be conceived."

Of particular interest in relation to Paliard's thought is the influence of George Berkeley and of St John of the Cross. Relevant also is the *De Veritate* of St Anselm (1967), in which intellect and will are both involved in the ultimate search for truth.

The influence of Berkeley is especially evident in Paliard's analysis of knowledge and of his discovery of the self as incessant activity. His article "L'illusion de Sinsteden et le problème de l'implication perceptive," and *Pensée Implicite et Perception Visuelle* (1949), and *La Pensée et la vie* (1951) show his awareness of Berkeley's *New Theory of Vision* with its emphasis on the heterogeneity of the

258

objects of the five senses, and also the very personal character of human experience. With his recognition of the relativity of experience, it makes it extremely difficult to establish a connection between experience and the universal principles of reason. Yet the search for knowledge which is fundamental to the human intellect demands that there be a connection, an ultimate unity which makes knowledge possible. Thus, the search for knowledge, according to Paliard, involves at the outset and at the conclusion a presupposition of unity in being, called Love or God. One may be struck here with certain similarities with the role of God "in whom we live and move and have our being" of Berkeley's philosophy.

The influence of St John of the Cross is also evident in Paliard's thought. The will has its purposes, but it also recognizes that other humans have wills and purposes. The result could be and often is a conflict of cross-purposes, and yet the fact that there are volitional beings seems to involve a natural necessity of unity of purpose for all wills. In the latter section of *La Pensée et la vie* (1951), Paliard presents the relevance of the experience of the mystic for philosophy. Even as the will advances towards its fulfilment, it experiences a Dark Night of the Soul, and yet the persistence of the act of willing carries with it the conviction of the promise of ultimate fulfilment. "Only those who aspire to God, whether they find Him in themselves, or whether they find Him absent, are the practitioners of the ontological argument." (1925).

In an article entitled "Prière et dialectique ("Meditation sur le *Proslogion* de Saint Anselme)" (n.d.), Paliard relates his examination of intellect and will more directly to the ontological argument. God belongs to no intellectual class and nothing can be compared to God. Therefore one cannot move from a consideration of essence to the existence of God. Rather what is involved is the designation of the uniqueness of the idea of God. God is the untranscendable, and therefore it is in vain to say that one is going from a subjective idea to objective necessity. It is possible for what is not, not to be. What cannot be can be thought not to be. What can be thought not to be is not the same thing as what cannot be thought not to be.

In this affirmation, human thought is not just affirming itself, but is pointing beyond itself and realizing its inadequacy and dependence. "That than which nothing greater can be conceived" is conceived but is not comprehended because it lies at the farthest bounds of both mind and will. "There is enough light to affirm God, but not enough light to make this affirmation a vision of God." (n.d.) The idea of God transcends itself. It is the ultimate principle of the

259

universe which makes possible intelligibility and the possibility of fulfilment of creatures. As such the reality of God is not remote but encompasses us in any search for intelligibility and in any hope for fulfilment.

Yet people become content with lesser truths and petty desires and close themselves off from "that than which nothing greater can be conceived". According to Paliard, the argument of Anselm requires an endless interaction of intellect and will in a spiritual dialectic which leads to God as the summation.

Paliard discusses the act of reflexion in relation to "that than which nothing greater can be conceived" more fully in an article entitled "La Conscience de Soi et l'idée de Dieu" (1943). Since the infinite is already present in consciousness as the condition of any affirmation, the idea of God is not an abstraction but the "expression of thought to reflect upon itself and to transcend itself." According to Paliard, if one seeks to become self-conscious and to understand oneself, it cannot be done by introspection or by intuition because that is an abstract perspective and the self can only be understood in act in the world. At the same time, as one seeks to understand any experience, there is a gulf always between subject and object, and again one is driven to reflexion to overcome the gulf. The process is an infinite one and when the infinite is perceived in reflexion, it is the condition of all thought which is affirmed only in reflecting upon itself.

God is not the supreme object because He is the condition of all thought. One is essentially a searcher for God, because one never attains God by reflexion, but one can only affirm Him as the ultimate source and sustainer of the profound aspects of one's condition. To reflect is at the same time to think God who conditions us and to think of the short-comings which make us realize that we are other than God. If self-consciousness perceives by reflexion its intimate relationship with God, if it recognizes the secret otherness which constitutes it, and if it is willing to go to the source instead of being enclosed within the self and seeking only self, it is open to "that than which nothing greater can be conceived." At the conclusion of his major work *La Pensée et la vie* (1951), Paliard writes : "It does not belong to reflexion to actualize the possibilities of desire but only to recognize them and to see itself as making confession of what it is not. It affirms without possessing."

In the light of this exposition of Paliard's position, it is appropriate to ask two questions : (1) Does Paliard correctly interpret St Anselm in the *Proslogion*? and (2) What is proved or what is achieved as a result of this exercise?

(1) It has been suggested that the argument of St Anselm is like one of those restaurants in France with the sign "on reçoit avec provisions". One brings to the argument whatever one wants and finds it there.

Yet St Anselm was not concerned with anything but with "that than which nothing greater can be conceived", and he specifies in the reply to the monk Gaunilo that that is quite unique. Thus the consideration of the existence of "that than which nothing greater can be conceived" involves a study of quite a different mode of existence from that of things. Paliard, in regarding God as the untranscendable, certainly reinforces this point, as do Barth, Hartshorne and Malcolm in stressing *Proslogion 3* and the notion of necessary being.

However, merely to give an exposition of the nature of necessary being is not consistent with Anselm's intention in the *Proslogion*. An abstract consideration of necessary being is far from the living God to whom Anselm addressed the *Proslogion*. It was Pascal who deplored the God of philosophers as being so different from the God of religious faith. So many philosophers, in assessing St Anselm's argument, apply their own *a priori* standards of Hume's logic and hence declare the argument invalid. Thus, Jonathan Barnes in *The Ontological Argument* states that "if Hume is right, *a priori* theism is false." Factual statements apply only to sense experience. All others are tautologies. Therefore, it is impossible for statements about God to be factual. Barnes hopes that as a result of his criticisms, theists will not appeal to the irrational.

E. Gilson, in *Reason and Revolution in the Middle Ages*, accuses St Anselm of being over-rationalistic. It is evident that Paliard, in his consideration of the conditions of knowledge, has not abdicated the use of reason. Indeed, he was critical of Gabriel Marcel for not stressing reason sufficiently.

At the same time it is helpful to recall the already mentioned distinction made by E. L. Mascall between logical and metaphysical necessity. Was St Anselm accusing the fool of being a bad logician or was something more profound involved? According to Paliard, what was in St Anselm's mind was not just a contradiction about the meaning of the word *God* but a contradiction which involved the very being of the fool. In denying the existence of God, the fool was carelessly denying that the world had any principles of unity and coherence, any intelligibility and structure, and any ultimate hope of human fulfilment. More profoundly than this, if the fool had reflected on his statement, he would have seen that his faith in his own rationality in making such a statement was parasitic on his faith in intelligibility which made it possible for him to have faith in his own statement. Thus, his very statement in denying God was dependent upon an implicit faith in God in being able to make any statement.

Aimé Forest (1959) suggests that Paliard writes in the spirit, if not according to the letter, of St Anselm. By his reflexive approach Paliard takes us into most profound aspects of the rationality of Anselm's argument, but also in the spirit of Anselm he points out the limitations of rationality. "That than which nothing greater can be conceived" involves not a definition of the nature of God, but an affirmation of the reality of God which lies beyond our human comprehension.

In this also, Paliard shows that the assertion of God's existence as presented by St Anselm is not at all opposed to the spiritual aspects of the *Proslogion*. Indeed the spirituality and the rationality go hand in hand. They complement each other in that the spirituality gives the reason a vision and an impetus while the rationality brings the spirituality down to earth and clarifies its claims.

The question is then that when so many see a dichotomy in Anselm is it possible that there is none and that the only way to grasp what Anselm had in mind is to see him as Paliard does? If this is so, as it appears that it is, does this point shed light not only on Anselm but on the whole of the metaphysical quest? This is not to insist on revelation as a prerequisite to metaphysics but it is to suggest a prerequisite of a natural faith and of an act of will.

What of the spirituality which is a basic characteristic of the *Proslogion* and which is so much a part of the thought of Jacques Paliard? Aimé Forest, in the Preface to Pierre Masset's *La Dialectique de la conscience chez Jacques Paliard*, (n.d.), writes of Paliard: "He begins with a concern more spiritual than practical, more metaphysical than moral ... One must seek for his basic inspiration in St John of the Cross; his final doctrine is a transposition of this." Is spirituality an unwarranted insertion of religion into philosophy or does it bring its own significance into philosophy? To answer this, it is important first of all to beware of the difficulty of comprehension of things of the spirit. "The wind bloweth where it listeth." However, in standing for the ultimate ineffability of reality to the human mind, the idea of the spiritual sheds light on that reality, indicating its richness, its inexhaustibility and also its infinity. St Anselm writes : "For how great is that light from which shines every truth that gives light to the rational mind? How great is that truth in which is everything that is true, and outside which is only nothingness and the false? How boundless is the truth which sees at one glance whatsoever has been made, and by whom, and through whom, and how it has been made from nothing? What purity, what certainty, what splendour where it is." (*Proslogion*, Ch. 14.)

The idea of the spiritual also sheds light on the one who makes the quest. Not only the intellect but a joint activity of intellect and will is required. However, this is not a basic issue in St Anselm, but it is in Paliard and this leads us to the second point.

(2) What is proved or is anything proved as a result of this exercise?

At this point, it is necessary to ask just what would constitute a valid proof for the existence of God? Particularly, after Kant's criticisms of all proofs for the existence of God, it has been necessary to re-examine this question. It is evident that in the pursuit of knowledge people may recognize many different sorts of proofs which vary according to the kind of truth involved. Thus a proof in mathematics may be quite different from a proof offered in the natural sciences and this again may vary considerably from a proof which may be offered in the social sciences. However, a proof for the existence of God offers some very special problems. As the ultimate principle of the universe, God cannot be treated as an object among other objects. As Being, which is the object of a living faith, God cannot be approached basically in terms of principles and ideas, but in terms of existing things. Also, as the Alpha and Omega, the Creator of all things, the Being of God is beyond the comprehension of any finite, human intellect. Now, how is one to demonstrate the existence of such a Being?

In an article on the wager of Pascal (1933), Jules Lachelier makes it clear that the force of the wager cannot rest on the mathematical odds involved which rely on the chance of infinite reward and therefore he asks what experience, what sign is there for a reality beyond nature? His answer is human thinking and willing are the best sign but they provide more of a hope than a proof and ultimately require a leap from the finite to the infinite. More strong than this is the view of Jean Guitton in "Note sur l'argument ontologique et sur la critique que Kant en a faite" (1937–8) who suggests that, contrary to Kant's position, an understanding of nature provides one with an intuition of a natural necessity to affirm the existence of God. Commenting on this article, Paliard states that the passage from nature to God could be called a prayer on the natural level and in reply, Guitton suggests that this is a kind of ontological argument because as one prays "Hallowed be Thy name, Thy will be done," one is asking God to be. However, this suggests that Paliard's position is merely one of wishful thinking and does not do full justice to the force of his argument.

In *Sur les chemins de Dieu* (1956), H. de Lubac points out that in concluding the existence of God as distinct from thought, the ontological argument opposes all that Hegelians have wanted, and this helps to bring out the profound meaning of the argument. He refers at some length to Paliard's interpretation of the argument and suggests that it is very similar to the traditional Thomistic way of affirming God from the contingency of things in nature. One knows that one is only through the untranscendable and one also knows that one is not the untranscendable. Though the terminology is quite different, there is a marked similarity in spirit between Paliard and St Thomas Aquinas.

As stated earlier, the ontological argument was not named as such until the time of Kant. The word "ontology" indicates a study of the essence of being and hence the term "ontological argument" seems suitable as a name for the argument as often presented. The name would also seem appropriate for the interpretation given by Barth, Hartshorne and Malcolm who concentrate on the unique essence of necessary being.

However, if Paliard is correct in his understanding of Anselm, and it appears that his view is truer to the total *Proslogion* than any other, then the name "ontological" is inappropriate. Paliard himself insists that his approach is metaphysical, not ontological, because what is involved is the assertion of being as the necessary presupposition and as the culmination of the human quest for intelligibility and fulfilment. One cannot know the essence of Being. It is beyond our comprehension. However, one must insist on the existence of Being (as the chicken coming before the egg) in order to make any sense of the human situation. It seems clear that Anselm in the *Proslogion*, as Paliard, was affirming God as the untranscendable. Being is the *Alpha* and the *Omega*, the beginning and the end.

Paliard insists that being is implicit in all of our judgements and assertions and in all of our activities. In that sense, being is believed in by any thinking being in a natural faith. In addition, however, being is also discovered as the ultimate goal of knowledge. In this way it is proved. But it is not proved by way of ideas, by universal concepts, but by the concrete realities of human life—hence the title of Paliard's major work *La Pensée et la Vie*. Pierre Masset in *La Dialectique de la conscience chez Jacques Paliard* (n.d.) makes this point very clear. "It is not mind that he studies, in the sense of pure thought, because that would not at all satisfy his sense of the concrete and of the human. What interests him is the concrete human consciousness, thought without doubt, but not at all pure, but immersed in a fleshly reality which values the body by which it exists; a consciousness involved in life, temporality and change through which it must find its path, seek itself and find itself."

Anselm, like Paliard, is concerned to assert the existence, but not the essence of Being (which is called God), but, as mentioned earlier, the reflexive philosophers go on to indicate how this assertion of Being sheds light on the human situation. M. Nédoncelle, in an article on three reflexive philosophers (1965), describes Louis Lavelle's position as being in heaven on earth, that of René Le Senne as being in purgatory, and that of Jean Nabert, the most Kantian of all, as being in hell. In comparison with these, one might describe the human situation in Paliard as that of a pilgrim. He knows that the ultimate goal exists but he does not know the nature of the ultimate goal; he does know that the route is a long and arduous one. According to Paliard, this argument of St Anselm, if it be called an argument, sheds much more light on the nature of man than of God.

The self discovers itself and understands itself, not by intuition, not in isolation, but as involved in a world. The French reflexive verbs bring out this point more clearly than does English usage, although curiously enough the best analogy for this found by Paliard and other French writers is that found in Berkeley of the self as a fountain which shoots out the water and then it returns to itself.

It is characteristic of Paliard in some of his writings to reflect on his early childhood and some of his past experiences, e.g. *Profondeur de l'âme* (1954), and there he finds a knowledge that was implicit in his early experiences which only became explicit at a later date. It is on this point that he makes some of his most important discoveries about the human spirit. For Paliard, a fact of consciousness is always a fact of knowledge and a fact of consciousness is a fact of implicit thought. Man always assumes himself to be in a real world; so that he does not bother to examine the meaning of reality but describes it and accepts it. According to Paliard, the task of the philosopher is to pay attention to these implicit beliefs of people about their experience and to see the permanent connection between these beliefs and the way these beliefs are explained. Thought and life are mysteriously bound together. Sometimes what we think important at the time turns out to be of no consequence and sometimes what we think is of no consequence turns out to be of fundamental importance. (See *Théorème de la connaissance*, (1938).

Sometimes we think we have answers which are complete; but, for Paliard, the dialectical process is an endless one. We set up idols in terms of scientific knowledge or of over-confidence in oneself but these idols only cut us off from the ultimate answers. Life is an endless quest and, according to Paliard, it is only by positing the infinite, or Being, or God, that one is able to gain a true perspective on the self and the world, the relationship between them, and the knowledge we have of them.

The self and all the world is finite, but also inter-related, bound together, and this ultimate bond is inherently personal. All of this is very reminiscent of St Augustine's "Our hearts are restless until they find their rest in Thee." Here is the core of the human side of St Anselm's "that than which nothing greater can be conceived." The nature of human experience puts man to the test. What is he capable of conceiving that takes him beyond comprehension to the utmost bounds? Here is the greatness of man to be able to conceive of God which makes him unique in all the world, but, as Pascal affirmed, it is also the source of man's wretchedness. The nature of reality is to stretch man to his utmost capacity of intellect and will, but so often people are content with something less, and fall below their assigned destiny. To think God, "that than which nothing greater can be conceived", is to arouse man from his complacency and to act in pursuit of his highest dreams and goals.

The human spirit is not static essence but a vital entity which constantly acts and reacts with the world around. However, the human spirit is always going beyond the immediate objects, seeking an ultimate fulfilment of one's intellectual hopes and dreams and also of one's feelings. Yet the idea of God is not a dream; for God lies at the root of all one's hopes and dreams and feelings. God is not ourselves but God is the root of all that we have and are. Therefore, according to Paliard, the only way to understand oneself is to posit the reality of God. Some may not call this God, but yet God is always there.

A most profound description of the human situation reveals a

266

being which cannot exist without assuming and yearning for the reality of God.

Dr F. Temple Kingston
University of Windsor
Ontario, Canada

BIBLIOGRAPHY

Anselm of Canterbury (1962) *Basic Writings*. E.T. by E. W. Deane. Intro. by C. Hartshorne. 2nd ed. La Salle Illinois: Open Court.
Anselm of Canterbury (1967) *Truth, Freedom and Evil*. Ed. and E.T. by Jasper Hopkins and Herbert Richardson. New York: Harper Torch.
Aquinas, Thomas (1945) *Basic Writings of*. Ed. A. C. Pegis. New York: Random House.
Ayer, A. J. (1973) *The Central Questions of Philosophy*. London: Weidenfeld and Nicolson.
Barnes, Jonathan (1972) *The Ontological Argument*. London: Macmillan.
Barth, Karl (1962) *Anselm: Fides Quaerens Intellectum*. E.T. by I. Robertson. Meridian Books.
de Lubac, H. (1956) *Sur les chemins de Dieu*. Paris: Aubier.
Forest, Aimé (1959) "L'argument de Saint Anselme dans la philosophie réflexive," in *Specilegium Beccense*, pp. 273–294. Paris: Vrin. Congrès International du IXe Centenaire de l'arrivée d'Anselme au Bec.
Foster, Michael B. (1957) *Mystery and Philosophy*. London: S.C.M.
Gilson, E. (1938) *Reason and Revelation in the Middle Ages*. New York: C. Scribner's.
Gilson, E. (1955) *History of Christian Philosophy in the Middle Ages*. New York: Random House.
Guitton, Jean (1937–38) "Note sur l'argument ontologique et sur la critique que Kant en a faite" in *Les Études Philosophiques*, pp. 23–29 and pp. 31–34. With reply by Paliard and others.
Hartshorne, C. (1965) *Anselm's Discovery: An Explanation of the Ontological Proof for God's Existence*. La Salle Illinois: Open Court.
Hick, John and McGill, A. (1967) *The Many Faced Argument—Recent Studies in the Ontological Argument for the Existence of God*. New York: Macmillan.
Kant, I. (1965) *Critique of Pure Reason*. E.T. by N. Kemp Smith. Toronto: Macmillan.
Lachelier, Jules (1933) "Notes sur le pari de Pascal" in *Oeuvres*, Tome II, pp. 37–65. Paris: Alcan.
Malcolm, Norman (1970) "The Second Form of the Ontological Argument" in *Classical and Contemporary Readings in the Philosophy of Religion*, pp. 446–463, ed. John Hick. Englewood Cliffs: Prentice Hall.
Marcel, Gabriel (1940) *Du Refus à l'invocation*. Paris: Gallimard.
Marcel, Gabriel (1952) *Metaphysical Journal*. E.T. by B. Wall. Chicago: H. Regnery.
Mascall, E. L. (1971) *The Openness of Being*. London: Darton, Longman and Todd.
Masset, Pierre (n.d.) *La Dialectique de la conscience chez Jacques Paliard*. Intro. by A. Forest. Montpellier, Paris: P.U.F.

Nédoncelle, M. (1965) "Trois approches d'une philosophie de l'esprit" in *Filosofia*, pp. 217f.

Paliard, Jacques (1911–12) "La connaissance, à la limite de sa perfection, abolit-elle la conscience?" in *Annales de Philosophie Chrétienne*, pp. 232–273 (Dec. 1911) and 327–379 (Jan. 1912).

Paliard, Jacques (1925) *Intuition et Réflexion*. Paris: Alcan.

Paliard, Jacques (1930) "L'Illusion de Sinsteden et le problème de l'implication perceptive" in *Revue Philosophique de la France et de l'étranger*, pp. 359–409.

Paliard, Jacques (1938) *Théoreme de la connaissance*. Paris: Aubier.

Paliard, Jacques (1943) "La Conscience de soi et l'idée de Dieu" in *Les Études Philosophiques*, pp. 50–57.

Paliard, Jacques (1949) *Pensée Implicite et Perception Visuelle*—Étude d'une optique psychologique. Paris: P.U.F.

Paliard, Jacques (1951) *La Pensée et La Vie*. Recherche sur la logique de la perception. Paris: P.U.F.

Paliard, Jacques (1954) *Profonduer de l'âme*, Paris: Aubier.

Paliard, Jacques (n.d.) "Prière et dialectique" in *Dieu Vivant*, #6, p. 53f.

Plantinga, Alvin (1965) *The Ontological Argument*. From St Anselm to Contemporary Philosophy. Intro. by R. Taylor. Doubleday Anchor Book.

XX

IS SYSTEMATIC PHILOSOPHY POSSIBLE TODAY?

M. Marković

I

LIKE ANY OTHER general question, the question about the possibility of a systematic philosophy covers a large number of different particular questions.

A first such particular question is : what does the word "possible" mean here? Is this the question about the *logical* possibility of a systematic philosophy? If yes, then the answer to the general problem would also be an affirmative one. There is nothing in the historically evolved idea of philosophy which excludes the possibility of building again the great systems in the style of Spinoza or Hegel. (Surely one can define the concept of philosophy in such a way that the answer to our general question follows analytically. But in this case both the question and the answer would be quite trivial.)

The more interesting question would, of course, be : is building up of philosophy in the form of an all-embracing system *really* possible in 1975? And the term "real possibility" means here that in present-day social life there are certain social forces (attitudes, accumulated experiences, beliefs, trends of thought, fears, institutions) which constitute boundary conditions of any present day creative activity in the field of culture. These actual forces exclude many conceivable forms of cultural life and reduce the enormous set of logical possibilities to a much more narrow subset of real historical possibilities. In that sense the question asked earlier actually is : Is it really possible to creatively build up philosophy as a systematic theory after Hegel and other contemporary philosophers have exhausted all possibilities in that direction and after all negative experiences with attempts of that kind? Is it really possible for systematic philosophy to become anything more than worthless, pedantic pseudo-creativity of retired academicians, unable to reach out into the world of living culture in an age characterized by intense experimentation, by criticism and analysis of existing forms rather than by efforts to create great new syntheses? We realize here that the question about the real possibilities is not purely *descriptive*. It is not the question whether, as a matter of fact, philosophical systems can be built, independently of or contrary to the big streams of the time, disregarding completely the fruitfulness of such endeavours. The question implies a value judgment : Can the rehabilitation of systematic thinking contribute something essentially fruitful to the development of contemporary philosophy? The real problem is then : What are the possible advantages, and what are the basic limitations of systematic philosophical thinking?

II

This leads us to the second preliminary question. There are many different ways of systematic thinking. What do we mean, then, when we ask about systematic philosophy? It is systematic philosophical thinking in the style of Spinoza, *more geometrico*, or in the Hegelian dialectical form, or in the tradition of logical positivism of young Wittgenstein and Carnap, or perhaps in the sense in which Stalin attempted to systematize Marxist philosophy?

One could propose a typology of the forms of systematic philosophical thinking on the basis of the following two basic distinctions : One the one hand, there are *static* and *dynamic* systems; the former expound synchronic relations within a given and completed body of knowledge (consciousness), the latter express diachronic relations among the elements-stages of an evolving process of cognition and historical consciousness. On the other hand, there are *absolute* systems (that claim to embrace the totality of being in a spatially and temporally unlimited way) and systems which are *relative* (in the sense of referring themselves to a limited field and a limited historical epoch or depending on logical properties of a particular form of language.)

When we cross both criteria we obtain the following four types of philosophical systems :

(1) *Absolute static* systems—as in Spinoza's *Ethics*;
(2) *Relative static* systems—as in Wittgenstein's *Tractatus Logico-philosophicus* or in Carnap's *Logische Aufbau der Welt*;
(3) *Absolute dynamic* systems, the best example of which is Hegel's *Encyklopedie der philosophischen Wissenschaften*;

270

(4) *Relative dynamic* systems—as in the above mentioned attempt of Stalin and his followers (Rosenthal, Leonov and others).

The essential limitations of all static systems is that they completely miss the historical dimension of consciousness and knowledge, and construe, therefore, the particular form of consciousness of a certain historical period as something frozen and merely given. Interest in the heuristic problem, in the conditions of emergence and development of ideas, is completely absent. A one-sided interest in demonstration, in logical derivation, prevails in a quite exclusive way. However what characterizes any formal logic procedure of demonstration is that some categories, some initial statements, some rules of derivation, must be simply postulated and not derived themseives as the products of the preceding historical development of culture. Now, as the philosophical critique of each system of this kind shows, the basic philosophical ideas generated by the method of postulation are invariably either naive or simply wrong. It was naive to believe that the basic assumptions of the system were universally valid and evident—therefore such an interpretation of the basic premises of a system was later given up. On the other hand, it was simply untrue to characterize *Protokolsätze* in Carnap's system or "Atomic statements" in Wittgenstein's *Tractatus* as the most elementary, simple data of consciousness and pictures of the elementary facts of the real world. Already at the time when these systems were created it was well known that those statements always formulated the results of selection and interpretation in the process of perception. Long before, Hegel had convincingly shown (in his *Phenomenology of Mind*) that any apparently immediate and concrete act of consciousness involved mediation through certain general and abstract categories (such as *Now, Here, This,* etc.). In such a way any system built up by the exclusive application of a static, formal-logical method has to freeze the epistemological processes—to put all history "into brackets", and to artificially build up a starting point. While this method contributes to revealing the architecture of a body of knowledge, it, at the same time, leaves obscure and hidden its true foundation as well as the structure of the historical process that brought it about.

Hegel's dialectical system has the great advantage that its categories are genetically derived from each other and not postulated in a dogmatic way. The logical structure is here identified with the pattern of spiritual history. However real history is open and has a real future that is not fully determined and predictable. Whereas an absolute system is closed and cannot tolerate anything that deviates from the ideal logical order—and is therefore considered irrational, unthinkable. A system of the Hegelian type is, at best, able to describe the structure of the past so adequately that real phenomena look rational and all that is rational seems to have its reality. And yet life is infinitely richer than any abstract system and invariably defies its constraints, its rules and "laws". As time passes, more and more "unthinkable" phenomena actually take place and then become the past. More and more real historical processes have to be characterized from the point of view of the system as irrational, accidental phenomena, as mere unhistorical deviations, as arbitrary, capricious acts. On the other hand the "thinkable", "historically necessary" and rational patterns of the system increasingly lose their relevance and applicability and turn into empty, dead constructions without any explanatory and predictive power. The sets of logical and real possibilities become increasingly desperate. Under these conditions the system no longer offers an adequate paradigm for the understanding of past history, let alone of present and future history. Dialectic is incompatible with the idea of an absolute system.

The attempts made hitherto to build up dynamic, non-absolute systems are of limited philosophical value. For our purpose it could be of some interest to notice that here a specific form of dogmatism is possible. In the system of Dialectical Materialism of Stalin and his followers there is a dynamic and historically relative object-theory coupled with a static and absolute meta-theory. The object-theory deals with movement and change in all material, social and psychic phenomena, and in particular it deals with the forms and laws of a progressive historical development. However, at the level of meta-theory the principles of meta-realism and dialectic have been postulated in a dogmatic way as eternal truths which do not allow any later revision in the light of subsequent experiences and discoveries.

Thus it seems that all the well known types of systematic philosophical thinking have very serious limitations. To the extent to which philosophy is relevant for and applicable to the problems of real human life every systematization, every attempt to identify the historical with the logical, seems to lead to a negation of the really historical and to a hypostatization of the abstract logical.

272

III

Is then a non-systematic, analytic, piecemeal method the only alternative for modern philosophical thinking?

Nowadays we already have a rich experience with modern analytical philosophy. It is in a profound crisis, both theoretically and socially.

The essential theoretical limitation of any non-systematic philosophical thought is its escape from the most difficult philosophical problems such as : establishing mediating links between solutions of problems that belong to different fields of philosophical inquiry, stating explicitly hidden premises, resolving existing inconsistencies among them, justifying them without such *circulus vitiosus* as begging the question.

When we, following one of the Cartesian rules, temporarily leave aside those most difficult problems in order to return to them later, this is a perfectly sound methodological procedure. But when we try to get rid of synthesis in the name of analysis and even turn this vice into virtue then there is really no reason to be permanently satisfied with this specific expression of philosophical laziness.

The following illustration should clearly indicate how much piecemeal approach in philosophy leaves to be desired.

It is relatively easy to analyse meaning in terms of truth-conditions of sentences, as many authors have done. It is also rather comfortable to discuss the problem of truth assuming that we already know what the meaning of "meaning" is. But one who has to build up a philosophical theory of both truth and meaning has to solve difficult problems of explicating at least one of the two without reference to the other. Separate treatment of the two allows one to gloss over that highly challenging task.

A similar situation rises when one deals with the concepts of *causality, necessity, law of nature*. When these are discussed in isolation from each other the most difficult problem of explicating at least one of them without reference to the other two is avoided. Thus part of the meaning of a cause is that it is a necessary condition. Necessity in the non-logical, empirical sense can hardly be explicated without reference to the laws that govern phenomena of the given field. But when it comes to the explication of 'law of nature' the idea of necessity will in most cases be either explicitly presupposed or smuggled in. And here we do not immediately notice *circulus vitiosus* only because it happens in isolated papers. The most diffi-

273

cult problems arise only when on attempts a systematic theory of determination embracing all three and many other concepts.

And, in order to avoid giving the impression that this sort of critique is relevant only to analytic philosophy, an example of lazy Marxist non-systematic humanist thinking will be given. In separate papers of Marxist humanists, even in those of one individual author, one finds, time and again, the following vicious circle: Man is being defined as a being of praxis and praxis as a specifically *human*, free, creative activity. Then freedom is interpreted as essentially (human) self-realization. But then self-realization is in turn taken to mean the actualization of man as a being of praxis. Mere awareness of a difficulty here creates a need for a more systematic approach.

A difficult class of cases is of those where the purpose of inquiry is not so much to give full philosophical analysis of a category in its various dimensions but to examine as thoroughly as possible only one of its dimensions. Such analysis could be technically extremely sophisticated and make quite a substantial contribution of lasting philosophical value. Such are the cases of Tarski's semantical theory of truth and Popper's theory of falsification. But in both cases something philosophically very essential is missing, precisely owing to the fragmentary character of the theories in question. Tarski's theory is fully elaborated for a formal language, which is not and will never be the language of philosophy. What is of general philosophical importance is his scheme for constructing specific theories of truth and the basic idea on which this scheme rests. And this basic idea is of very little informative value: A statement is true when it is satisfied by all objects (*Gegenstände*) to which it refers. The analysis stops here. But the most difficult question arises when we ask: What does it mean to be an object? Very often we accept something as an *object* (for example, we begin to speak about positrons, mesons, neutrinos, hadrons, beryons, quarks, gluons as really existing subatomic particles) only when we know that some corresponding statements are *true*. If one chooses not to build up a systematic philosophy of both *truth* (which is an epistemological problem) and *object* (which is an ontological problem) there are two ways to avoid vicious circle:

(1) to postulate one of them,

(2) to assume the attitude of complete tolerance and declare that everybody is free to use one of them in whatever way he wants.

The former could lead to unnecessary multiplication of assumed entities: only within a system could their number be reduced to a minimum. The latter leads to complete relativization of concepts:

once anything may be considered an "object" if one chooses, so also any statement may be considered true that is satisfied by such an object.

A striking example of the incompatibility of the results of non-systematic inquiry in different fields may be found in Popper's philosophy, where one compares his epistemological theory of falsification and his recent ontological theory of the third world. On the one hand we can never know whether a theory is true ... we can only test it and establish that it is false if it is in contradiction with statements which formulate data of experience. And this falsifiability is the essential characteristic of scientific statements; it furnishes the criterion of demarcation between science and metaphysics. On the other hand, there is a world in addition to the world of material objects and the world of psychic processes, which is constituted by—among other things—the meanings of all our statements. However, if falsification is really possible, such a world is unthinkable. In what sense can the meaning of a factually false statement have an objective meaning, independently of psychic processes in erring individuals?

With respect to social problems the standpoint of a piecemeal analysis does not encourage a bold and imaginative critical approach. The criticism of isolated elements, parts, dimensions of a system can lead only to modifications and limited reform of the system. Thus, behind a non-systematic philosophy an ideology of the preservation of the *status quo* is often hidden. In order to transcend the *status quo* one has to see given historical reality as a whole and has to ask the question of the total condition of men in the existing historical situation.

IV

The preceding analysis leads to the following conclusion : Non-systematic thinking about isolated problems is only *one phase* of the philosophical inquiry, that phase in which separate elements and abstracted relations among them have to be studied and described. Without this phase a philosopher is always tempted to try and speak about the whole (the world, human mind, historical situation at a given time) in a *direct* way, without mediation—therefore superficially (when the talent is small) or mystically (when a genius is in question). Nevertheless the results of this indispensable analytical phase are unfinished products. It is necessary to establish links among them, to continue search where it was stopped, to look for deeper

K

common grounds where two particulars were mutually derived from each other. The initial abstract totality was decomposed and carefully studied piece by piece in the analytical phase. Now the time comes to attempt a synthetic reconstruction of the whole, which by now should emerge as a relatively concrete, systematic totality with apparently distinct levels, dimensions, elements and relations among them. What, in contrast with the age of Hegel and other great system-builders, would be utterly naive is not the very aspiration to systematize all philosophical knowledge and culture within one tradition, but the illusion that all traditions could be shown to be only special cases of one, and, furthermore, that such a system exhausts all possibilities of future development.

A modern systematic thinker hardly has any alternative but to accept the plurality of the great existing streams of philosophical thought and to regard a systematic philosophical theory as, at best, the most adequate approximation to the immensely rich and complex real structure of the world.

Since Hegel it is no longer possible to believe that one philosophical system can embrace all other systems and trends as mere incomplete truths, as special moments of the absolute truth expounded by it. Surely some theories are richer and more complex than others and do embrace their solutions of certain philosophical problems as the special cases of its own, more general solutions—this helps us to avoid relativism and to introduce an important criterion of evaluation of different alternative philosophical approaches. But when we compare most important present day trends : empiricism, phenomenology, Marxism, structuralism, we notice immediately that they do not all deal with the same problems and that, therefore, some statements that are considered true within one trend are not incomplete truths but irrelevant, pointless, within the other. Part of the empiricist tradition has always been a strong interest in the problem of validation of knowledge, much lesser in the problem of its growth and non-existent in the problem of the transition from one paradigm to the other. The latter was traditionally considered an issue that does not belong to philosophy but at best to psychology and sociology—an issue that escapes rational consideration. Marxist dialectic, on the other hand, tends to throw light precisely on this point in the history of knowledge, offering the principles that regulate precisely this discontinuity. On the other hand a Marxist tends to completely leave aside what a phenomenologist is doing when he tries to describe phenomena as they look to a completely neutral, unprejudiced, value-free mind. They both might search for objectivity but one finds it in the suspension of all previous beliefs, the other in the search for universal potential characteristics of human nature, in suspension of particularly wherever it is incompatible with that basic human universality. What the phenomenologist has to try to say about ideal objective essences introspected by an unbiased, non-committed thinker cannot always be incorporated into Marxist theory even as a partial truth : the Marxist does not believe either that there are such ideal essences, or that there are unbiased, non-committed thinkers; therefore to him phenomenological descriptions make sense only when he takes them to be something quite different from what they pretend to be : expressions of the state of mind of people unaware of the prejudices and values that direct them.

It is interesting to note that even within one great tradition there might be such great differences between more specific orientations that systematic organization of ideas within one will leave outside its scope essential elements of the other. Russellian ontology is irrelevant for a purely linguistic orientation within the empiricist tradition. In a similar way within contemporary Marxism ontological interpretation of dialectic in the style of Engel's *Dialectic of Nature* looks obsolete and pointless to a humanist who sees dialectic only in history because only from the human point of view does it make sense to speak about progress, and transcendence.

This plurality of possible perspectives for philosophical systematization should not be confused with mere pluralism, in the same way in which relativity allow overlapping and a ground common to all. In the same way in which relativity of space and time goes together with equal absolute validity of laws in all systems, so relativity of human perspectives goes together with the assumption that there is just one world in which we all live and one universal ground for referring to individuals of different generations, races, nations, sexes and creeds—as members of one human species.

The task of giving a systematic account of that one world and that one universal human ground of all particular cultures and individual endeavours is the task of the whole history. What is needed is a progressive ongoing totalization. To think systematically does not mean, therefore, to construct one "final", "perfect" system but to keep building up an unfinished series of systematic theories that follow each other in time and transcend each other.

Systems have their life-pattern which need not coincide with the life-pattern of the informal, unsystematized philosophical current which gave them birth. Precisely those features which constitute

277

the basic limitation of a poorly organized and not fully spelled out thought may also be the source of its surprising recurrence and longevity. Vagueness, metaphoricality, ambiguity, conciseness of language which reaches the point of obscurity, gaps, inner contradictions, absence of mediation, wild ungrounded projections into the future—can utterly compromise a mediocre theory but also prolong the life of a powerful one by challenging the imagination of posterity and making room for ever new reinterpretations and reconstructions. By being systematically spelled out a philosophy takes the same risk as the lover who allows his beloved to know him too well : both lose all their magic and become too clear, too vulnerable, too open to criticism.

At the beginning a system is a daring, impressive piece of new architecture that fully reveals all the secrets of a new mind in working. After some time, at best, it becomes a part of the given established culture : its secrets are being taught in the high-school.

Then the time comes when it has only an historical interest and sometimes becomes a part of enslaving tradition. Every system will be surpassed by life sooner or later. It has to be transcended; its essential inner limitation abolished; its still living elements incorporated into a new whole. The principle of history eventually prevails over that of structure.

Surely it could be objected that this series of systematic philosophical theories does not yet constitute the movement of spiritual life and of historical praxis; that this would be only a series of states of peace, of standstill. But that is what thought in general is, at best. Any concept, any statement, any rule or law is only a moment of peace in the eternal flux of phenomena. In that sense a philosophical system also is only a frozen structure of the constantly changing world. A series of systems, which transcend each other and constitute the steps of a progressive conceptualization of human self-consciousness, is the only possible synthesis of history and structure.

V

Two resultant points require illustration :

(1) That the systematic building up of a poorly organized body of philosophical views could considerably improve it by stating explicitly hidden premises, by justifying dogmatic assertions, by mediating among unrelated categories, by resolving concealed contradictions.

(2) That transcendence of one systematic theory by a richer, more

adequate and general one is essentially the abolition of a limitation of the former; that it involves, therefore both continuity and discontinuity between the two.

Any effort to systematize Marx's philosophy would have to solve the following problems :

(1) Marx intended to develop a strictly and thoroughly *scientific* theory of existing capitalist society and its transition into socialism. He also, very early developed a radical humanist critique of alienated labour and of any form of social organization in which human individuals are reified and an enormously rich human potential wasted. This critique is based on a very optimistic conception of human nature and its implications sound utopian. How to reconcile the scientific and the utopian dimension in Marx?

(2) Marx established a number of laws governing capitalist society and believed that they are inexorable, completely independent of human consciousness and will. On the other hand he developed an activist philosophy of history the basic premise of which is the conviction that men make history and change circumstances under which laws hold. How to resolve the apparent contradiction between economic determinism and activism of men—the being of praxis?

(3) Materialistic epistemology, which Marx emphasized so much, ever since *German Ideology* of 1845, tends to reduce consciousness to a reflection of given material conditions, eventually to a superstructure of the existing economic infrastructure. On the other hand Marxian dialectic obviously involves normative elements : development is "progressive"; contradictions have to be resolved in a certain way in order to give rise to "higher" forms of being; some features of social life are "negative" and will have to be abolished. But where do these normative elements come from? How to reconcile them with a materialistic idea of consciousness?

(4) Revolution is the key problem of Marx's theory. Marx realized that a social revolution, a total transformation of all social relationships, presupposes the existence of a very big social group that is strongly motivated for radical change, that is interested not in establishing its own particular clan rule but in an universal human emancipation, and that has enough energy to wipe out the ruling class resistance to change. Very early, in 1843, Marx came to the conclusion that only the proletariat satisfies all these conditions. However, in his opinion, the proletariat is the most oppressed, the most alienated class; its misery can only increase in the course of capitalist development. Consequently according to the principle of materialism its consciousness will be only a rebellious, oppositionary

consciousness aiming at immediate improvement of its working and living conditions. However, Marx never stopped believing that precisely this class will become the subject of the most profound change in the whole of history, and will organize the new market-less, state-less, clan-less society on an entirely new basis.

How is this transition from the "class in itself" to the "class for itself" ever to be achieved?

The only way to solve these and other apparent inconsistencies is to systematically reconstruct Marx's theory, starting with his basic ontological-anthropological assumptions about the human being as a being of praxis. This involves a fundamental distinction between actual existence and the potential structure of human nature. The latter is constituted by a number of latent capacities and powers which are there, as a result of the whole preceding biological and social development, but need not be actualized : such are in the first place, capacities for free, creative, intentional activity. Under conditions of class society, of capitalist production in particular, these capacities are blocked and wasted on a mass scale. But at the same time, the ground for their actualization is being prepared through industrialization, rise of material productivity, wealth for material needs. To the extent to which human potential is arrested and human persons reduced to things there are objective, inexorable laws analogous to those in nature. They can be studied scientifically, with an accuracy approaching that in the natural sciences. It follows, then, that strict determination is not something that prevails in the whole of history but only in the phase characterized by private property, commodity production, market exchange, the political character of the public power. Scientific theory of capitalism becomes therefore, a part of a more general, critical humanist social theory which supplements the empirical study of reified behaviour (according to fixed laws) with an exploration of optimal historical possibilities of the whole epoch. All the normative elements (such as the concepts of "optimal, positive versus 'negative' overcoming" etc.) are derived from the fundamental structure of human nature, where Marx does not allow the distinction between the descriptive and the value elements : both constitute "human essence". "The utopian" in Marx follows from the value elements of human nature (man is essentially free, creative, social, open for an unlimited development of his senses, intellectual powers, needs ever new ways of acting). It is important to note, however, that the utopian is not here an arbitrary projection of conceivable, "reasonable" forms of human life but the implication of what in the opinion of Marx *there really potentially is* in human nature. The utopian in this sense is not incompatible with the scientific. When the latter is taken in a more general sense it involves the exploration of both manifest and dispositional properties of objects, therefore it embraces the function *both* of description *and of critique* (critique of the actual from the point of view of the potential).

The existence and development of such a critical science provides part of the explanation for the emergence of the radically critical, revolutionary consciousness of the proletariat. To the extent to which an intellectual liberates himself from the ideological mystification and illusions of the ruling bourgeois class which he is supposed to serve, to the extent to which he really searches for objective universal truth, he adopts the standpoint of universal human emancipation, which is also the standpoint of the proletariat. It is true that workers are objectively conditioned only to struggle for better working conditions and that they cannot elaborate alone a sufficiently sophisticated revolutionary theory (which requires the mediation of the whole preceding culture); but they can instinctively recognize one and respond to it where it appears. As human beings they remain always potentially free and no matter how heavily conditioned by the material circumstances of their daily life they retain the capacity to generate an awareness of their long range interests and thus to understand that a revolutionary theory expresses precisely those interests. Then a transition from a class "in itself" into a class "for itself" takes place. New subjective determinants emerge which are no longer the reflection of immediate material (economic, political) infrastructure, but the reflection of a much deeper infrastructure in the very basic potential of human nature. The historical process no longer has the character of blind inescapable determination but of conscious, purposeful self-determination.

When a modern systematization removes all or most of the flagrant apparent ambiguities and inconsistencies in Marx's theory, one basic weakness still remains in the very fundamental assumptions about the character of human nature. These assumptions have in Marx the character of theoretical statements about human *essence*. The essentialist language here obscures the fact that a philosopher who speaks about human nature does not only say what as a matter of fact man *is*—as the result of previous history—but also what he *could be* and what he *should* be. These statements are therefore both descriptive and normative, both theoretical and practical. Now if they are not merely theoretical but also practical, if they are not only basic assertions about what human nature is and must be, but also basic commitments to create historical conditions under which some human dispositions ("positive", "good" ones) would be favoured and freely developed and some other dispositions ("negative", "bad" ones) would be blocked and slowly modified, then historical necessity in the deterministic sense has to disappear both at the level of empirical science (object-level) and at the level of philosophy of history (meta-level). Otherwise men would be free to make their history but they would not be free to be free; they would rather be condemned to be free. As in Hegel, history would have only one direction : human beings *must* be disalienated, institutions like private property, commodity production, state, church, etc. *must* be abolished, then people *will have to* become free, creative, and social; capitalism *must be* overcome by communism. So at the meta-level of philosophy freedom disappears, and unity of theory and praxis disappears too. The essentialist language of Marx's anthropology and the rigidly deterministic conception of the philosophy of history are incompatible with his principle of the unity of theory and praxis. But the latter is more important than the former; it is more characteristic of Marx's thought as a whole. In fact, precisely this principle expresses the fundamental novelty of Marx's theory : essentialism and rigid historical determinism are just remnants of the preceding tradition (Hegel, Feuerbach). That is why they have to be considered a *limitation* and to be transcended.

A new systematization has to start from the meta-meta-principle specifying the nature of basic meta-principles and stating that assertions about human being are, on the other hand, the result of the objective study of the patterns of human behaviour in history; but one, on the other hand, the result of our basic practical commitment to reinforce some of these patterns (such as self-determination, creative activity) and to discourage others (such as aggressivity, acquisitiveness, egoism). Thus even if we continue to speak about human *essence* or human *nature* it will be clear that our statements are both descriptive and normative. Then whatever we say about transcendence or alienation in history, about human self realization and forms of new rational and just society, becomes the expression of the *optimal* historical *possibility* and not the expression of inexorable historical necessity. And even if we continue to speak about historical "necessity", the term will not refer to what *must happen* (independently of human consciousness and will) but to what human individuals and collectives *must do if* they don't wish their civilization to perish or to waste its potential.

This approach to systematic philosophical thinking lays sufficient emphasis on history, it does justice to the obvious tendency to pluralism in the present day world, and it avoids relativism.

It remains open for history because, while building a new systematic theory, the author is already aware of its incompleteness and the revisability of its very basis : universal human dispositions are changeable, historical, and the inner conflict among them allows several ways of resolving them. On the other hand, conditions of actual human existence also change and the conflict between them and universal dispositions obviously is a dynamic factor. Which opens room for a plurality of coexisting systems and a dialogue among them.

Relativism is avoided, however, because all those more or less subjective philosophical constructions ultimately acquire their meaning and value in a confrontation which is objective and invariant for all philosophies—the confrontation of *real* human beings and the *real* world which ultimately, *a posteriori* shows best what are the practical implications of the one philosophical orientation or the other.

Mihailo Marković
Serbian Academy of Sciences and Arts
Belgrade, Yugoslavia

XXI

ULTIMATES AND A WAY OF LOOKING
IN PHILOSOPHY

H. D. Lewis

> *"There is a general rule in philosophy that whenever the phrase*
> *'immediate and ultimate' comes up, one reaches for one's*
> *analytical gun. It probably means that one has just run out of*
> *steam in explaining what one is trying to say."*
>
> (Bernard Williams in *The Listener*, 3 July 1975)

BY "ULTIMATES" for the purpose of this paper, I do not understand, in the first instance, some one supreme being or some alleged final source of all other conditioned existence—the infinite, the absolute, the transcendent, the unconditioned, God, or whatever term or description be thought appropriate. Not that I consider these notions unimportant for philosophy, or want to exclude them from what I want to maintain here about ultimates. They would in fact provide one excellent example of what I have in mind and provide a variation on my main theme which is significant and instructive in some ways. But what I am concerned to put forward holds irrespective of whether one is disposed to consider seriously the idea of some supreme existent or reality along the lines indicated, and I am anxious not to confuse the present issue or give a wrong impression of what I am mainly concerned to advance at the moment.

For the same reason I must also make it clear that I am not concerned with the idea of some basic philosophical principle which we need to recognize before we can make proper progress with other questions, or some key idea which will unlock all the other mysteries, evolution, relativity, a self-representative series etc. Indeed I am very little attracted to clues of this kind in philosophy and suspect that many have been badly led astray by them. I do indeed believe that philosophers, like all others, have to respect one basic principle, name the principle of non-contradiction and would defend this, in the proper place, against suggestions that it may be conventional

284

or limited in its application. But while I hold that we must respect this principle I would make no further claim for it or suggest that other philosophical ideas may somehow be educed out of it.

The place of the "Form of the Good" in Plato's philosophy, provides an interesting half-way house which may be worth noting here. On the one hand, "the Good" is an ultimate which is not established by argument but by a glimpse or noesis. Nothing is known in the vision of "the Good" which can be communicated in any other way. The vision is all, but it is only within the reach of suitably equipped and accomplished philosophers. It does, however, once achieved, provide a means of exhaustively understanding both the inherent necessity of the other forms and their essential inter-dependence. It is the prime source of philosophical wisdom. At the same time, little in the conduct of Plato's general treatment of various philosophical questions is directly affected by the notion of "the Good". *Ex hypothesi* it could not be, for the discussion is not addressed solely to the few who have come to the ultimate attainment. Most of the time Plato continues as the rest of us might. In the account of "the Good" as something which is apprehended peculiarly for itself, and in the insistence on a peculiar philosophical flair for doing this, Plato is taking the course I especially wish to commend. That the "glimpse" has implications for further questions is also important. But I do not subscribe at all to the notion of one supreme insight, however fine and distinctive, from which the proper understanding of all other issues is made manifest. The major philosophical questions must be taken on their merits, whatever the ramifications there may also be between them. Nor am I thinking, along the lines of Plato, of a quite exclusively philosophical insight. What the philosopher apprehends in the cases of what I here call ultimates, is what is usually evident to all in the common course of experience. What is peculiar to the philosopher is his appreciation of the distinctiveness of the awareness involved and the way to treat it intellectually without lapsing into misleading aberrations.

But having paid our respects in these terms to Plato, let us now return from this historical excursus to our proper task. What I particularly want to claim is that, in a number of central philo-sophical contexts, there is a point to be reached where further explicit consideration ends and we can do no more than note the way things are and declare them to be so. This does not, as should be obvious, concern ordinary matters of fact which we may note and record for our usual purposes from day to day. But it is on the other hand not just a way of talking about the world or the way things are in general; it is in the first place an appreciation of the way things are, of what we ourselves and the world around us are like and, in that way, of what we may also say or affirm.

The main point is that, in all philosophical discussion, we reach a stage where further analysis and argument is at an end, not because of our own failings and limitations, but from the nature of the case and unavoidably. Argument may indeed end because of the stubbornness or the seeming inanity of one's opponent or some blind spot or bias to which even the most reflective may be prone in subtle ways. "There is no point in trying to argue with him", we may say, or more politely, "We must agree to differ". It is not our aptitudes or temperaments that prescribe the sort of finality or terminus with which I am now concerned, but the nature of the philosophical enterprise itself. A point is reached where we see, or seem to see, the way things are and can only declare this, though much will indeed turn on the care and precision with which the declaration is made—perhaps that is where peculiar philosophical skill is most evident, and this in turn helps us to appreciate the persistent preoccupation of philosophers with words and their equally evident fear of words. Words are our tools but they seem to be never quite right or appropriate for us. We seem to hit on the right words but then in no time it seems to be all wrong.

One embarrassment in the view of philosophy which I am seeking to outline is that the last thing a philosopher would wish to be accused of is an unwillingness to go on arguing his case. It is by discussion and argument that he exists, they are his life blood. Our patience may easily run out with certain kinds of discussion, but to give up discussion and argument is to give up our practice. We must continue on the "long and circuitous route" and not seek an easy resting place or "a short way". Dogmatism and unreason are what we most wish to avoid, and when the philosopher meets them in others he is understandably affronted and dismayed. That much intellectual activity of a sort, in politics and theology for example, is just an elaborate ringing of changes on initial dogmatisms is a solemn enough warning, of which, one would hope, philosophers stood in little need. But dogmatism and the closed mind take their course sometimes in very subtle ways and no one can be wholly unmindful of the hold they may have on us, the sceptically-minded as much as the rest. No philosopher likes to be accused of unreason or of "knowing all the answers" or of giving up the discipline of hard and continuous thinking and of listening properly to what others have to say. It becomes him more ill than any to have recourse to subterfuge, prevarication or similar ways of scoring an easy victory, and for that reason he will not take it lightly to be thought to lack openness and flexibility of mind and to just "dig his heels in" and take his stance in serene assurance that he is right. To be troubled becomes him better, a certain sort of doubt is part of his attitude of mind and he knows well how hard it is to find any adequate resting place at all in his subject.

This has in turn a tendency to induce its opposite, namely the almost total refusal to commit oneself, either by not putting pen to paper, except perhaps for wholly negative criticism, or by inventing curious philosophical moves which involve no subscription to any positive content, an evasion which seems to keep us genuinely engaged with our problems while remaining sublimely superior to the seeming futilities of others. Some play the safe game by rigid adherence to a fairly simple policy like strict empiricism. But while caution is estimable, indeed indispensable, where it is so easy to *say* the misleading thing even when on the right course, we must not give up the philosophical task of indicating how things in general seem to us to be, about ourselves and the world; and this will involve commitment, for the time at least, to some positive views. My present contention is that we must not be deterred, by the fear of dogmatism or, like J. S. Mill, of being "found out", when we come to the point where we can only affirm how things seem to be without adducing further considerations or arguments.

The danger is, I must repeat, that this requirement be invoked before it is inevitable or proper from the nature of the case, either out of intellectual indolence (and we must remember how very demanding and trying genuinely close philosophical reflection is bound to be) or from fear of refutation. I would not impute either of these motives, at least in any overt form, to so tireless a philosophical thinker as Norman Malcolm, but I have elsewhere[1] noted how he makes things easier for himself by resorting at an inappropriate point to Wittgenstein's celebrated and very proper insistence "that it is an important thing in philosophy to know when to stop". Malcolm will not have it at all that dreaming is some kind of waking state, an immediate vivid impression the moment we awake. But he will not have it either that the dream is anything that goes on, while we sleep, though there is no doubt that "people really do have dreams". We tell the dream but the dream is not the telling. Just then what is it? Here Malcolm tells us we have "to stop", and I have insisted, with perhaps some impatience, that he is not entitled to stop there. The question just cries out for an answer, and Malcolm seems to be "stopping" because no further move is possible to him (he is in a complete impasse) when there certainly ought to be. He retreats into silence when it is not reasonable to do so.

Malcolm is in no way alone in this. For while it is important (that is the main theme of this paper) to know that we must stop and when to stop, it is only too fatally easy to stop at the wrong place or where it is convenient. This has happened in some celebrated ways. Let me note some examples.

One of the pioneers and architects of recent realism, especially in its English variety, is Cook Wilson. How much he is read today is hard to tell, though he seems always mentioned with respect. I think it would not be hard to show that his genius has presided far more than is realized over the course of philosophy at Oxford during this century, even though the strict allusions to him may not be very extensive. He held[2] that there were certain things we undoubtedly know without further reason. These include the existence of the external world, the self, other minds, causality, God, a formidable list which leaves little scope for the sceptic. How far this is meant to extend to particular items is not always clear, but some of Cook Wilson's closest followers certainly meant it in that way. I have discussed the views of one of them, R. I. Aaron, elsewhere.[3] Aaron is forced to the peculiar position of maintaining that while in all matters of fact we are fallible, I can affirm now that I *know* that a bird is singing outside my window, though I may have later to affirm that it was an imitation and that I did not know this. The course that Cook Wilson himself took was to say that, in all the contexts in question, there could be "philosophic doubt"—I know that there is a "table before me", as Berkeley has it, but thought about illusions and perspectival distortions etc. cause me to doubt this in some rather special way which leaves the original certainy quite unaffected. It is not easy however to see just what this amounts to. Berkeley was as certain as any that there was a "table before" him. His normal reaction would not be in the least affected. But he was all the same denying something substantial in his famous immaterialism. External things would not for him have any genuine reality when not perceived. This is certainly at odds with a widespread impression, and while we may or may not incline to Berkeley's view or some variation on it, the questions raised in this context, from ancient times to Berkeley and later, cannot be settled out of hand by invoking an initial or basic certainty not to be affected by further philosophical thought. It may be that there has to be some form of realism in our view of the external world, and I imagine that there would be few today who would go with some post-Hegelian idealists in dissolving the world into a "system of relations". We encounter the world of nature, we do not make it, it is in some sense there. But before we take our stance on this or any rival claim we have to do a great deal of hard philosophical thinking to discover what sort of stance we are forced to take. Cook Wilson and most of his followers are stopping too soon, to the serious detriment of philosophical thought.

A similar comment is invited by much in the course of the twin form of realism about the external world, namely the philosophy of common sense as practised by G. E. Moore and those he inspired. No one would now agree that it will do to hold up our hands and declare that here are two external things. Indeed few have shown a more subtle grasp of the complexities of the problem of perception than Moore, as readers of his *Some Main Problems of Philosophy* will be well aware. In one place he suggests that the external object may be just a point, a far cry from the impression generally conveyed by the famous British Academy Lecture, "Proof of an External World".[4] The main point here again is that we must be careful where to stop and not indulge ourselves with the comfort of a resting place, or seem to do so, before we have earned it by exhausting all the appropriate philosophical considerations in the first place.

Of course we all know after a fashion that there is an external world and we have every confidence in much that we believe about the "furniture" of it and what happens to it. But this is the beginning not the end of philosophical reflection, and the ghost of Berkeley (and many perplexed thinkers before him) is not to be laid by just invoking this day to day assurance. To retreat on that is a prime example of stopping at the wrong place.

Nor is it possible, as some have tried, to avoid being involved in any issue of commitment by simply considering how the verb "to know" is most commonly or advantageously used. It may well be that, for most purposes, the proper course for me to take is to say that I *know* that my elbows are resting on this table and, indeed, a host of things not so immediately plain, that a boy is mowing my lawn away from the window, that King's College is in the Strand, etc. extending to much that I know about the past. It would be misleading to say "I believe" in these cases. If I said *that*, as evidence in court, I would be thought to prevaricate, and the advocate could well ask me sharply to say did I or did I not *know* that the boy I had engaged and whom I glimpsed from time to time was cutting my lawn this morning. It would be pedantic to start to qualify, and yet, in all

289

these matters, there is an element of fallibility. We have, with reason, been certain and proved wrong. Shall we then decide to say that we *know* only when there can be no possibility, not even the most remote, of error? My point is that nothing of real philosophical importance hinges on this. Linguistic conventions depend, or should depend, on convenience, but the situation which the philosopher seeks to understand remains unaffected.

We have in short to say something, or take some stance, in the study of perception—or give up philosophical study of it altogether. The world around us is not made in our thought, it is in some sense "there", we have to take it as it is and come to terms with it, disagreeable and pleasant features alike, we "encounter" things and they make their "impact". This is the strength of the realist case and common sense philosophy, though whether the best way to deal with this is to say that something is "given" is a moot point. My present insistence is that it is not enough to invoke the obvious reality, in some form, of external objects and our practical certainties. This is the start, not the stopping place, and I would not care here, in this peculiarly tricky subject, to say where I think we must stop—though I think I shall not find Berkeley very far from my elbow when I do so. Common sense realism has certainly stopped too soon in the past.

The same goes, though a good deal more obviously, for the appeal to ordinary language and the paradigm case. It may be a useful way of bringing out something that is lacking in the sense datum theory to say that we do not see patches of colour flash past at the races, we are watching horses. But to say that, *and no more*, is just to give up. There are problems, very exciting ones too, connected with perspectival distortion, the working of our physical organs, nerves, brains etc., which are evident to the most elementary student, and we cannot just sweep these away, to say nothing of reverie and dreams, by noting that what we see are chairs, horses, people and not patches of colour or sensations. Likewise, the free will problem is not settled by noting that we would clearly say that we are free, in some sense, most of the time. I am free now in the sense that I am not in prison, I write these words of my own accord since no one is guiding my hand, or again in a different sense because I have no aversion to writing in this way or some like psychological hindrance, or yet again because there is no law against it. To disentangle these various uses closely is a proper task for philosophy, and there has been much careful work in this vein of late. It is also important to consider what sort of freedom is involved in our accountability, by no means an easy task and certainly one not to be settled entirely on the basis of linguistic practice. But here again I would maintain that a point must be reached, in respect for example to the implications of moral accountability and of our exercise of the appropriate freedom, where we just have to affirm how the matter seems to us.

Likewise, elsewhere in ethics, Professor Toulmin, on one occasion, poured great scorn on the alleged "inner eye" by which W. D. Ross claimed to come to know things in ethics, only to close his paper with the insistence that the important thing in ethics is to appreciate that we know some things without further reason. There may, or there may not be, ethical intuitions. But *ex hypothesi* this is not a matter to be itself settled by argument. We must reflect on how we do come to say that certain things are wrong or right or good. That, however, is in no way a simple matter of sitting in one's chair and noting whether flashes of intuition happen to us from time to time, like twitches of pain. To suppose this is the unworthy travesty to which much fine work in ethics has been exposed. The kind of thinking that goes to settling these matters is very special, and before we reach the point of saying, with or against the intuitionist, that this is how it now seems to us, a great many subtle considerations, including what we might say in this or that circumstance, are relevant. There are also alleged fallible intuitions, and when we have gone through all the appropriate motions we may find that a term like "intuition" has misleading associations and is best replaced by another—"insight", "judgment"[5] etc. But none of this precludes there being some point where, not from philosophical weariness or desperation, but from what the situation philosophically calls for, we have to exercise some final judgment and stay with it as long as things seem so to us.

I myself strongly favour the view that, at some point in ethics, intuition must be invoked. But I also think that, once this was clearly appreciated by oustanding thinkers earlier this century,[6] notably G. E. Moore, there was a lapse into the besetting philosophical sin of making this notion do more work than it should. Intuitions were apt to proliferate, to the serious discredit of the concept. This seems to me to be a further case of philosophers stopping too soon or too conveniently at the wrong place. That is how I would judge the controversy, very much alive at the moment in a very different garb, between intuitionists like Ross and utilitarians like Moore or Pickard-Cambridge. In both cases some kind of ultimate was invoked and it is of interest that Moore, while surrendering under attack the attempt to establish non-natural properties by arguments about the "naturalistic fallacy" etc., still clung to the notion of a distinctive insight into a non-natural quality of goodness. The dispute was as to where this insight came about, for Moore in the assessment of worth and, perhaps, in the general duty of maximizing good, for Ross in this and the apprehension of other *prima facie* duties, like truth-telling and keeping promises, which had also to go into the final reckoning.

There is no easy solution to this problem. On the one hand it seems odd to suppose that we ought to do something which will not produce most good on the whole for those affected, on the other we have compunction about disregarding promises made to the dying man, etc. and we feel there is something in the view that "a promise is a promise" etc. I believe that it is not impossible to bring the latter under the utilitarian principle if we think hard enough about subtle aspects of the cases where the strain is felt; and if I am right in this and in inclining more to Moore's "agathistic utilitarianism", then it would seem that the intuitionists (of the Ross variety) and their "consequentialist"[7] descendants now, are just stopping too soon when they should go on thinking still harder to locate the precise point where a special insight or intuition is to be exercised. The distinctiveness of ethics which we find it impossible to avoid, however hard we try (and the more tough-minded as much as any), seems to make an insight of that sort inevitable somewhere. The point is, just where?

Let me now refer to problems about persons. First a word about "other minds". Cook Wilson regarded immediate and certain knowledge of other persons as a prime example of the sort of basic certainties he had in mind. In one respect he is clearly right. No one seriously doubts that we have knowledge of other persons; the solipsist is a figure of fun and does not even take himself seriously— as was underlined in Bertrand Russell's oft repeated pleasantry about the solipsist who was surprised that her view was not shared by more people. But this tells us nothing about the mode of this awareness. One sees, in a way, the point of Cook Wilson's famous jibe about not wanting "inferred friends". We want our friends to be close and intimate and our companionship simple and easy. But when all has been said in this vein—and that would be a theme in itself—the fact remains that we do not know other minds as we do our own, we must have some basis for what we believe about one another. Usually, and in close relationships, this involves mainly observation of one another's bodies. But it is the body that I strictly observe, and on that basis I learn, easily and spontaneously as a

292

rule, about thoughts, feelings, sensations and so on. I do not strictly observe another's pain, I find the indication of it in what I see or hear.

I have stressed this a good deal elsewhere, it is a point on which philosophical opinion could be a good deal firmer. Strawson[8] may speak to his heart's content about watching someone "coiling a rope" and Aaron[9], reflecting the initial persistent Oxford realism a little more explicitly, may say very boldly that I know my friend is there because I *see* him. But all that I strictly observe is bodily appearance and behaviour. I do not properly *see* the thoughts and intentions, though in many cases I have no doubt or hesitation whatever about them. I know that the fisherman passes the rope through his hands as he does to coil it, but I know this, without consciously pausing to infer it, as the obvious explanation of the movements of his hands and the picture of his body and his situation. It is the thoughts and intention that I learn about, but, very obviously it seems to me, in a mediated way.

It is worth noting here a curious procedure of many philosophers today who, impressed by the fact that there never is any real doubt about the existence of other minds, however liable to error we may be in particular cases, feel that this requires them to give at least a partially physicalist account of the nature of person. They feel that the inferential element brings in a degree of uncertainty. It would leave at least a remote possibility that solipsism is true. How this can be eased by falling back on a requirement of bodily continuity is not as plain as might be thought. For there again some sort of uncertainty may creep in. But without looking at this in more detail (I have again noted it more fully elsewhere[10]), we may list this also as a case, and in some ways a peculiarly significant one since not so overly realist, of taking a common sense or day to day conviction as a final insight or closure point, however desperate, from the writer's general view, the course it prescribes, rather than persist with further reflection.

These considerations seem to be underlined by the fact that, however happy we may feel in one another's company and serene in our mutual understanding, we may also be badly in error and completely misunderstand what our friends and others are about. The further we go from actual bodily presence, the greater seems to be the likelihood of error. If this were not so historical problems would be greatly simplified. Cook Wilson himself, and the strictest of his followers, could hardly have believed that what I know about Julius Caesar and the philosophical thoughts of Plato came about

293

through immediate contact with their minds (there would be no "Socratic problem" if things happened that way). I know what I do know here from books and related evidence, and the position in principle seems no different in less remote contacts and when people are physically present. There is physical mediation by which I know what is not physical.

Followers of Martin Buber sometimes yoke themselves somewhat unequally with common sense and tough-minded realists on this issue. Elsewhere[11] I have expressed my regard for Buber and indicated fairly closely what are some of the important things which his treatment of the "I-Thou" relation reflects. It is a great pity that those who invoke his views and find them suggestive do not think more closely about their true import. But one thing seems to me certain, namely that there is not a direct contentless relation with persons (man or God) which is quite distinct from knowledge about them and need not involve it. Indeed I doubt whether the idea of such a relation is meaningful. The facile invocation of it, as an easy way of evading tough philosophical problems, is one of the most conspicuous theological counterparts to the "short way" with difficult questions in various forms of common sense realism in recent philosophy. One hopes its day is over.

These matters are in no way affected if we find that the evidence for telepathy and related phenomena is strong or conclusive. Whatever happens in telepathy I do not think it even conceivable that it should involve the same knowledge of other minds as we have of our own. Often a vision of certain events significantly correlated with their so happening is involved, and the mediation here is evident enough—we do not strictly see the shipwreck or hear the cry as those on the spot do. But even if visions or voices of this kind are not involved there must be some other way in which the absence of the normal physical mediation and evidence is met. I have myself, in my book *The Self and Immortality*,[12] discussed the possibility that communication between totally disembodied creatures might take a quasi-telepathic form through some intrusions into the course of our own thoughts of ingredients we might have reason, by their substance or the mode or occasion of their happening, to ascribe to some outside influence we might learn in due course to recognize. But the mediation in its own way is equally evident here. To deny this is to stop, in our philosophical reflections, at the one point where it is most inappropriate to do so.

I believe, in short, that the search for an ultimate, in the way I now use this term, in our knowledge of other persons, is a most wasteful and delusive pursuit of a philosophical will o' the wisp. For a reason to be stressed more in a moment, I think it inherently impossible to know the mind of another, man or God, in the same way as one basically knows one's own thoughts or sensations expressly in having them. But this brings me to the contrasted case of our knowledge of ourselves which is the main context in which I wish to high-light and stress the central theme of this paper.

For what has to be said of self-knowledge is radically different from what has to be said about knowledge of others. There is indeed a great deal we may know about ourselves from evidence or observation, our own and that of others. I discover where I was and what I did this time last year by looking in my diary. My friends, and presumably a psychiatrist if required, could tell me much about the sort of chap I am. But there is a more basic form of self-knowledge, namely that by which I know that my particular thoughts and other mental states, and thereby my traits of character, are mine. Two distinct points need to be sorted out here, and both of them provide prime examples of what I understand by ultimates in this paper.

The first concerns the nature of experience itself. This is sometimes said to be neutral, as between a corporealist and non-corporealist account. Everyone agrees that we do perceive, argue, resolve etc., but this, it is said, proves nothing. Thus Professor Flew, in admitting[13] that my understanding my wife's call that lunch is ready is decisive in my going downstairs, urges that this leaves the corporealist view unaffected, and Roger Squires[14] firmly denies Robert Kirk's claim that sentience depends on private access. I know of no argument that will settle this question, any more than the debate with more old-fashioned materialists, if the latter are consistent enough. On the other hand, nothing seems plainer to me than that seeing, hearing, pondering, resolving etc., while they have behavioural and dispositional aspects, are essentially non-extended, non-physical on-goings. The simplest stock example is having pain. However "physical", the pain itself is just not a state of my body, but what I feel. But if I am asked to adduce a reason for this I am at a loss, and I marvel that anyone should request a reason for what seems to me so evident in itself. The appeal to our consciousness of pain, or any other experience, seems quite conclusive here, but if it is denied and arguments requested to show why the pain we admittedly do have, and our thoughts about it, must be thought altogether different from physical processes, then one is put out of court before the only possible plea can be made. The thoughts that I put on paper now cannot themselves be located though much that concerns and conditions them can. If this is not plain in itself I do not know what is, and I could hardly fail to do my case the gravest injustice if I took up the challenge to adduce further arguments for what I maintain. What could they be that would not give the case away? And yet it seems so manifestly clear a case.

The same goes for the claim that will be more widely contended, namely that the processes in question, sensing, perceiving, arguing etc., are "owned" or "belong" in some way. The precise term does not matter, and one is not quite happy with any, but I do know quite clearly what I mean when I say that I, and not someone else, am having these thoughts and sensations now. This has nothing directly to do with our separate bodies, or the different contexts in which these thoughts might be had in different cases. Quite irrespective of any distinctness of this kind, there is what I am almost tempted to call the brute fact that *I* am having these thoughts. That is an ultimate of which no further account appears possible.

Take again the stock and fairly simple example of pain. I know, in my own case, both that there is pain and that I am having it. In the case of others, a reason is in order. I may hear a scream and conclude that someone is in pain, and wonder who. I do none of this in my own case. I may indeed wonder whether I or someone else has been wounded—whose blood is flowing, whose crushed foot is that. But if I have not been too numbed to feel the pain then I know that there is pain, with no possibility of pretence or delusion, and that *I* have this pain. I know both things in one and the same experience, and both are beyond doubt. But knowing that the pain is mine is more than knowing that there is the pain. I know that beyond doubt in having the pain.

Not many, at the moment, would deny that it would be absurd for anyone to look for reasons to help him decide whether he or another was in pain, or whether he was in pain at all. What could he do? Trust his own report, look at his bleeding limb, listen to his own screams? Quite obviously all that is absurd. I just know that I have this pain, whether or not I can describe it properly or know the true cause of it. But many who would not oppose me on this seem curiously reluctant to accept the implications or the proper force of it. This is how Professor Zemach is able to declare that Strawson, "in spite of his rejection of the Cartesian ego, is basically a Cartesian".[15] Zemach himself seeks the answer, ingeniously enough, in "an assembly of this experience with other things".[16] But is not this quite plainly the wrong tack from the start, whatever may be said about the alleged "assembly" or its importance? It is not a case of Zemach, or any other, not being quite clever enough, not developing his own line to the best effect. He is from the start attempting the impossible. I know from the start that my awareness of myself is not that sort of thing. Similarly Shoemaker admitting, indeed stressing, that there are no criteria of self identity etc. goes to great lengths to avoid the proper import of this.[17]

The view is not, incidentally, as Zemach suggests, that we know "*a priori*" that "my experiences are mine", though that may not be out of place as an account of Strawson. Or, if I do know *a priori* it is because I know in the first place, in having any experience, that I am having it and what this means. The problem is of course to say what it means, and this, I suspect, is why many are reluctant to own to a Cartesian view. They fear a philosophical dead-end, or of naively (perhaps for suspect vested interests, moral or religious, not appropriate in a tough-minded age) affirming something for which they can make no further case. It is at least expected that something should be said about the self so invoked.

Professor Antony Flew brings this sharply to a head in the closing pages of his reply to my own paper at the Joint Session of the Mind and Aristotelian Societies.[18] He writes :

"But though the Lewis investigation is properly philosophical, it is still about how we might know, and when we might be entitled to claim to know. Yet the primary question here is precisely what we should know if we knew that this incorporeal substance at time two was the same as that incorporeal substance at time one."

and again :

"In part my difficulty arises because those who argue on this assumption never seem to make any but the most perfunctory attempt to show that it is true. One of my hopes of the coming discussion is that someone will indicate the lines in which they think this might be shown."

Professor Flew's hope was not fulfilled, at least not by me. But I warmly applaud, and did at the time, the unambiguous and sharp way in which he points up the central issue. What he says, with typical incisiveness, is what many say and feel about a Cartesian style dualism, and perhaps this will become also a "Flew's Challenge". It does indeed seem awkward to have to say, in response to questions like his, there just is nothing we can say. Is not this just burking the issue? We clearly should be able to say something. Otherwise as Professor Bernard Williams put it to me in the BBC debate about the same time[19]—I seem to be "running out of steam". That is of course infuriating, as, in a way, it is quite true. There is nothing more of any substance to be said. But this is not, whatever one's limitations, because of philosophical ineptitude. From the nature of the case no answer can be given.

The force of the temptation to provide an answer is almost overwhelming, especially as much ingenuity can be provided in trying to do so. But ingenuity is not philosophical wisdom, and if we have reached an ultimate the proper course is to admit it. That does not mean that the ingenious explanations have no point, they may illuminate something by the way and also help us to appreciate better just what the appropriate reticence really involves; and there is indeed a great deal around the edges of the subject that can be said, and should be. We can stress the awkwardness of seeking the right terms, allow for the dangers of terms like "ego" "substance", even "subject", go over the moves which preclude us from saying too much while still saying something enormously important and distinctive, note the level at which a person *can* be described and identified—by himself as well as others—in terms of his appearance or his psychological traits, or his history, what he is like and what has been the course of his life etc. All this is appropriate and important, and even when we come to the crunch over the question, "But what is it for this appearance and these likes and aptitudes etc. to be mine?" we can indulge in the skilful handling of pointers or "slantwise" considerations ("assembling of reminders", some would have it) by which we come to appreciate better what it is that we ultimately claim just to "see". We shall understand better, for example, that what is being invoked is not something occult, or something which only a few can come to know in special conditions (like appreciating poetry or music or having some transcendental vision). We shall likewise learn how misleading it is to think of the self or person as just a presupposition, in a Kantian or any other style, much less a remote "thing in itself". A person is what someone is and knows himself to be.

There is, in short, no mystery-mongering. Nor is there an arbitrary or a dogmatic taking up a stance, much less a lapse into a non-philosophical brute acceptance. There is all the subtlety in the world involved, *of its own kind*. Indeed, this is just where the finer philosophical skills are displayed, and where the old insights have to be presented anew without the misleading accretions acquired in repeated and too familiar statement. The perils of the wrong sort of confidence are only too evident in the bewilderment of critics, indeed the parodies and travesties to which sound philosophy is so easily exposed, and which puts the premium in debate on the skilful teaser. Plato must have suffered a great deal in this way, not at the hands of just stupid and undiscerning philistines, though there were some around as always, but from truly philosophical minds who had not the peculiar philosophical persistence and high merit to stay with the philosophical task of "turning the eye of the mind to the light" and going on looking in the appropriate philosophical way, aware all the time of the insidious charm of words and how fatal it is to be too wholly under their spell. What is right when you say it becomes almost immediately misleading.

The caution in all this is of first importance, and it has been as brilliantly displayed in fine philosophical work in the East as much as in the West. Time will not allow me now to illustrate this in the way I had hoped. The affinities between the more overt scepticisms of the East and of the West can be crudely presented in a way that takes away the true significance of both. But subject to a very necessary warning against cheap exploitation and listing of superficial resemblances, I would like to emphasize how much philosophical wisdom may be deepened by attending, in an informed and reflective way, to those aspects of Oriental thought and religion, where caution is struggling with explicit utterance in a profoundly philosophical way of looking at the world and ourselves. To highlight the ultimates in philosophy is in no way to encourage philosophical stupefaction and staleness. If we seem to know all the answers we give the wrong impression. The "right way of looking" like the vision of God, if the comparison may be made without impiety, has to be recovered, re-conveyed, recultivated and constantly cleansed of the accretions it generates itself. It is also, in itself and in other ramifications, supremely rewarding, and the vistas it opens out, the new philosophical destinations to be reached, can only be glimpsed by those who foresake the easy triumphs for the strains of maintaining a peculiar way of looking at provokingly elusive things which can only shine, like the Good Will, by their own light.

Professor H. D. Lewis
King's College
University of London

NOTES

[1] *The Elusive Mind*, p. 140.

[2] See especially "The Existence of God", *Statement and Inference*, Vol. II. For more detail see Chap. 12 of my *Philosophy of Religion*.

[3] "Realism and Metaphysics", *Idealistic Studies*, September 1974, pp. 2–11.

[4] G. E. Moore. *Philosophical Papers*, pp. 127–150.

[5] In his contribution to *Contemporary British Philosophy*, Series 4, (Ed. H. D. Lewis) Professor R. M. Hare comes round to the invocation of what he calls "judgment".

[6] They had of course been anticipated in essentials by others, like Richard Price.

[7] "Consequentialism" is a fairly new term. The theory is opposed to utilitarianism, but insists all the same that we must look to the consequences. If this means that we must consider what our action will bring about it is too general to be significant. It excludes absolute prohibition, but what else? Its advocates have not yet made it sufficiently clear how their view differs from Ross's doctrine of *prima facie* duties. For an informative discussion see "It makes no difference whether or not I do it", Jonathan Glover and M. Scott Taggart, *Proceedings of the Aristotelian Society*, Supp. Vol. XLIX.

[8] *Individuals*, p. 111.

[9] *Knowing and the Function of Reason*, p. 75.

[10] In the discussion of A. J. Ayer's views in my *The Elusive Mind*, pp. 251–259.

[11] *The Elusive Mind*, chap. XIII.

[12] Chap. 9.

[13] *Proceedings of the Aristotelian Society*, Supp. Vol. XLIX, p. 242.

[14] *Proceedings of the Aristotelian Society*, Supp. Vol. XLVIII, pp. 162–163.

[15] "Strawson's Transcendental Deduction", *Philosophical Quarterly*, p. 123.

[16] Op. cit., p. 125.

[17] As I tried to show in my *The Elusive Mind*, chap. X, but the point will, I think, be more apparent when the papers prepared by Shoemaker and myself for the Symposium on Immortality at the Conference on Reason and Religion (Royal Institute of Philosophy) are available.

[18] *Proceedings of the Aristotelian Society*, Supp. Vol. XLIX, pp. 244–245.

[19] *Listener* as above.